"Mark Travis is the only practical teacher of directing I've ever met — and simply the best. I learned more from him than I did in four years of film school!"

Cyrus Nowrasteh, Writer-Director
The Day Reagan Was Shot

"A comprehensive and inspired examination of craft. A must read for any serious professional."

Mark Rydell, Director
On Golden Pond, James Dean

"It is rare to find a reference guide that has as its primary focus the director as creative artist and visionary. For the experienced director, THE DIRECTOR'S JOURNEY is an invaluable reminder of why the journey was first undertaken: for the beginning director, it is a compass that will hopefully set the course for the rewarding explorations to follow."

Asaad Kelada, Director
Who's the Boss?, Family Ties

"Writers and actors will weep with relief that this book was written. Mark Travis has written more than a practical guide; he has evolved an enlightened, egoless, and effective approach based on communication and the drive to create the most authentic, powerful work. I recommend it."

Judith Claire
Entertainment Career Counselor

"With an astonishing clarity Mark Travis articulates the techniques and skills of film directing. Not only does the beginning student find invaluable guidance on all stages of the directing process, but the experienced director will learn rational explanations for many of the things he may have only been doing intuitively."

John Badham, Director
Saturday Night Fever,
War Games, Blue Thunder

MICHAEL WIESE PRODUCTIONS
www.mwp.com

Since 1981, Michael Wiese Productions has been dedicated to providing novice and seasoned filmmakers with vital information on all aspects of filmmaking and videomaking. We have published more than 50 books, used in over 500 film schools worldwide.

Our authors are successful industry professionals — they believe that the more knowledge and experience they share with others, the more high-quality films will be made. That's why they spend countless hours writing about the hard stuff: budgeting, financing, directing, marketing, and distribution. Many of our authors, including myself, are often invited to conduct filmmaking seminars around the world.

We truly hope that our publications, seminars, and consulting services will empower you to create enduring films that will last for generations to come.

We're here to help. Let us hear from you.

Sincerely,

Michael Wiese
Publisher, Filmmaker

DIRECTING
FEATURE
FILMS

THE CREATIVE COLLABORATION
BETWEEN DIRECTORS, WRITERS, AND ACTORS

MARK TRAVIS

Published by Michael Wiese Productions
11288 Ventura Blvd., Suite 621
Studio City, CA 91604
tel. (818) 379- 8799
fax (818) 986-3408
mw@mwp.com
www.mwp.com

Cover design: Objects of Design
Book layout: Gina Mansfield Design
First edition final copy check by Bernice Balfour
Second edition material edited by Brett Jay Markel

Printed by McNaughton & Gunn, Inc., Saline, Michigan
Manufactured in the United States of America

This is the second edition of *The Director's Journey*
Copyright 2002 by Mark Travis
First Printing, May 1997

Library of Congress Cataloging in Publication Data

Travis, Mark, 1943-
    Directing feature films: the creative collaboration between directors,
writers, and actors / By Mark Travis.
          p.   cm.
Rev. ed. of: The director's journey. 1997.
    ISBN: 0-941188-43-4
    1. Motion pictures -- Production and direction. I. Travis, Mark,
1943- Director's journey. II. Title.
    PN1995.9.P7 T76 2002
    791.43'0233--dc21

                                                                    2002001432

We are grateful to the following for the screenplay pages which are included:

Forrest Gump
Based on the novel by Winston Groom
Screenplay by Eric Roth
Pages 36, 37A and 38
Copyright 1994 by Paramount Studios

Diner
Screenplay by Barry Levinson
Pages 1 and 2
Copyright 1982 by MGM Studios

American Beauty
Screenplay by Alan Ball
Pages 31-33 and 102-104
Copyright 2000 by Dreamworks LLC

DEDICATION

To my father, W. Willard Travis, who always encouraged me to reach for the stars.

You were the first to open my eyes to the wonders of storytelling as you sat on the edge of my bed, night after night, during my long illnesses. Each evening you improvised a new chapter of our novel that made my mind reel with the power of your imagination as you took me on a magical adventure.

It was your quiet but firm support, as I chose this "irrational" profession, that gave me the courage to hang on. You were the first to tell me that I had a book in me. I resisted it for ten years.

Then there was that one phone call two years ago when I was despondent and discouraged. I reached out to you; you were still there with your incredible support after all these years of struggling.

And, finally, it was your last word to me as I leaned over your bed and told you I had finished the book. You reached up, patted my cheek and managed to get out "congratulations". Supportive to the end.

Bless you, Dad. I love you. I miss you. This is for you.

TABLE OF CONTENTS

ACKNOWLEDGMENTS

Writing this book was a two-year journey, but it has been a lifetime of experience and relationships that has resulted in these discoveries. I am deeply grateful to all who have helped shape the sensibilities that inform this work.

First of all, Mr. Barker, my high school English teacher, who convinced me I could write. Whitney LeBlanc who convinced me I could direct. Asaad Kelada who guided me through those first idealistic college years. Paul Treichler and Meredith Dallas who supported my dreams, and Antioch College which allowed me to find my own way. The instructors at the Yale School of Drama who encouraged me to trust my talent and study the classics: Gordon Rogoff, Robert Brustein, Stella Adler, Jonathan Miller, Nikos Psacharopoulos, and Bobby Lewis. And Harold Clurman and Mark Rydell who infused me with a passionate love for the craft.

Theatre West, which gave me a place in Los Angeles to experiment and grow. And all the members of Theatre West who for years tolerated my obsessions and supported my dreams. Linda Marsh and Margie Peters who had enough confidence to hire a first-time television director and sufficient humility to actually enroll in his first directing class.

Ronnie Rubin of UCLA Extension who was willing to take a risk on a new teacher. Selise Eiseman and Gary Berg of The Directors Guild who were equally courageous in hiring this one-time film director (but many-time theatre director) to teach other directors the art of communicating with actors. And again to Selise who said to me two years ago, "You have a book, you must write this down."

To E.W. Swackhamer for your constant support and for always convincing me that what I did mattered. I miss you.

A special thanks to all of my directing students. We created this book together. Without your enthusiasm, curiosity, and consistently probing questions, much of this would not have materialized.

To several students who were generous enough to read early drafts and give me invaluable advice, thank you: Josh Aronson (for being a most loyal friend and inspiring collaborator), Jeff Boortz (for having the courage to do it "by the book"), Evan Crooke (for embracing the process and for your thoughtful notes), Fred Johntz (for your insightful critique on the first draft), Juliette Marshall (for your encouragement after reading the first faltering chapters), and Marty Pasetta, Jr. (for being a great friend, collaborator, and constant inspiration). A debt of gratitude to several mentors and advisers who were kind enough to read this work in its early stages: John Badham, John Bailey, James Burrows, Judith Claire, Mark Johnson, Asaad Kelada, Carol Littleton, Michael Pressman, Mark Rydell, and Robert Wise.

To Michael Wiese — loyal friend, courageous student, and astute publisher — for having the confidence that I could indeed write the book. Thank you for your patience as I struggled with those ever elusive deadlines.

Finally, the most special thanks to my adoring, supportive wife and favorite actress, Dianne. You constantly supported me during the two years it took to write this book, as well as the twenty years and many productions of experimentation, trial and error, success and failure. You and I have worked together in eleven productions (theatre, television, and film) and your constant feedback from the actor's perspective has helped me mold and define my skills as a director. Thank you, Dianne, for being a tough critic, a compassionate collaborator, and always believing in me.

PREFACE

When I was asked to write this book I was at first thrilled and honored, but all that soon turned to dread. I had been directing for over twenty years, studying even longer, teaching for nearly five, and could conceive of no way to organize all I had discovered and learned into a linear comprehensible form.

But the idea intrigued and challenged me. One of my frustrations as a teacher, coach, and consultant has been my lack of opportunities to share this knowledge with a large number of people. Even in intensive weekend workshops and seminars, there are always territories that have to be left unaddressed or unexplored.

Now I sit here two years later staring at this 300 page opus with feelings of pride, sadness, regret, and dissatisfaction. I'm proud because I got to the end of the journey and covered the topics I wanted to address. I'm sad because like any creative journey there's an unwillingness to let go, to let the child live on its own. The regret and dissatisfaction are much more serious. I still feel as if I haven't completed the task, that there are more aspects of the process that could be addressed. Each chapter felt like it could be a book all on its own.

Most significant is the loss of the one-on-one relationship. I want to be there when each of you reads this, to engage you in a dialogue; to discuss, explore, and make new discoveries. Much of what I have learned about this process called directing has come through interaction with my students. They have forced me to examine, comprehend, and articulate that which is often intuitive or instinctual. Every day I learn something new.

As directors we all crave the collaboration, we yearn for that artistic rush that happens when our energies are combined with another's and the results rocket beyond our own expectations.

Writing this book has been like making a movie, and now that it is in release I can only sit back and wonder what the journey is like for each of you.

My final frustration is knowing that in the weeks and months to come, as I am directing, teaching or consulting, I will come upon yet another aspect or example of this process I wish I had included (this has happened already and I'm not liking it). My only solace is to consider this book a work-in-progress, a living, growing entity, that may be amended in the years to come.

I welcome your responses, questions, suggestions, and critiques. Already I have had the pleasure of learning how this book assisted several directors, writers, and actors. This feedback is important to me. I need to stay in the collaboration. Please feel free to contact me through the publisher, Michael Wiese Productions.

Enjoy the journey.

Los Angeles
December 1996

NEW INTRODUCTION

It is now five years since *The Director's Journey* was first published and, as predicted, I found myself teaching and lecturing and saying things that I wish were in the book. New questions would arise requiring new answers and suddenly chapters loomed in front of me. While teaching in Tokyo, Berlin, Munich, Cologne, London, and cities throughout the United States, I would hear myself saying, "I wish this were in my book" more and more often. So I vowed that I would make the effort to expand the book and address many of my new thoughts, questions, and discoveries in the world of filmmaking. The result: Chapter 10, Reconsiderations and Recapitulations; Chapter 11, No More Acting, No More Directing; and Chapter 13, The Ultimate Collaboration: Directors with Directors. Plus these thoughts:

Filmmaking is not a precise science. It's not even an imprecise science. It's a craft, an art form. Nobody knows how it really works. We all guess. We all speculate. There are moments of blazing clarity when we think we've discovered some infallible truth about the process — and we rejoice. With great pride we announce our discovery to the world as if we had discovered a tenth planet. Then, a few years later, after more filmmaking, more successes, more failures, more frustrations, anxieties, victories, and disasters — we realize that the truth wasn't quite so infallible. In fact, it may be wrong or misguided. Now we make no bold announcements. We just pull our baseball caps down a little lower over our eyes and hope no one notices. And we move on.

Los Angeles
January 2002

Original Introduction

The storyteller sits at the edge of the circle, the flames from the fire leaping, playing shadow games on his face. His listeners sit patiently, politely, attentive. The storyteller can feel the tension, all eyes on him, waiting for him to begin, waiting for the first few words that will start them all on a journey together. The moment arrives, the moment when the story must commence. The storyteller picks his words and his tone carefully. "Once upon a time . . ."

Word by word, images begin to form. Colors, movements, characters appear and in the mind of each listener a similar yet personal movie begins to play. The words flow, the pictures grow. The minds of the listeners sweep through the void, leaving ribbons of colors and images, rainbows of moods and emotions growing like wild flowers out of the verbal imagery.

The agreement is simple. The storyteller creates a verbal outline, paints a picture, and then the imagination of the listener fills in the rest. It is a contract, a collaboration of the highest artistic order.

This is storytelling in its purest form with a direct link between the storyteller and the listener. There is a vibrant interactive relationship at work. The storyteller adjusts and modulates the telling of his story according to his listener's responses. And the listener gets as much of the dynamics and the subtext of the story from being in the presence of the storyteller as he does from the story itself.

* * * * * *

1

"Cut, print. Let's set up for the close-up," the director instructs the crew. Two dozen people scurry in different directions and set about their individual tasks while crew members move the camera, lights, and props. The director prepares the actors for another take with slight variations. Within a few minutes the cast and crew are ready. After a brief rehearsal the cameras and recorders roll again and another small piece of the story is recorded.

This is storytelling the hard way. Piece by piece. Moment by moment. Laboriously recording different elements. There is no contact with the listener, no interplay between the two parties, no collaboration. So the director has to assume both roles. The director has to picture an audience sitting in a theatre months from now and imagine their response, their reactions, and the feelings that are generated within them. She has to create a collaboration where there is none. In each of the three times the story is told (in the writing, in the production, and in the postproduction) the director has to both guide the telling of the story and be the surrogate audience.

To complicate matters, a director does not get to tell the story all by himself. In many ways it would be easier if he did. It would be simpler if the director were the one who wrote the script, played all the parts, recorded the scenes, designed all the scenery and costumes, edited the final product, and supplied the music. That's what the fireside storyteller does. It's easier when it all comes from one source, one sensibility, one vision.

But now in order to reach a larger audience and because of changing life styles and technology we elect to tell our stories through other mediums — theatre, radio, television, and film. And we find that our efforts are simultaneously thwarted by and assisted by the technology of each medium. Suddenly there is a script, a written description of the story to be told. And there are individual actors to portray each role. Then there are designers, producers, and a variety of other artists including cameramen, audio recorders and mixers, special

2

effects coordinators, editors and composers. All of these people are there to assist in the telling of the story, but with each new individual comes an individual point of view, a singular artist with a talent and a vision. Each artist usually has experience and ability in his/her individual craft well beyond that of the director and thereby can enhance the telling of the story. Yet, how do we bring all these talented artists together into the process of formulating one story, one singular vision, so that in the realizing of the final product it will feel as if this story has been told by one person? How can we bring our final product to our listener and have the listener genuinely feel as if she is in direct communication with one storyteller, that this is genuinely vision, so that in the realizing of the final product it will feel as if this story has been told by one person? How can we bring our final product to our listener and have the listener genuinely feel as if she is in direct communication with one storyteller, that this is genuinely a one-on-one relationship? We know that the combination of all these talents in the process of telling a story can certainly rise above the potential of any one of them, but we also know that the attempted collaboration of all these artists can turn into collision and that the individual efforts may not combine to make a product worthy of the effort.

The director, as captain of the ship, has the task of creating an environment and casting his film (and by casting I mean all artists on the film, not just the actors) in such a way as to assure the best possible collaboration.

It is often said that casting is 80 percent of making a film. This is only partially true. Having a clear vision of the film and establishing and maintaining an environment in which those that you do cast can do their best work in alliance with the other artists — that is 80 percent of making a movie.

In this book we will be focusing primarily on the medium of film while mindful of the similarities in theatre, television, and even radio. We are making the following assumptions: the existence of a script, the use of actors to portray the various characters that people the script, and the role of the director.

The prospect of directing a film is overwhelming. Not only is it not very clear or even agreed upon as to what a director does, but there are very few guidelines or programs for the learning director. There is no particular structure or manual that comes along with the job. When you start directing a film you are suddenly face to face with every aspect of the project — the script, the writer, the producer, the actors, the designers, editing, music, locations, studios, previews, schedules, etc. It feels like a tidal wave coming at you.

But when you sit down and start to contemplate the directorial process you begin to realize that it need not be so overwhelming. There are certain definite steps that need to be taken in the process. There is a logic — a sequence — an order.

The directing process is actually a process of discovery leading to decisions. It goes from the general to the specific in a very logical and organized fashion. It is a process of eliminating choices. While a very personal journey, it is also a series of collaborations, intimate and vibrant relationships with other artists that will eventually bring everyone to the point of mutually creating one piece of work.

For the director the process is a long conversation, first with the script, then with the writer, the producers, the designers, the actors, and others. And, most importantly, with himself. It is this series of conversations and dialogues that lead to the artistic expression that is the film.

Before we plunge into the process of directing a film (play or teleplay), we need to formulate a point of view about the directorial process and the role of the director.

THE ROLE OF THE DIRECTOR AND THE CREATIVE TEAM

Throughout the course of the making a film a director enters into numerous creative relationships with writers, producers, designers, cinematographers, actors, editors, composers, and others. The director relies on each relationship (and the talent of each collaborator) to contribute an important aspect of the film. The director cannot make the film without these people, without these creative relationships. This is what I call the director's Creative Team.

The director's job is twofold. First, she needs to formulate a vision for the film. Second, she needs to communicate that vision, that concept to every member of the creative team in such a manner that each artist will be inspired to make her best contribution to that vision. That's it. That's about all a director does. That's all she's allowed to do. That's all she's required to do — formulate a vision, communicate a vision.

In Chapter 1 ("The Director and the Script") we will discuss how that vision is formulated. Or rather, how the director, in relationship to the script, *begins* the formulation of a vision for the movie. We will also examine that delicate relationship between the director and the script — an interactive relationship that is constantly being challenged as it continues to grow.

In Chapter 2 ("Terms and Definitions") we will examine the common vocabulary used by actors, directors, and writers when discussing characters and how it reflects script structure and analysis.

In Chapter 3 ("Working with Writers") we will discuss how the director discovers the *writer's* vision for the film and then how, through a collaborative process, the director begins to blend the two visions into a more cohesive one and thereby establishes a strong working relationship with the writer.

In Chapter 4 ("The Script Breakdown") we will see how the formulation of this vision begins to determine and affect many of the mechanical aspects of the telling of the story, including design, locations, movement, and even character arcs, relationships, objectives, and adjustments. Also we will begin to see how the formulation of this vision will affect the director's selection of the creative team.

In Chapter 5 ("The Creative Team") we will discuss the methods of selecting the creative team based on the vision the director has for the film. We will consider ways of communicating and working with this team in order to establish and maintain healthy collaborative relationships.

In Chapter 6 ("The Casting Process") we will examine various approaches that can insure that you select actors that will bring vitality to each character and will be eager collaborators.

In Chapter 7 ("The Rehearsal Process") we will explore in detail many techniques that you can use to create a unified acting ensemble and establish healthy working relationships between the director and the actors that will result in performances that support and enhance your vision of the story.

In Chapter 8 ("Production") we will see how your creative team (including the actors) can be molded into one forceful storytelling unit, and we will outline various ways of establishing and maintaining strong lines of communication with all members of the creative team, both collectively and individually.

And, finally, in Chapter 9 ("Postproduction") we will examine various methods of communication with your postproduction team. In the last phase of the making of the film your vision will be severely tested and challenged. And as your choices become more limited and definitive it will be your ability to maintain your vision and your lines of communication that will insure that your film fulfills your expectations.

THE DIRECTOR'S WRITING PROCESS

As we look more closely at the role of the director we need to consider two very important aspects of directing:

(1) All A Director Has To Do Is Talk.

That's it. Talk. Communicate. As a matter of fact, that's usually all a director is <u>allowed</u> to do. Look at it this way, a director (who is not a screenwriter) doesn't write the script, design, act, operate the camera, physically edit the film, or compose the music. Yet, the director is in charge of all of that. The director is a communicator, an inspirer, a visionary. The main thing we do as directors is we talk and we talk and we talk. Consequently the most important skill for a director to develop is the art of communication. It is through the often limiting communication of speech (and writing) that the director does all his work. He can only pass on ideas, visions, impressions, with the objective of inspiring his creative team so that they can realize his vision through their individual disciplines.

(2) The Director Must Be A Writer.

I am not talking about the director as a writer of the script, but rather the director employing the tool of writing as an important element in her communication with other members of her creative team and, equally important, with herself. Writing to the creative team will help clarify your thoughts and your vision and establish a clear line of communication with each member of your team. We will deal with this in more detail in Chapter 5. At this point we need to discuss establishing a clear line of communication *with yourself* through your writing and how this will help clarify and solidify your vision of the film.

The most important relationship you will have in the entire creation of your film is with yourself. It is *you* who are making the film. It is you that you have to please. Everyone is going to turn to you for answers, for decisions, and the only person for you to turn to is yourself. Despite all its collaboration directing is a very lonely job. You only have yourself to rely on so you must be clear in your vision. And an essential step in that process is writing to yourself.

THE DIRECTOR'S NOTEBOOK

During the course of preparing for and making your movie, you will be keeping a journal, a private accounting of your work, not to be shared with anyone except yourself. I call this the director's notebook.

Your personal journal is the heart and soul of the director's notebook. During the course of your film, you will be making many entries in your notebook (or notebooks by the time you're done). These notebooks serve as your communication link with yourself. They will keep you on track.

We will be seeing concrete examples of this writing process throughout this book.

FORMULATING THE VISION

Even though it may appear that this is a two–step process, (formulate the vision and then communicate the vision) these two steps actually overlap. They occur simultaneously and they are interactive. The process of communicating the vision will affect the formulation of the vision. And, how the vision is formulated will affect the nature of the communication.

So how do we formulate a vision? Where does this vision come from?

Go back to storytelling. It's just you, the listener, and the story. You know from your soul how you want to tell the story and the impact you want it to have. Your vision is already formulated because you picked this story in order to have a certain affect on your listener. This is pure communication, one-on-one.

The vision has to come from the story itself and why <u>you</u> want to tell it. In Chapter 2 we will explore various relationships you can have with your script, and how these relationships will assist you in shaping your vision. Remember, a vision for the film is not something that is imposed upon a script. It emerges from the script and stimulates you, the director. This relationship with the script is the genesis of your directing process and a crucial step in the realizing of your film.

But what about the writer, you say. The writer is your collaborator (one of many) but the writer is not the script. It is not your job to carry the writer's vision but rather the vision of the script itself. In Chapter 3 we will explore the complexities of the director/writer relationship. The relationship between writer and director is a delicate dance, a shaky marriage. It has to be entered cautiously and respectfully, and maintained with firmness and flexibility. It is your job as the director to set the tone for this and all other collaborative relationships in the making of your film.

In subsequent chapters we will explore your relationships with other collaborators in the creative team (designers, cinematographers, editors, composers, etc.) and how you can employ their talent in the telling of your story. These are all very delicate and vital relationships that must be nurtured and respected. It is in these relationships that the world of the film is created, recorded, and reassembled.

But the most important relationship you will have is with the actors. No matter how brilliant the script may be, no matter how beautiful the production design, the lighting, the cinematography, the editing and the music, if the events that you and the actors have created are lacking then the entire film will suffer. In Chapters 6, 7, and 8 we will explore in great detail that tricky and elusive relationship between the actors and the director. Remember, filmmaking is a very simple process: you create an event and then you record it. If the event isn't worth recording, then all the camera angles, designs, editing, and music won't make it any better. But if you have created a worthy event, then even the simplest recording and rendering will suffice.

Now it's time to start. And the only place you can start is with the script, the source of all information and inspiration.

CHAPTER 1

THE DIRECTOR AND THE SCRIPT

You're a director. You're handed a script to direct. What do you do? Many directors begin their process by working immediately with the writer and the producer and by considering casting possibilities, budgets, locations, crews, and other related matters. However, by doing this they bypass one of the most important relationships a director has in the realizing of a film — the relationship with the script itself. This is a relationship that has to be encouraged, nourished, and carefully monitored.

But first, what is a script?

You're handed 100–120 pages of typed material, including descriptions, dialogue, and characters interrelating that we are expected to translate into a film (or a play or teleplay). A script has been defined as a blueprint, a plan, a guide, a skeleton, or a map — but it's more than that. A script is a living breathing force that has reached a specific stage of development. It is an expression, a result, and a mere suggestion of something else — a film.

The novel is an end in itself. It is intended to take the reader on a journey that will stimulate the reader to visualize the characters, situations, and locations. As we transport ourselves into the world of the novel we create all the visuals, the sounds, the smells. But a script is intended to stimulate the reader to see the play, teleplay, or screenplay on the stage or on the screen. It is intended to stimulate the imagination of the reader with the notion that the reader will participate in the next stage of the development of this idea. Therefore it is only a suggestion, a hint, a prodding device. It is very difficult to read a script without

11

thinking about how this movie could or should or would be made. For one reason it's very difficult because the format of a script is always reminding us of the mechanics of filmmaking (fade-in, dissolve, cut to, interior, exterior, day, night, etc.). It is also difficult because most of us who read scripts are reading them with the constant question in the back of our minds: "Is this something I want to make?" or "How would I make this?"

The script is also a result. Just as the dialogue in a scene is the result of the interrelationship between the characters, the script is a result of all the writer's energies, aspirations, frustrations, dreams, and desires that have led to and informed this story. It only <u>implies</u> what has gone on before or what is happening <u>under</u> the scene — the needs, desires, and emotions that have been or are operative that <u>caused</u> these words and this behavior. But the causes lie buried, hidden, and it is our job as directors to dig them out.

The writer writes <u>from</u> the passion, needs, desires, and emotions of the characters but in the script we only see the character's <u>resulting</u> behavior and words. So the script is not so much a blueprint as a footprint — the image that was left behind as the beast passed through the jungle. But what made the beast choose to go this way? Was he running to or from something and why? Or just wandering and exploring? The director has to dig below the surface to find the cause of these behaviors. And there is not just <u>one</u> probable cause, there are many.

It is important that you see the script as a <u>result</u> of the behavior of the characters and understand that your job in the making of this film is to create an environment wherein those <u>results</u> will organically occur. It's not your job to take this script and make it *seem* real. It is your job to create a dynamic between actors/characters that will *be* real, thereby eliciting the desired results (the script).

Not only is the script (the behavior and words and actions) a result of the characters needs, desires, and passions, but it is also the result of the needs, desires, and passions of the writer. The writer brought forth this work in response to some deep-felt convictions. Before you attempt to carry that vision forward, you, as the director, must retrace the writer's process in order to connect to the source of those passions, and convictions.

As the director you need to identify and comprehend the impulse that initially prompted the writer to create this script. And you need to locate that urge, desire, or passion within yourself that is your emotional connection to this work.

How can we genuinely find and stimulate those impulses, notions, ideas, and passions within ourselves that will inform and fuel our enthusiasm for this project? First, don't think about it. Sometimes our best thinking gets in the way of our best work, and certainly too much thinking gets in the way of our best intuitive work. Second, form an intimate relationship with the script without imposing ideas upon it or obligations upon yourself. You need to allow the script to become a part of you — a partner, a collaborator.

There are three basic steps that need to be taken in order to establish your primary relationship with the script.
1. Reading the script — the script wash.
2. Identifying your passion for the material.
3. Determining what the script is <u>really</u> about.

STEP ONE: READING THE SCRIPT - THE SCRIPT WASH

You've already read the script one or two times, and now I'm suggesting that you read it in a very different way. It is important to remain open, unbiased, uncritical, and nonjudgmental. It's what I call "letting the script wash over you." This is not the time to judge, rewrite, cut or add, design scenes, think of casting or locations. Just allow the script to have its full impact on you.

This is a crucial step in the beginning of a long (and hopefully fruitful) relationship between you and the script. A relationship doesn't get more intimate than this. You need to allow the script to get inside you, to stimulate you, please you, anger you, strike a nerve. You want to find the passion that will carry you through the next year or two that it will take you to make this movie. Let the script be your guide to that passion. It will constantly inform you and fuel your imagination, energy, and vision.

STEP TWO: IDENTIFYING THE PASSION

As you are reading the script, record your impressions, reactions, and feelings in your director's notebook without judging them or the script. If you feel bored or restless, put it in your notebook but don't try to analyze it. If you're excited, pleased, frightened, intrigued, or angry, write it down. Don't get into fixing or editing, just read and respond. It's not quite as simple as it seems because it is difficult for directors to resist the temptation to analyze, fix, judge, or rework the material. We want to stage scenes in our mind, cast roles, and design camera moves and editing patterns. But it is crucial at this point that you do this very intimate, very personal work in a naive manner, putting aside your agenda, craft, and needs. Allow it to be extremely personal. You'll be thrilled and intrigued with the results.

Now, having let the script affect you and having made a record of it in your director's notebook, you are ready to respond. It's time to bring your reactions and experiences to the script. Start talking back. Write to the script, to the characters. Tell them what you think of them, of their actions, and their behavior. Be honest.

This dialogue is <u>not</u> intended to be in the form of a critique. This is <u>not</u> the director suddenly imposing a vision. This is you, as an audience member, genuinely responding to the material. You are establishing a viable and vital relationship between you and the story. Think of the script as a new friend, someone you want to get to know, and someone that you want to get to know <u>you</u>.

The more detailed the writing, the more connected you will be with the script. Don't sit down with preconceived ideas, just write. Be impulsive! Be spontaneous! Write! Don't think, don't intellectualize, just write.

This writing is not meant to be shared with anyone. You don't even need to read it yourself. What is important is that you establish this dialogue with the script and maintain it throughout the making of your film.

> For example: My initial reactions to my first reading of *Forrest Gump* (the first draft screenplay after having read the novel): I'm shocked. Where I found the novel to be interesting and intriguing, it seemed to be totally void of the magic in the screenplay. In the book I found myself pitying Forrest. He was such a big lump of a man stumbling through life, like a Lenny (from *Of Mice and Men*), but my pity had little empathy in it. I really wasn't too concerned about what happened to him, and his brushes with historical characters seemed totally contrived and just clever. But in the screenplay I found myself seduced by Forrest. I couldn't help but like him and admire him. Now I want to go on this journey with him. I may even want to be like Forrest. When I finished the book I was relieved, glad to have the journey over. When I finished the screenplay I wanted to start the journey over again.

These initial reactions were important to me. It made me realize that Eric Roth (screenwriter) had defined something within Forrest that had connected with me in a visceral way. And if he (Eric) could do that to me then I could do that to the audience. The power of a story well told.

> Note: Throughout this book we will be using two established screenplays and films (*The Fugitive* and *Forrest Gump*) as models.

It is important to state at this point that we are not trying to come up with definitive decisions as to the values or interpretations of these films under discussion. What we are examining here is a process of analysis that is intended to lead you, the director, to your own interpretation and personal identification with the material. The fact that three different directors would make three very different (and possibly all very valid) versions of the same script is what makes this entire art form so exciting. It is what certainly makes the theatre such a live and vital art form and why different productions of the same play can each carry a powerful yet markedly different message to an audience. It is sad that most films are given only one production. Wouldn't it be fascinating to see a Scorsese production of *The Player* or a Merchant/Ivory production of *Age of Innocence?*

I suggest that you familiarize yourself with *The Fugitive* and *Forrest Gump*. At minimum, rent the videos, but if you want to get the greatest value from this book, read the novel of *Forrest Gump* and the scripts for both films.

As we proceed with these scripts (and others that we will refer to), remember that the analysis is mine. You may or may not agree with me, but that is not the point. Our focus is on the process. Apply the process. Come to your own conclusions.

STEP THREE: THE CORE QUESTION

The most important question you are going to ask concerning the script is, "What is it really all about?" This is the core question. We will be asking this question of many other elements of the script (the acts, sequences, scenes, characters, events, etc.) at a later date, but at the moment we are asking it of the script itself. We know what the events are, the scenes, the relationships, but what is the internal theme or premise that is driving all of this? How does this story of total strangers affect and touch each of us personally? What is the writer really trying to say underneath it all? Are there universal truths here? Universal experiences, attitudes, beliefs? There is a heart and soul at the core of every good script, and it fuels every aspect of the script. You just need to find it.

It often happens that the writer isn't totally aware of what's pulsing at the heart of the story. Many times writers, and some of the best writers, are coming from such an organic subjective place and are so true to their impulses that they have little awareness of the universality of their work, or how the work is truly affecting their audience. There have been times I have told a writer what he or she has written, either in the entire script or a particular scene or sequence, and the response will be "Really? That's what I wrote?" This is not to put the writers down in any way. Not at all. It is said with the deepest respect for writers and their craft. Writing and acting are the two most vulnerable, dangerous, and exposing endeavors within this art form. They need and deserve our deepest respect. But we do have to understand that the process of writing is markedly different from that of directing. And because writing at its best is personal, intuitive, and subjective many writers create without awareness of the resonance of their work.

Let's look at *The Fugitive* for a moment with the purpose of determining what it is <u>really</u> about.

Written by Jeb Stuart and David Twohy and directed by Andrew Davis in 1993, *The Fugitive* is a remake of the television series of the same name. It is the story of a very successful doctor, Dr. Kimble (played by Harrison Ford), who is wrongly accused of the murder of his wife and is intent upon proving his innocence. And we have an investigator, Lt. Gerard (played by Tommy Lee Jones), whose sole objective is to capture Dr. Kimble regardless of his guilt or innocence. A pretty simple story. A chase story. But is that what *The Fugitive* is <u>really</u> all about? Just one man trying to prove his innocence and another trying to catch him? If we look deeper we will find a story about honor and pride, integrity and tenacity — a story about ethics, both personal and professional. Dr. Kimble could easily leave town after he escapes from that spectacular bus and train crash, but he chooses to stay. Why? Why would he take the risk of being shot, killed, or incarcerated for life just to save his own reputation and the esteem of his relationship to his murdered wife, when he could quite easily escape? The core of this story lies in the core of our main characters.

Let's look for a moment at Dr. Kimble. What do we know about him? He's a doctor of some distinction, highly respected, and has a happy marriage that is full of passion, romance, trust, and youthful fervor. He is not (as far as we can tell) an adventurer. Dr. Kimble is a man in the public view and very comfortable with this, an honest man with no dark clouds or questionable past. As a model citizen he has most likely had no run-in with the law. Any one of us would like to have him as our doctor, friend, or neighbor. We would like to be like Dr. Kimble — happy, successful, respected, and respectful. Here is a man with no worries. Until one day . . .

Then suddenly he is tested. The test itself does not matter, but the severity of the test does — and this is a brutal test. So, how is our model citizen going to respond? How would each of us like to respond were we in his place? What are his priorities? This is not so much about proving one's innocence as it is about proving one's self. There is a code of ethics that is being tested and it is not the success or failure of the actions taken that really counts but rather the actions themselves. Dr. Kimble chooses to risk everything he has to clear his name and his marriage. *The Fugitive* is about placing your reputation, the reputation of your family, and the belief in your own innocence and integrity above your own safety and future.

Think of it this way. How often have any of us been falsely accused of murdering our wife or husband? How often have we had to put our life at risk in order to prove our innocence in such a situation? Chances are there are only a handful of audience members out of the millions of people who saw or will see *The Fugitive* who can relate to it on that level. Now look at it another way. How many of us have ever been falsely accused of an action and that accusation has put our reputation at risk? And how many of us attempted or <u>wished</u> we had attempted to clear our names of this false accusation? I would question any audience members, adults or children, who claim they have never been in that kind of situation. Suddenly, *The Fugitive* relates to all of us, and only because we have looked beyond, or beneath, the surface story to find out what this story is <u>really</u> all about.

Let's look at Lt. Gerard. What do we know about him? Lt. Gerard is a man of singular vision, tenacious, a bulldog. When he has a job to do he doesn't stop until it's done. He listens to everyone but follows only his own advice. He doesn't question the morality or the ethics of his job. He is unconventional, difficult, yet compassionate and considerate. He abides with no variance from the means he has chosen. <u>By whatever means necessary</u> might be his code. When Dr. Kimble says "I'm innocent," Lt. Gerard says "I don't care." He knows it is not his job to pass judgment, but rather to catch his prey by whatever means necessary. He is insightful, intuitive, and even with a loyal following, basically a loner. We get the feeling that he is respected for his work but not necessarily for his person.

Now, at the beginning of the story Lt. Gerard has absolutely no personal relationship with (and very little knowledge of) Dr. Kimble. All he knows is that Dr. Kimble has escaped and it is his job to catch him. As a matter of fact, it is simpler for Lt. Gerard if there is no personal relationship -- just the hunter and his prey. Gerard will not stop until he has Kimble, dead or alive.

So, from Lt. Gerard's point of view, what is this story about? Catching an escaped criminal? On the surface, yes, but below that it is more. Remember, in each story, every character is being tested in some manner and the test for Gerard is not whether or not he can catch Dr. Kimble. He is being tested far beyond his expertise as a detective. No one would blame him for giving up the chase after Dr. Kimble jumped out of the culvert, presumably to his death. Lt. Gerard, however, has a higher standard that he has to answer to, and this higher standard exists only within himself. So, again, we have a character that must answer to himself and his own code and <u>must</u> maintain that relationship with himself, or he will die. Perhaps you are thinking this sounds a bit severe, but that is the nature of these characters. And that is the way we must look at them. They are not going to necessarily physically die if they abandon their own ideals, but such abandonment would cause severe damage to their sense of self and self-esteem.

Lt. Gerard is doing more than trying to catch Dr. Kimble; he is attempting to maintain and even strengthen his sense of his own value, not just as a detective but as a person.

What we're looking for here is not the details or the events of the script, but the forces that drive our protagonist and antagonist — their passions and needs, their priorities and values. We are looking for the values that we can all relate to, the universal core of each character.

> I don't know what it would be like to be unjustly accused of my wife's murder. But I do know what it is like to be unjustly accused and I take great pride in my sense of morality and fairness. I empathize with Dr. Kimble.

> I don't know what it would be like to be pursuing a convicted murderer. But, like most adults, I have a job to do. Sometimes simple, sometimes difficult. I take great pride in doing my job well, in completing an assignment. So, I do understand Lt. Gerard's position, and his attitude, his sense of responsibility. And I admire it.

THE EMOTIONAL CORE

The point is: We cannot proceed with other work on the script until we have established an understanding of the morality, the values, the very essences that are driving our primary characters (and thereby our entire story). As we do this work, we are identifying the very core of the project, the heart and soul of the story — the emotional core. It is the director's passion for the story plus the passions, needs, desires, and drives of the main characters that will inform every decision the director makes. When you are in trouble and are trying to answer the difficult questions, go back to the emotional core.

When decisions and choices are made with disregard for the director's passion and the emotional core, the project will begin to veer off track.

> Anecdote: I was sitting in a Warner Bros. executive's office discussing the most recent cut of my film, *Going Under*, an adult comedy that the executive wanted to recut for a younger audience. We were viewing some of the scenes on the executive's office television monitor (not an advisable idea). After viewing one brief scene he turned to me and said "Now, that's funny. They'll find that funny. Leave that in." I turned to him, having grave reservations about his assessment and asked, "Do you find that funny?" "No", he answered without hesitation, "but they will. That's what they find funny." I knew I was in deep trouble. This man, who was not a filmmaker, fashioned himself a surrogate audience for teenagers, although to the best of my observation he shared little with them. We were making a comedy that he didn't find particularly funny, but he was convinced that he knew what our potential audience would appreciate.

Regardless of what studio executives, producers, and marketing people say, I don't believe that you can make a film for an audience with whom you do not share certain sensibilities. Please your sense of humor, honor your morality — then and only then will you make a film that will touch others, and go beyond mere entertainment.

Make the movie <u>for you</u>. This seems like a simple and obvious idea, but it is actually a profound notion, one that in the months to come will keep you grounded. Some people, with all the best intentions, will try to get you to make the movie that will please them. Listen to them — and then follow your own heart.

Identifying the emotional core of your script is the first step toward making the movie that <u>will</u> please you.

With each element of the film, each event, each character choice, say to yourself, "What do I want? What pleases me? How do I want to see this?" If you can do that and answer the questions honestly, then you will stay on track. You will stay in touch with the emotional core.

Here are the questions you must avoid asking: "What do <u>they</u> want? What will please <u>them</u>? How will this affect <u>them</u>?" Or even worse: "What does <u>he or she</u> want? What will please <u>him or her</u>?" This hypothetical him or her being some studio executive, producer, writer, or any other person associated with the project. You're not making this film for them, any of them, individually or collectively. If <u>they</u> want it a certain way, let them make their own movie. You have to make yours. That's your job, and the only reason you're there. You have been hired because you have the sensibility, sensitivity, willingness, desire, ability, and ultimately the courage to make the film <u>your way</u> - for you!

We see films every day that have been marketed for a particular audience — and they feel that way. They may work to a certain extent, but there is always a feeling of compromise and it leaves us all with an emptiness. The film will slip away from us shortly after we leave the theatre. But look at a film like *The Crying Game* or *Pulp Fiction* or *The Player* or *The Professional*. Look at the works of Scorsese, Coppola, Allen, Sayles, Altman, Stone, and Bergman. These are films that were made to please the filmmaker and it shows.

So now you've completed these three initial steps:
1. Letting the script wash over you.
2. Finding your (the director's) passion for the material.
3. Determining what the script is <u>really</u> about.

The initial relationship between you and the script has been established. You have a bond, a contract, an obligation between you and the story. You are now ready to explore telling the story.

TELLING THE STORY

Telling the story is a process that you can employ from now until the film is completed. Without the script in front of you, start at the beginning and tell the story to a friend, an associate — anyone who has not read the script. This may sound like an unusual exercise but in the telling of the story you will begin to embellish certain scenes, certain moments. You may find that you skip certain scenes or events, and you may find yourself working extra hard to make certain events or story points clear. Be aware of these alterations and embellishments, when your listeners are engrossed and when you are losing them, which story points capture their interest and which seem redundant or unnecessary. You are the storyteller and these are your first audiences. Trust your instincts and their responses. They will guide you if you will let them.

This process can be employed throughout the making of the film, even while in production and postproduction. Keep testing your abilities to tell the story and the strength of the story itself as you relate it verbally to the uninitiated listener. You'll be pleasantly surprised.

We are now back to the one-on-one relationship that we emulated, the storyteller and listener. And as we approach this ideal storytelling situation we have to be cognizant of the role of the listener, our audience.

THE AUDIENCE

The audience is an integral part of the storytelling relationship. It is more than a receptor and like any other character, has its own particular needs and desires. It wants to be entertained, intrigued, captivated, and kept involved. If we lose our audience's interest and involvement then the relationship between the storyteller and the listener will suffer and may eventually die.

Within the audience is the deep-seated need for resolution. They want the good guy to catch the bad guy, the two lovers to get together, the innocent man proven innocent, the guilty party punished, etc. We all want that. We all want resolution and balance. But, paradoxically, the moment we get the resolution we so desire we lose interest in the story.

When you are telling people a story in person you are in direct relationship with your listeners. It is a give-and-take. You get immediate responses. You can tell when they are interested and when they are bored. You know when they are engaged, irritated, intrigued, or frustrated. And, like a good scene partner, you will adjust to their responses. You will do what the best storytellers do: keep them intrigued and interested by not giving them the resolutions they want, yet without frustrating, irritating, or annoying them. It is a fine line we walk when the story is on that dangerous edge. It is much easier to stay there when we are in direct and immediate relationship with our audience. Theatre has that immediacy; the actors on stage can actually gauge and adjust to the audience's reactions, and every performance will vary because of that. But in the making of a film, we have no immediate audience. We, the directors, have to become the surrogate audience.

Once we have established a viable bond between the director and the script, and have created a flexible yet dynamic understanding and appreciation for the story to be told, we are ready to include the writer in our process.

Chapter 2

Terms And Definitions

The terms that are defined and discussed below are those that most writers and actors use and will understand. Regardless of an actor's training, or the genre of script, there are certain basic requirements for every character in every script. If these requirements are ignored or violated you will end up with a script, story, or character that is incapable of holding an audience's interest.

The Three-Act Structure

Most stories, plays, teleplays, novels, and screenplays follow some variation of the three act structure. This does not mean that there are necessarily three discernible acts (with the curtain falling as in theatre) but that there are three essential stages of our protagonist's journey. We can define the structure of our story by looking at the arc of our central character.

In the first act our central character is taken from a life of innocence, naiveté, and predictability into a world of stress, conflict, challenge, and uncertainty. During the course of the first act our protagonist usually has a choice, whether or not to continue the journey. If he chooses to return to the uncomplicated life, then our story is pretty much over. If he chooses to take on the challenge (or is forced to continue the journey), then our protagonist reaches a point where there is no turning back. This point of no return is the end of our first act. Our antagonist (or intervening character) appears in the first act heightening the danger and conflict for our protagonist.

Dr. Kimble, from the life of successful and respected doctor, is tried and convicted for the murder of his wife. He is on his way to prison when a series of accidents and attempted escapes (by others) leaves him suddenly free. He runs but is faced with a major decision: run for your life or return and prove your innocence. Lt. Gerard is on his trail and he knows it. They have their first face-to-face confrontation (in the dam culvert). Dr. Kimble throws himself into the rushing water. Presumed dead by all (except Lt. Gerard) he takes the dangerous road, the one that could cost him his life. He changes his identity and heads back to Chicago where his fame is now an obstacle. He makes a commitment to prove his innocence and clear his name (and his wife's). There is no turning back.

The second act takes our protagonist into uncharted waters, the world of the unknown. This phase of the journey has ever increasing obstacles. The closer our protagonist gets to his objective, the more danger he faces. This is usually the longest phase of the journey as our protagonist and antagonist are constantly being tested. As we approach the end of the act our protagonist is faced with another major decision: a choice which could irrevocably change the course of his life.

Dr. Kimble learns that it is his associate and friend, Dr. Nichols, who is ultimately behind the death of his wife and that he, Dr. Kimble, was the target. Suddenly the stakes are higher, the risks are greater, and even though Dr. Kimble has identified and located the one-armed man, Sykes, his job is not done. Facing Dr. Nichols openly and publicly is the ultimate challenge.

The third act plunges our central character into the abyss as he races toward the conclusion of the journey and (usually) success.

Dr. Kimble confronts Sykes on the subway. There is a fight and Kimble leaves Sykes handcuffed to the subway car. He heads for the hotel where Dr. Nichols is accepting an award and he confronts him directly, openly, publicly. Gerard is pursuing Kimble and Kimble is pursuing Nichols. Kimble needs to prove his innocence by implicating Nichols, and he will do so or die trying.

This is a fairly typical three-act structure. If you look closely at most well-crafted plays and screenplays, you will discover a similar structure.

Each act contains a certain number of sequences and scenes. And each sequence or scene contains a certain number of events and behaviors. What we want to examine is how the characters and their objectives function in the telling of the story.

OVERALL OBJECTIVES

Each character, every character, has an overall objective (see Diagram 1) that she is attempting to complete or achieve during the course of our story. This objective spans the entire time of each character's involvement in the story.

Objectives are always expressed as verbs. They are active. They always imply an action that needs to be taken.

Examples of objectives: to convince, to find, to change, to persuade, to seduce, to hurt, to heal, to blame, to discourage, to shame, to deny, to attack, to teach, to ridicule, to threaten, to destroy, to test, to empower.

OVERALL OBJECTIVE

| ACT ONE | ACT TWO | ACT THREE |

Diagram 1. Each character has one overall objective that remains consistent for entire story.

27

Using *The Fugitive* as an example let's take Dr. Kimble (Harrison Ford's character) and Lt. Gerard (Tommy Lee Jones's character). In *The Fugitive*, Dr. Kimble's overall objective is *to prove* his innocence in the death of his wife. It's that simple. For Lt. Gerard his overall objective is *to capture* Dr. Kimble. Again, very simple. But in their simplicity, these overall objectives are all encompassing. They encompass all that these characters are involved in for the entire film.

Often a character will not achieve her overall objective, but if the character does, then that character's storyline is finished and she is no longer necessary to the main story. If it happens to be the protagonist or antagonist whose overall objective is achieved, then the story is over. It's time to roll credits and go home.

Take a look at the final moments of *The Fugitive*. Dr. Kimble has finally located and captured the one-armed man who did kill his wife, thereby proving his innocence, and Lt. Gerard, finally aware of Dr. Kimble's innocence, has just captured Dr. Kimble. And when these two overall objectives are coincidentally achieved at about the same time we (the audience) all know the movie is over, and the credits roll. All through the movie we have been championing Dr. Kimble to find the one-armed man and prove his innocence and we have been championing Lt. Gerard to capture Dr. Kimble (although not before he catches the one-armed man) and achieve his goal. But as soon as either or both of them accomplish these tasks, we're finished with the movie.

> A note on the audience / story relationship: Regardless of what a lot of studio executives and producers will tell you, it is not our job to give the audience what it wants. Let me explain. True, the audience wants a good story whether it's a thriller, a mystery, a love story, or science fiction. Basically they want a well-told story, but a well-told story involves refusing to give the audience what they want. As the audience is watching *The Fugitive* they want Dr. Kimble to escape, find the one-armed man, and prove his innocence. But as soon as this happens the audience will lose interest in the

story. So, the longer we keep the audience from getting the resolve they desire, the longer we can keep them with our story.

Consider a typical love story. The two lovers are destined to be together forever. And we want that. We want them to be together, loving, caring, with lives uncomplicated by stress and danger. But if you give that to us in the first reel or two of the film you'll lose us. The longer you deny us the satisfaction and tease us with the possibility of a satisfying ending, the longer we'll stay with you. We'll moan and groan with every plot twist that seems to take us further away from <u>our</u> objective, but in the end we'll thank you for it, because it will be a story well told.

It's important to understand that the audience, from the outset of the story, is quickly aware of the overall objectives of the main characters. We get behind these characters and their objectives very quickly and passionately. And we want our characters (whether heroes or antiheroes) to succeed. But, if we can't discern the overall objectives of our main characters, or find these objectives unworthy or trivial, we will lose interest in the story. We have all had the experience (too often unfortunately) where we have just simply lost interest in the film we are watching. However, it's not the film itself we are losing interest in but rather the characters and their overall objectives.

Each character has an overall objective that carries him or her for the length of time he or she is in the story. I put it this way because some smaller characters achieve their objective before the story is over. All this means is that their participation in the story is over, and they no longer function as necessary elements.

As we break the story down into acts we can see that each character has an objective for each act (see Diagram 2). The objective for each act is more specific in nature than the overall objective. For example, Dr. Kimble in *The Fugitive*, in order to prove his innocence, has to escape and return to Chicago. That's the first act. In the second act he has to identify and locate the one-armed man, and in the third act he has to confront his best friend who betrayed him and eventually prove his innocence.

OVERALL OBJECTIVE

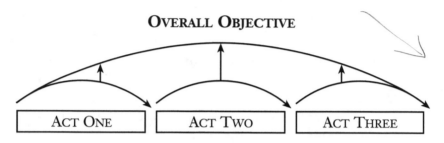

Diagram 2. Each character has one objective for each act and this objective is an attempt to fulfill the overall objective of the entire story.

The important thing about the objectives for each act is that they must support the overall objective. The objectives must be specific steps in a valid attempt to achieve the overall objective. If they are not, then they won't work for the story and we (the audience) will lose interest.

As we continue to break down the script into smaller sections (sequences, scenes, and even beats), we will see that within each section each character has a specific objective (see Diagram 3). Each of these objectives <u>must</u> be a valid attempt to achieve or fulfill the overall objective for the act. Otherwise it doesn't belong in our story.

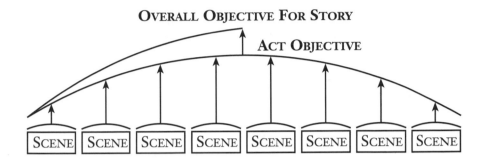

OVERALL OBJECTIVE FOR STORY

ACT OBJECTIVE

SCENE SCENE SCENE SCENE SCENE SCENE SCENE SCENE

ACT

Diagram 3. Each character has one objective for each scene which is attempting to fulfill the objective for the act which in turn is attempting to fulfill the overall objective for the story.

Take a simple event in *The Fugitive*. Dr. Kimble buys hair dye and shaving equipment (objective? to change his appearance) in order to return to Chicago (objective? to get to the hospital) in order to examine hospital files (objective? to identify the one-armed man) in order to clear his name. If the smaller but equally important objectives are not being pursued in order to achieve the larger objectives, then they don't belong in our story.

OBJECTIVES (INTERNAL AND EXTERNAL)

Objectives fall into two categories, internal and external. External objectives can be defined as those objectives that we are aware of by simply observing the behavior of the character. They are the objectives that are pursued through the character's action. Dr. Kimble dyes his hair and shaves his beard. The external objective of changing one's appearance is very clear. But at the same time there may be internal objectives operating. Internal objectives have more to do with the inner workings of the character, his own struggle within himself and often with himself. As Dr. Kimble is dying his hair and shaving his beard, he may be dealing with an internal objective of overcoming fear or humiliation. He may be struggling with a sense of self-betrayal. Or he may be struggling with his own sense of guilt and self-hatred.

31

There can be a myriad of things going on inside the character while we are observing the outward behavior. Quite often there are two objectives operating, one internal and one external, and it is often the struggle between these two that creates the wonderful complexity of the character. The external objective is what we see and observe happening, and this is very much under the watchful eye and control of the director. The internal objective (and internal obstacles as we will see) is very much the world of the actor. This is where the actor "writes" his own material and creates his character. We will examine this more thoroughly in Chapters 6, 7, and 8.

OBSTACLES (INTERNAL AND EXTERNAL)

Drama is created out of conflict and obstacles are the key to conflict. Without obstacles there is no conflict and thereby no story. Obstacles are the obstructions that our characters face in attempting to achieve their objectives. If there were no obstacles, the characters would achieve their objectives in a nanosecond. Seriously. No obstacle, instant success — and then the story is over. We all deal with obstacles every day. They are a natural part of life.

Obstacles come in three categories:
  1. Other characters.
  2. The environment.
  3. The self.

Other Characters

These are the most common and most easily perceived obstacles. Characters are always obstructing each other. It is the cross-purposes of characters that keep them in conflict, and thereby hold our interest.

Example: A husband and wife are discussing the future of their daughter. The child is not doing well in school and both the husband and wife agree that some changes have to be made. The husband feels that their daughter is just being obstinate and that privileges should be taken away until she performs better. The wife feels that the school is inadequate and wants to send her to private school. The husband's objective is to convince his wife that his solution is the best choice. The wife's objective is to convince her husband that her choice is the best. Each character is the obstacle to the other. As a matter of fact, and this is often the case, the objective of each character represents the obstacle to the other. If the husband and wife agreed on a common solution, there would be no conflict and probably not much of a scene. But because they are obstacles to each other we now have conflict and a scene can evolve.

The Environment

The environment itself is an obstacle: when you're trying to get from one location to another on a busy, crowded street; when it is raining; when you have to climb the mountain; when the train is late; when the room is too big or too small; when there are too many things in the room so you can't find what you are looking for; when the bridge is washed out; when the power goes out, etc.

Example: The husband and wife are still arguing about the future of their child. But now let's place them in a crowded elevator. Suddenly the environment of strangers around them becomes an obstacle that they share. Or, let's place them in a car, the husband is driving, it's rush hour, and he's impatient. Now the environment of the crowded highway is an obstacle to the husband, but maybe not to the wife. Maybe she's finding the slow pace of the traffic pleasing to her, conducive to her objective, giving her more time to talk to her husband. But he finds the traffic an obstacle because it interferes with his concentration on his objective. Now let's place them in their living room. There are dirty dishes and glasses

33

left over from a small party. The wife feels the need to clean up the room even as she has this discussion with her husband. The dishes are an obstacle to her, they interfere with her concentration, although they may not affect the husband at all.

As you can see from the above examples the change of a location or the elements within a location can significantly alter the nature of the environmental obstacle.

The Self

Internal obstacles are those aspects of a character which inhibit the character's progress toward the objective. They are the subtlest and frequently most powerful obstacles. Character and environmental obstacles are easily defined. Internal obstacles are more elusive and open to interpretation and their existence may only be suggested in the script.

> Example: The husband and wife are still arguing about the best solution for their daughter. The husband, as we mentioned before, places much of the blame with the daughter. But let's assume for the moment that it was the husband who insisted that their daughter go to this particular school because of financial reasons which he never mentioned to his wife. He still has these financial concerns and is unwilling to address them with his wife; he knows that the school choice was an incorrect choice but he can't admit it. All of these feelings of guilt, shame, and embarrassment become internal obstacles for the husband. Without this history and without these feelings the husband would be operating in a very different manner. But the internal obstacles actually operate to keep the husband locked to his objective of blaming the daughter.

> Or, looking at it another way: Let's assume the husband has been bragging to his friends about how bright his daughter is and how

they don't need to send her to a private school since private schools are only for mediocre students and that good students, like his daughter, can do well in any school. Now the husband has a different set of internal obstacles to deal with, and this can significantly alter the nature of his performance.

Let's look at the wife. Suppose that the wife's mother has been berating her for not placing their daughter in a private school and that the wife has always felt a bit of shame about it. Or let's suppose that from the wife's point of view the husband has always been a penny-pincher when it came to their daughter. She is afraid to discuss these feelings with her husband but is determined to protect her daughter. These feelings would fuel her objective, but her fear of discussing her feelings becomes an obstacle. Perhaps the wife fears that she is always too demanding with her husband and she ought to be more lenient. This fear is clearly an obstacle if she also genuinely believes her solution is the best.

It's important to understand two points: First, these internal obstacles are not written specifically into the script, they are *implied* by the script and by the behavior of the characters. Second, the internal obstacles are the arena of the actor. This is where the actors do their best, most significant, and most personal work. With the slightest adjustment of an internal obstacle, the scene will be altered. We'll deal with this more in Chapters 6, 7, and 8.

MEANS

Means are the ways in which the character/actor attempts to achieve her objective. Objectives are expressed as verbs. Means are expressed as adverbs. For example: quickly, seductively, casually, forcefully, boastfully, distantly, aggressively, calmly, etc.

It is the means that define the action in the scene.

> Example: Our husband is trying to *convince* his wife that it is indeed the child's fault (and not the fault of the school) that she is not doing well. There are many ways he could attempt to convince her. He could be forceful and domineering because that has worked in the past. Then again he could choose to be compassionate and reasonable, or he could choose to approach his wife seductively and coyly. Or he could be submissive, beaten, and put-upon.

> These are all means. The objective remains the same. The dialogue in the scene remains the same. But the manner in which the character/actor chooses to pursue the objective can vary greatly. Again we are in the working arena of the actor; that is why I characterize this as the character/actor. These are choices the actor (in conjunction with the director) is making. Often the means are only implied in the script. A character does not have to stay with one means for the entire scene and it is actually the shifting between different means that can give the scene and the character new dimensions (see Adjustments on p. 38).

ACTIONS

An action is a means made active. It is the actual physical and behavioral manifestation of the means. An action is a result of the objective plus the obstacle plus the means to overcome the obstacle.

> Example: If our husband has elected to be forceful in his attempt to convince his wife, what action, what behavior will most clearly demonstrate and communicate this forcefulness? Perhaps it begins to affect his manner of movement, stance, or physical attitude. Perhaps his voice will take on a new timbre. Or perhaps he is more demonstrative even to the point of throwing his

weight around, throwing things, threatening. Or, with the same means, he may demonstrate his forcefulness by planting himself in his chair at the head of the table and refusing to move until he gets his way. These are very different actions even though we have the same objectives, obstacles, and means.

The wife may have elected a means of displayed patience, choosing to wear her husband's resistance down. But what action can she take? She could choose to be very attentive, yet calm and determined. She could also choose to involve herself in one of her favorite soothing pastimes such as knitting or planting. Or she could choose to just sit quietly, attentively, patiently listening to her husband. These are all very different actions with the same objective, obstacle, and means.

The action is a manifestation of the means.

INDEPENDENT ACTIVITIES

An independent activity is a character's involvement in a specific behavior that has it's own purpose, it's own objective. Ironing, straightening the room, washing dishes, knitting, reading a book, or playing with a dog — these are all independent activities. They may or may not have anything to do with the central action of the scene.

Example: Our wife, while totally intent on persuading her husband to adopt her plan, has elected to fold the laundry during the scene. This is an independent activity. The manner in which she folds the laundry will tell us much about what is going on with her emotionally. If she is folding in a light-hearted fashion, almost playful while her husband is bellowing at her, we will feel that she is not affected (or won't allow him to see that she is affected) by his behavior. If she is folding the laundry in a very tense and precise manner with all her energy focused on each crease as her husband is bellowing at her, then we will feel her tension and discomfort.

Again, we are in the arena of the actor. But, as we will discuss in more detail later, it is crucial that the director understand these various forms of expression and how each aspect of the actor's process affects the other.

ADJUSTMENTS

An adjustment is a change of means and/or action. When a character is attempting to achieve an objective, the longer the character stays with a particular means and does not overcome the obstacle, the bigger the obstacle becomes. When the character determines that the approach he is taking will not produce the desired results the character (consciously or unconsciously) makes a change, an adjustment.

> Example: Our wife, still intent upon convincing her husband that their daughter should be in a different school, has initially elected to approach her husband in a calm and rational manner (means). But part way into the scene it becomes clear to her that she is not getting through to him and she will have to change her approach (adjustment), so she shifts to a sterner more demanding attack (new means). Then perhaps a little later in the scene she finds that this sterner attack is counterproductive because her husband is now becoming belligerent (his adjustment), so she shifts into an impatient and distant mood (her second adjustment).

The above example may seem a bit mechanical and calculated, but I am sure you can see how this works. Remember, these attributes are merely reflective of how we all behave in our daily existence. We all select means to achieve our ends, display various actions, get involved in various independent activities, and constantly make adjustments as we find the obstacles growing in front of us. It is important to note that much of this work is done intuitively by the actor, although some actors make these choices consciously and with much calculation. More about this in Chapters 6 and 7.

PUBLIC AND PRIVATE LIVES

Every character has a public side and a private side. All characters go through their day attempting to present themselves the way they want to be perceived. We all do this. We all want to present our public self so that people will think of us the way we desire to be seen. But underneath this public persona is a private self — the real person. And this private self can be, and often is, diametrically opposed to the public persona. It is this difference between the two selves that often creates the inner conflict in a character, the private self generating the internal obstacles. It is the struggle between these two selves that often leads to great performances.

> Note: the creation and control of the private self is the work of the actor. Again, the nature of this private self is often suggested by the script, but it is up to the actor to fully create this aspect of the character.

> Example: Let's assume that our tenacious wife is presenting herself as being calm, controlled, and extremely rational. We may have no idea that under that exterior is lurking a woman who is agitated, frenzied, and irrational. She may be hiding it that well. Her husband may not even know, but she knows because she can feel it. The husband may be presenting himself as confident and perhaps even a bit arrogant. But underneath he may be feeling uncertain and a little ashamed. This may be what is creating the internal obstacles and causing internal conflict.

Windows Of True Nature

Even though we want to present only our best side, there comes a time when the private self slips through. We have all had experiences when suddenly we see a new side of someone, when unexpectedly a radically new behavior slips through, sometimes only for a moment. Perhaps it was due to the stress or the importance of the moment that some hidden aspect of this person was suddenly revealed. And then, just as quickly as it arrived, it is gone, hidden again. This is what we call a *window of true nature* — a moment in time when the private self slips through and is suddenly exposed. It is usually not the intention of the character and often the character is not totally aware of what has happened. But what it affords us, the audience, is the opportunity to witness a deeper layer of the character.

> Example: Our husband and wife are in the middle of their argument. He is confident and arrogant (hiding his uncertainty and shame) and she is calm and rational (hiding her agitation and impatience). Then, in a brief moment, she suddenly snaps, loses her cool for only a word or two — "*Harold, please!*" — and we see the anger that has been residing under the calm exterior. And then it is gone. Harold, whose confident exterior has now been threatened by her brief outburst, responds with a weak and submissive "*I'm sorry!*" and then a moment later he composes himself and the cover of confidence returns. These are both windows of true nature.

Besides exposing the true nature of a character, these windows also indicate much about the conflict between the private and public. If a window opens only under severe stress and it takes energy for the character to close the window, then we can assume that the conflict between the private and the public is significant. If, on the other hand, the window opens easily at any time and the character can close the window easily, then we can assume the conflict is lesser. Either way the conflict is there.

Note: Once we, the audience, have witnessed a moment of true nature from a character we never view that character the same way again. Even though that character may return, with all conviction and clarity, to the same objective and means and actions that he/she was previously involved in, we have a new insight into his/her personality. We have witnessed a piece of the private self.

There is a wonderful scene in *The Fugitive* where Lt. Gerard (Tommy Lee Jones) is alone in his office, looking out his window over the cityscape of Chicago. It is one of the rare moments that we see him alone, but what we glimpse for a moment is his sense of isolation, his loneliness. And as he looks over the sprawling Chicago below him we even get a slight feeling of his frustration and a touch of sadness. All interesting insights into the private self of this very complex man.

Again, and this can't be stressed too often, with all of these above terms we are talking about the arena of acting. This is where an actor creates, fine-tunes and controls a character. In Chapters 6, 7 and 8 we will be discussing this in more detail as well as how a director can work with these tools in an appropriate manner.

CHAPTER 3

WORKING WITH WRITERS

The writer is potentially your greatest ally in the entire filmmaking process because the writer's point of view is closest to yours. The producers (who would like to think they share that position) really have too many other areas of concern (budget, schedules, finances, studios, actors, designers, the crew) and therefore are unable to share that singular vision in the telling of the story. The actors are only with you for a part of the process, and their point of view is through their characters. The writer is the only other artist strictly concerned with the telling of the story in the best way possible. You need an ally who shares your concerns and who will be an objective third eye.

If it is your intention (and I certainly hope that it is) to take your writer on the entire journey with you, then you need to establish a solid collaborative relationship from the outset.

THE WRITER / DIRECTOR COLLABORATION

Writers should write and directors should direct. It's that simple. The writer has brought the project to this point and now the director is joining the journey. It is not the director's role to take over the process, or to supersede or replace the writer in any fashion. It is the director's job to guide the writer (and the script) through the rest of the process to the completion of the film. The writer's function is to maintain a writer's point of view on the script and the story. It is very important that you and the writer maintain your individual roles and that neither attempts to supersede the other. As in a good marriage or any healthy relationship, the two parties have their distinctive roles to play, separate but supportive.

Expressing Enthusiasm

The first rule of working with a writer is to express enthusiasm.

Think for a moment about the writer's process. The writer had an idea, a notion, a burning question that needed to be answered and this idea was nurtured into a story that eventually became the script you have been reading. During this process the writer considered and either rejected or accepted many possible characters, events, conflicts, and revelations. The script has possibly gone through several rewrites before it was released to be read by you and others.

Writing a script is very much like raising a child — from conception through gestation, the birth, the nurturing process, the struggles and the joys, and finally the relinquishing of the child to the world. The writer shares many of the traits of a proud but nervous parent. We need to approach this "parent" with an enormous amount of respect, appreciation, and admiration. The first thing to do when you are responding to the script (the "child") is to express genuine enthusiasm.

This initial expression of enthusiasm cannot be a false sentiment because, if it is, then your relationship with the writer will eventually fall apart. If there is nothing of substance in the script which genuinely excites you, then you should not be attempting to enter into this relationship. If you do not have enthusiasm for the entire script (in other words if you have serious reservations about some aspects of the script) but there is sufficient enthusiasm for you to pursue the project, then be honest, tell the writer what you are enthusiastic about, whatever it may be (the theme, the characters, the intentions of the project, the relationships).

From the beginning you need to establish a relationship of mutual respect and trust, where no one dominates (the same holds true when working with actors). It must be a relationship based on the notion that through shared mutual interest, passion, desire, and collaboration, you will be able to achieve a result that surpasses either of your individual abilities. This relationship needs to be initiated and maintained by you, the director.

THE WRITER'S VISION VS. THE DIRECTOR'S VISION

It is important to understand and accept that writers and directors see the work (the script, the story) from very different perspectives. The writer's tools are story, structure, conflict, characters — all expressed through language. The writer works diligently structuring the story, developing character histories and backgrounds, arcs, working out the act breaks and the turning points. The writer works from emotional impressions and impulses, sensing intuitively where the material should go, what scenes should be explored and rendered. More often than not the writer's characters tend to take over, speak for themselves, the writer serving as a conduit for the characters' expression.

The director's tools are more three-dimensional and interactive. Telling the story with elements of design, movement, camera, music, and most importantly the behavior of the actors (characters), the director develops feelings, emotions, and relationships that exist on many levels. With a vocabulary that includes colors, movements, visuals, lighting, sound and human activity, the director translates the writer's work from the language of words to the language of behavior. It is the director's job to take what is implied or suggested by the script and turn it into credible human behavior, to create living, breathing, three-dimensional characters on the screen (or stage) that will bring us to a deeper understanding and experience of the story.

Keep these differences in mind. Understand that each collaborator in your film comes from a different perspective and does not necessarily share your concerns, point of view, or agenda. Each artist comes from the strength of his craft which needs to be recognized, nurtured, and honored by you.

Take time with the writer to explore your individual sensibilities. Get to know more about each other before you begin to work on the script.

DISCOVERING THE WRITER'S VISION

For the moment you and the writer need to put aside the crafts of writing and directing in order to get in touch with the personal passions and core issues that are compelling both of you to tell this story. Remember, the craft that is the mirror of your soul is also the mask. It's time to go beneath the craft and get into the heart of the artist.

Each of us, as we express ourselves through our art, reveals aspects of ourselves. Our feelings and our life experiences are informing our choices, coloring our perceptions, directing and guiding our expression. This is usually not conscious but intuitive. Our life experiences, the harsh and the beautiful, the glorious and the painful, the pleasing and the disappointing, shape our expression.

Even if a writer is drafting a screenplay based on a subject matter that is truly foreign to him (or contrary to his life experiences), his life experiences will still inform his choices. A writer could be crafting a script such as *Lethal Weapon* — a "buddy" movie — and even though he may have had no experiences in such escapades or adventures as his two protagonists, his choices in the relationship of these two men will be deeply colored by his own life experiences, his own buddy relationships whether with a brother, a friend, his father, uncle or someone else. Most likely it will be a combination of all of these relationships that will inform this new relationship he is creating.

A writer will often craft fantasy relationships, whether desired or feared, and not necessarily recreate relationships she has experienced. The new relationships may be a projection of what she wishes would have occurred rather than what *did* occur. The point is: you need to get beyond the story and get to the source: the life experiences that are informing the story.

If we, as directors, don't at least make an effort to understand the writer's perspectives (as informed by her own life experiences), then we will have a hard time understanding and collaborating with her.

This exploration with the writer is done primarily through the key relationships within the story.

Identifying Key Relationships

Relationships are at the core of every story. Without relationships we have no story, and in every script there are key relationships that are the foundation of the story. For example in *The Fugitive* we have: 1. Dr. Kimble and his wife, 2. Dr. Kimble and his profession, 3. Dr. Kimble and his peers (especially the doctor who betrays him), 4. Lt. Gerard and his career 5. Lt. Gerard and his surrogate family (his crew) 6. Lt. Gerard and Dr. Kimble. And there are more.

It is through our understanding of the writer's personal point of view of each relationship that we can begin to see the writer's personal vision.

Talk with the writer about these relationships, not in terms of the script but in terms of his/her own experiences. Talk about husbands, wives, and significant others — about careers, mentors, bothers, sisters, co-workers, peers and adversaries, and how you and the writer have experienced these various relationships. This is more than a probing of the writer's personal life, it is a sharing of two lives. By showing your willingness and desire to share your own experiences with the writer, you create a safe place. Never ask a writer to go anywhere that you are not willing to go.

Listen carefully as the writer tells you about his experiences. Get to know the prejudices, fears, desires, and dreams. Remember that this is the sensibility that is informing the story. Be aware of where you agree and where you differ. Again, we are not trying to achieve synthesis but rather a comprehensive understanding between you and the writer.

As you tell the writer of your experiences and your opinions, watch her reactions. Listen to her responses. Besides exploring your individual thoughts and experiences, you are also developing an awareness and sensitivity to each other.

Once you have a sense of what it is the writer *really* wants to say and you can place that in conjunction with what you want to say, you will feel the journey beginning. A vision will begin to be defined. You and the writer (and eventually the actors) are the keepers of the vision, and this is where the journey starts.

ESTABLISHING THE GENESIS OF THE STORY

Behind each and every script is a very personal objective. The writer is driven by the burning desire to answer some personal questions or resolve personal issues through the realization of the script.

At this point you don't want to impose your personal identification with the story on the writer, but rather take the writer back to where he originally got the idea for the story and then move forward through his process to the point of the completed script.

You can simply ask the writer, "Where did you get this idea? What prompted you to write this script?" and you will get a quick answer. But often it is not enough. When we probe more deeply we often find that there is a burning desire within the writer to explore some more personal issues through the writing — and that is what we are look-ing for, the personal issues. We want to get beyond and beneath the intellectual and cognitive or commercial reasons for the script.

Some writers will resist your probing into this very personal territory. They are not like actors who are eager to explore their own issues in order to come to a clearer understanding of the script and their own personal identification with it. Writers usually want the script to speak

48

for itself, and often it does, but you need to understand the writer's personal identification with her story.

Proceed in a very respectful and cautious way. Go on the journey together. Demonstrate that you are willing to be as open and honest in your expression as you ask the writer to be and you will create a trust that is more important than anything else at the moment.

The writer has only one opportunity to have this story told and at the moment it's with you. This is not like producing a play where there can be several productions of the same script. With a film there is one production and one production only. So when the writer turns the script over to you, it is often with trepidation. You need to instill confidence that you will handle this "baby" with as much love and attention as the writer has. And you must let him know that you intend to respect and honor his intentions in every aspect in the realizing of the film.

This does not mean that you are necessarily going to give the writer control over the film or render every aspect of the film exactly as the writer sees it. It only means that you will honor his intentions as you interpret them.

You are a translator, an interpreter, but you have to make your own film. It will most likely not be the film the writer sees in her mind. That would be the writer's film - a different film because there would be a different director. But — and this is very important — it does not necessarily mean that there has to be a separation between writer and director. It does not mean that you and the writer eventually have to part company because your views of the film differ. If it is understood from the beginning that you, as the director, are going to make your film of the writer's script while honoring, understanding, and incorporating to the best of your ability and sensibility the writer's intentions, then there is a greater likelihood that your collaboration will flourish.

Once you have established the genesis of the project, work forward and discuss the various stages of the writer's process. Identify the writer's journey from original concept to the completed script. Read earlier drafts of the script, discuss the various stages of development. As best you can, comprehend the journey the writer has taken so far.

MELDING THE WRITER'S VISION WITH THE DIRECTOR'S VISION

The likelihood that you will find the writer's vision for the script to be identical with yours is very remote. Don't look at this as a problem or disadvantageous in any way. This will almost always be the case and quite honestly it is an advantage. Like in any healthy, balanced relationship between two strong, determined and creative people, there will be a system of checks and balances wherein the combined efforts of the two will certainly surpass either individual's sole effort.

Listen to your writer, the ideas, the impressions, the visions. Don't discount them no matter how absurd or impractical they may seem. Remember, they come from a source of truth, the passion that originated this script. If an idea seems ridiculous, understand the intention of it and the desired effect. At this point the intention and the desired effect of an idea are much more important than the idea itself.

> For example: Let's say the writer has written a particular scene between the two main characters that you feel is not only unnecessary but also impedes the development of the two characters and their relationship. Perhaps you feel that you need a totally different scene at this point. First, try to understand where the writer is coming from. Don't just dismiss the scene as a bad idea or poorly written. Get to the notion behind the scene. Go to the source. Chances are you will eventually come to a place where you agree, not necessarily on the scene in question but at least on the impetus that brought the writer to the creation of the

scene. And if you find that you don't agree on the impetus or the core reason for the writer's selection, then you have come to a more basic disagreement and *that* needs to be discussed.

Make sure that in your disagreements you are discussing a core issue. Disagreeing over the quality of a scene has no value if you don't agree on the function of the scene itself.

POINT OF AGREEMENT

When you disagree on a basic issue in the story or how you see the story rendered, stop and back up. When you hit a *point of disagreement*, back up until you find yourselves at a *point of agreement*.

> For example: Imagine that you each have a very different point of view about the nature of a certain key character in your story. Let's say that the writer sees this particular character as a deceptive, lying cheat, a person who cannot be trusted. And perhaps you see this person as an unfortunate pathological liar who should have our sympathy and empathy, a character that could eventually gain our respect, even our trust.

Obviously this difference in perception will affect the story in a significant way. Rather than arguing about the character and your individual visions, go back to the genesis of the character. Determine as best you can why and how the writer determined the role and function of this character in the story.

Go back to a *point of agreement*. Find a place in the development of this character where you and the writer can agree. Perhaps you agree on the function of the character in this story and your only difference of opinion is in the general behavior, or how other characters see this character. When you find a point of agreement start working forward again. You now have a greater chance of agreeing on the rendering of the character itself. It may be that one of you may eventually come around to the other's point of view. Or you may reach a compromise. Or you still may disagree on the nature of the character, but since you do agree on the function of the character you will decide that this function will remain intact. Perhaps you will tell the writer that you can experiment with the character in the casting or rehearsal process, testing both of your visions. Or perhaps the writer agrees to consider some rewrites on the character in order to bring it closer to his vision or your vision. This is collaboration.

GOING FROM THE GENERAL TO THE SPECIFIC

It is important when working on the script, whether it is with the writer or with the actors, that you always go from the general to the specific. When discussing the script (or a character) start with the overall script, the overall arc of the story or the character, and work your way down to the specifics.

The steps involved, going from general to specific:
1. Discuss overall themes and premise of screenplay
2. Discuss overall events (major events) of screenplay and how they reflect the themes.
3. Discuss overall characters (starting with major characters) and how their arcs reflect themes of story.
4. Discuss sequences, scenes, and finally specific moments.

Note: In Chapter 7 ("The Rehearsal Process") we will discuss how this process is used with the actors and in Chapter 9 ("Postproduction") how it is also employed while editing.

Your first analysis of the script with the writer will begin by discussing the overall structure of the story. Look at how it moves in its large strokes, the acts, then the sequences, then the scenes, and eventually work yourself down to the specific moments. Just as we go back to the emotional core of the story to ground ourselves when we are examining the *function* of any aspect of the script, we also need to go back to the overview of the entire story when considering the *reworking* of any aspect of the script.

Start with the story's overall premise and make sure you and the writer are in sync. Ask yourselves, "Is this the best way to tell the story? Is this the proper first act, second act, third act? Does this sequencing of major events in the story support our premise?" If so, then we can begin to examine the finer details: the sequences, the scenes, the individual moments.

You don't have to agree on everything. As a matter of fact, where you disagree is where you may eventually discover new insights, deeper meaning, and greater potential. Having different points of view concerning the purpose of a particular scene or character could lead you to discover a third and more significant purpose for that particular scene or character. You may discover elements within the scene that are throwing one or both of you off track or misleading you. You may find that a certain character's behavior within the scene is setting up expectations or being interpreted by one or both of you in such a way as to create misunderstanding.

You may decide that a rewrite is not necessary and leave the scene as is. But whatever you do it will be an informed decision, not an arbitrary one.

As you go through the script with the writer, stay with your vision. The struggle between you and the writer (and between you and the actors, designers, and others, as we shall see later) is vital to the growth of the project. Fight for what you believe in, but at the same time be open and available to the other point of view. If there is something the writer is trying to communicate and you don't see it, be honest and say so.

Remember, if you don't get it, chances are a great percentage of the audience won't either. The story has to work for you in order for you to translate it to the actors and then to the audience.

53

As a director you are *not required* to have all the answers. However, you do have to ask all the right questions and make all the decisions!

On the other hand, when the writer confesses that she doesn't see eye to eye with your vision or your interpretation of a scene, make it your job to make your vision crystal-clear. Don't say, "You're the writer and I'm the director and you'll see it when it's on the screen." Chances are there are some assumptions or misconceptions in your points of view that are clouding the issue, and once you work through these even you will be clearer on your concept. Differences of opinion are healthy and can lead to greater discoveries. Welcome the challenge. Out of resistance comes growth.

THE PROCESS OF REWRITES

Rewriting is a very delicate and difficult process (as I am so keenly aware as I rewrite this book). As writers, we are always aware that our work can be improved, but it is always a question of how. The *objective* for the rewrite is usually pretty clear. The *obstacles* may be a bit vague, but we are aware of them. It is the *means* that is often totally elusive. How do we rewrite our work in order to achieve the clarity and the impact we desire? And what could we lose in the process? Every change in a script alters it. There is a gain and a loss. Astute writers are aware of what will be gained and what could be lost from the alteration.

It is in the rewrite that your relationship with the writer can become strained so you have to approach this phase cautiously and respectfully. There are several aspects of this process that have to be considered:

1. Determining where you feel rewrites are needed — "black holes" and "what ifs"
2. Determining the writer's ability to rewrite
3. The director-writer relationship during rewrites

54

4. If the writer can't deliver the needed rewrites
5. Bringing on a new writer
6. Readings

DETERMINING WHERE REWRITES ARE NEEDED

Black Holes

In your telling of the story or even in the first readings of the story you probably began to notice snags in the storyline — bumps that you had trouble getting over or moments that you just couldn't explain away. Maybe there were adjustments in the characters that seemed unmotivated, or arrivals and departures of characters that seemed forced or contrived. Perhaps you didn't feel properly prepared for a certain scene or sequence every time it came up, or maybe a certain character seemed to lose his drive (objective) at a key point. I call these "black holes."

Black holes are moments in the story that seem so out of line with the rest of the story that we get stuck and are unable to continue with the story. We stop and try to justify or rationalize the particular moment, event or information (or lack of information) that has us baffled.

A black hole only becomes a problem when the moment in question is essential to the telling of the story. If it is not essential, then it can just be removed or eliminated through a simple rewrite. But if it is essential then we have to deal with it in a different manner.

Black holes come in many forms. It could be a piece of information in the story that just doesn't jive with the rest of the story or a character who seems to appear too conveniently. This character may help the story move forward but also may leave the audience baffled. A common black hole is when a character suddenly spews a piece of information and we wonder where or how she obtained this information. More subtle are the black holes that go against the nature of the character itself; i.e., a moral character who suddenly lies, an ill character who is conveniently strong when needed, a determined character who suddenly becomes submissive. Often this will occur for only a moment (long enough to achieve whatever is needed in the furthering of the story) and then it will be gone — but so will the audience. The suspension of disbelief lasts only so long.

As directors, we are always on the outlook for black holes in our story and it is our job to resolve them. There are basically three ways to deal with black holes: ignore them, cover them up, or point a finger at them.

IGNORING THEM.

You can choose to ignore the black hole with the hope that the audience will never notice. But if *you* have noticed it then there is a great likelihood that a great part of the audience will notice as well.

COVERING THEM UP.

You can cover up a black hole by creating a smoke screen. This is very often done. Look closely and you will notice how music or editing or special effects or just the high energy of drama will cover up some of the biggest black holes in cinematic literature. But again, if the audience suddenly gets the feeling that a great wall of wool is being pulled over their collective eyes they get very suspicious — and they pull away from the story.

This happened for me in a very important sequence in *Forrest Gump* — the cross-country running. We are led to believe that Forrest, with a great pain in his heart, ran zigzag across this country for 3 1/2 years, never stopping. He became a folk hero, created many notable quips and sayings ("Have a nice day", "Shit happens"), and even attracted a following of fellow runners. And then one day he just stopped running (as he tells us in his narration) and decided to go home.

This, for me, was a huge black hole. It abandoned the reality of the film. It violated the world of *Forrest Gump*. It ignored the function of a key element in Forrest's character — his reason for running. Forrest runs to avoid pain and humiliation. The dramatic choice of having Forrest engage in an extraordinarily long run after Jenny has abandoned him is perfect. He is running from pain, but the pain is *inside him* and he can't run away from that. In the film (and in the script) they chose to make the running about Forrest engaging in another extraordinary event, that is, about him becoming a folk hero. They felt the black hole and were trying to cover it up with the beard, the excessive running, the following. However, these choices were no longer serving the overall objective of our main character. These events have nothing to do with Forrest's desire to connect, to have a family.

This should not have been a public moment, but rather a private moment. If the sequence had been treated as Forrest learning *to connect with himself*, of Forrest learning that he can't run away from himself, then it would have worked brilliantly. It is the major turning point in this movie — the one that trusts us into the final act. Forrest needs to learn that *he is enough* before he can achieve his objective of the connection, the family. This could have easily been achieved with the running and narration. Right after this sequence Forrest, still sitting at the bus stop, learns that he is only a few blocks from Jenny's house. A key moment! He is that close to his objective!

POINTING A FINGER AT THE HOLE.

This method, if done properly is foolproof. You simply acknowledge that there is a black hole. Let one of the characters bring it up. If it is a sudden change in behavior on the part of one of the characters that is creating the black hole, let another character mention it as being uncharacteristic. If it is a piece of information that is conveniently coming out that creates the black hole, let that be acknowledged. If the story is taking a convenient leap from one assumption to another with the hopes that the audience will follow, acknowledge it. Once the audience is aware that *you* are aware of the black hole and that *it is all right with you*, then they won't get stuck.

What Ifs

Another area for rewrite exploration is where you feel that objectives, obstacles, means, or actions haven't been fully explored within a scene. This is where we go into the "what if" mode. We ask ourselves, "What if this character did this or that instead of what she is doing? What if she didn't stay in the room, what if she stayed longer, what if she pursued her objective in a different manner. . . etc." Remember, we are not talking about changing the events of the screenplay or the outcome of the scene, but rather exploring the manner in which the scene might be played in order to emphasize or clarify the character's objective.

Let's take a key moment in *The Fugitive* and explore the "what if" possibilities.

Dr. Kimble is in the hospital, disguised as a janitor, and he has just obtained the information he needs. The objective for the scene has been accomplished! He sees a young boy, in critical condition, being misdiagnosed. He stops. He is asked by one of the doctors to wheel the boy into an examining room. Dr. Kimble is torn between his obligations as a doctor and his need to escape. He wheels the boy into an elevator, does a quick examination, makes a note on the patient's record and wheels him into an <u>operating room</u>. He even gives the attendant specific instructions. He takes the time and places himself in greater risk.

58

It is pretty clear what this scene is all about but have we really explored the internal conflict? What if someone sees Dr. Kimble make the examination? What if Dr. Kimble leaves the patient for a moment (tending to himself first) and then gets pulled back? What happens if someone recognizes him — or thinks he does?

All we're doing here is exploring the range of possibilities in our head. Often we will find that the scene works best just as it is, but we will know that it does because we have taken the time to explore other options. All we are doing is rehearsing in our heads and exploring in our imagination.

DETERMINING THE WRITER'S ABILITY TO REWRITE

Different writers rework their material in different ways and with varying degrees of success and thoroughness. There are some writers who love to rewrite and with the suggestion of an adjustment in a character will get so caught up in the process that the entire script will be altered (maybe way beyond your intentions). Some writers feel that their script is perfect and needs no adjustments whatsoever. Some will, at the request of an adjustment to a scene or a character, change two or three lines and consider that sufficient. Some writers can make the adjustment suggested but have little awareness of the "ripple effect," or how that adjustment will affect other scenes or other characters. Suffice it to say that the nature of rewriting for writers covers a wide range, and it is your job as the director to determine how your writer works.

It is best to test the waters with a small rewrite. Pick a scene which is not reaching its potential and where you feel you can clearly articulate your vision. Communicate your needs to the writer in the following manner.

1. Discuss the scene in question with the writer. Make sure you both concur as to the purpose of the scene in the overall structure of the film. Go back to a point of agreement. If you don't come

from a place of common understanding then the discussion will start from a point of disagreement and it will be difficult to resolve the scene to the satisfaction of either of you.

2. Bring the writer to the point where you see the scene not fulfilling that purpose (if it did fulfill the purpose then you wouldn't need a rewrite on the scene) and concur on the fact that it indeed does not fulfill the purpose.

3. Discuss the possible adjustments that can be made in the scene. Trust that the writer will pick up on your vision, energy, and point of view and will begin to see the possibilities that can be solutions to the problem you have addressed.

4. Let the writer rewrite.

Give the rewrite a chance. Read it several times. Seeing a rewrite is a bit like seeing a new cut of your film. At first it is a shock and perhaps nothing seems right because chances are the rewrite is nothing like what you had imagined — only because you imagined how <u>you</u> would have rewritten it.

I have found that sometimes a writer will give me exactly what I asked for in a rewrite — word for word. Perhaps I have even acted the scene out, improvising dialogue, and the writer put it down verbatim. You would think that I would be pleased, that it would be exactly the scene I wanted, but often that is not so, because the tone of the new scene is not the tone of the writer. It is not coming from the writer's sensibility anymore, it is not the writer's voice. It is my voice and it just doesn't sound right.

In a similar way, the voice of the writer may not sound right to you the first time you read the scene, but like in the script wash that we discussed in Chapter 1, let the new scene wash over you a few times. Give the new scene a chance to be heard for what it is. Then respond.

Sometimes it is helpful for you and the writer to read the new scene out loud. This will give you a chance to hear the scene and the writer a chance to give voice to what he has written. Give it a chance and then respond honestly.

WORKING WITH THE WRITER ON REWRITES

It is the director's job during rewrites to maintain objectivity at all times, while at the same time being the subjective passionate storyteller. It's a delicate balance between being totally involved in the telling of the story and remaining objective enough so that you become a valid judge of the work.

As you enter the rewrite process, remember that you don't have to go into the rehearsal process with the perfect script, but you do have to go into rehearsal with a script that is not going to hamper you or your process with the actors. You need a script that you know you can make work in its present form. This is crucial because once you cross that threshold into rehearsal other forces take over; the storytelling process begins to roll along with an increased momentum and this energy begins to carry everyone along with it. Make sure you are ready to take the ride.

If the script was perfect (and I guess that means that every nuance, every emotion, every plot development, every character adjustment was clearly and fully delineated), then what would be left for you, the director, and the actors to do? As a matter of fact, if the script did achieve this perfection it might be a fascinating script but it might prove to be a burdensome, redundant, and overly actualized movie. What you need in the script in just enough detail to stimulate, inspire, and challenge you and the actors and the other collaborative artists.

61

Remember, the script is *not* the film. There is a level of the story that is achieved only in performance and another level that is finally achieved in postproduction. It is your job as the director to bring each moment to completion in the final stages of the filmmaking process. It is not necessary to have the scene fully realized on the page. We will discuss this more in Chapters 7, 8 and 9.

So, when you are looking at a scene or sequence, ask yourself whether or not the elements you think are missing can be achieved in performance or editing. Will some of the other disciplines such as music or sound effects help complete the scene? This is important because you want to leave a certain percentage of the film open to interpretation, to the accident that can happen in rehearsal or in production or that can be created in the magic of postproduction. It is your job to take the script to its final expression. It is not the job of the script to *be* the final expression.

With the rewrites you must go from the general to the specific. Even though I have suggested above that you take one scene and use that scene to examine the writer's rewriting abilities and techniques, you must begin the rewriting process by discussing the entire story first. Make sure both you and the writer have agreed on the premise, the theme of the story, and that you are coming from the same perspective, the same passion. Go back to the point of agreement on the entire story. Examine the story structurally (see Chapter 4 for script breakdown). It does you no good to rework a scene or a sequence if in fact there are overall structural problems. Look at the overall objectives of each character and then the obstacles. Look at the major adjustments; make sure that the large strokes are working for you before you begin picking at the smaller moments. The general to the specific.

THE RIPPLE EFFECT

Be aware of how a proposed rewrite will affect other aspects of the story. A well-written story is a fine web of detail, character, and event; one small change can alter other details and this fine web may begin to unravel.

This is called the *ripple effect*. Some writers are more adept at seeing the ripple effect than others. Some work so subjectively within the characters that they lose sight of the overall picture. You, as the director, need to be aware of the possible ripple effects that the writer may overlook. This is a very healthy relationship between you and the writer; the writer is subjective while you are objective.

REVIEW: THE STEPS TO REWRITES

1. Express enthusiasm.
2. Approach rewrites carefully. Working with the writer is similar to working with the actors — you're treading on sensitive personal ground and you need to step cautiously.
3. Test the rewrite waters with the writer.
4. Try one scene.
5. Be aware of the writer's response to your suggestions.
6. Be wary of overenthusiasm or rigidity.
7. Go back to a *point of agreement*.
8. Make an effort to understand the writer's reluctance to make change. You may gain greater insight into the script by understanding the writer's reluctance than forcing her to see your point of view.
9. Be the devil's advocate to your own suggestions, especially if you feel the writer is too eager to accept them.
10. Be aware of the ripple effect.
11. Go from the *general* to the *specific* and back.

What we want is a healthy journey down the middle of the rewrite road — you and the writer, side by side — a healthy give-and-take. Defend the writer's work if you feel he is too eager to throw it out. Challenge the work if you feel he is too rigid. And then, challenge your own suggestions. This is collaboration.

Remember, if the writer had not wanted to enter this process of collaboration she would have written a novel.

IF THE WRITER CAN'T DELIVER THE REWRITES

There are many different opinions about the role of the writer in the filmmaking process. Many directors and producers will simply dismiss the writers from the process and even bar them from the set, from dailies, and postproduction. Others will be more protective of the writers and their role in the filmmaking process.

> I once heard a comment from a top director upon reading an interesting script: "Who shall we get to do the rewrite?" without ever meeting or discussing the script with the original writer. I guess the assumption was that this must be the best the writer could do or that since the script was not fitting with the director's current vision then someone else will have to rewrite it. This is not an isolated example, it happens often. Fortunately, most directors are more respectful of the writer.

I am of the opinion that if the writer was capable of bringing this script to its current level, enough to arouse my interest, then the writer is most likely capable of bringing it to the higher level that I envision.

In theatre the attitude is very different than it is in film and television. The playwright is the sole owner of the work, forever. No one purchases a play or options it. (We are not discussing the optioning or purchasing of the films rights to the play.) A producer can only license a play. Therefore, a playwright is never replaced. As a matter of fact, a playwright, according to the Dramatist Guild agreements, gets director approval. The playwright, except in extreme or abusive situations, is never banned from a production. When I read (as I recently did with Anne Rice's *Interview with a Vampire*) of a screenwriter being removed from a project prior to production and then not seeing any aspect of the film until it is complete, I am baffled. What is the point of this? Anne Rice said that she saw elements in the film that she never wrote, that confused her, and oddly went totally against the grain of her original concept (both her book and her screenplay). Now I am more than baffled, I am disheartened and angered. One of the most vital, valid, and valuable collaborations in the whole creative storytelling process has not only been damaged but destroyed.

Where do we as directors get the idea that our singular vision of a story is so much more valid than that of the original writer that it becomes necessary to totally extricate this writer from the project? What are we saying? We constantly hear the cry about there not being enough good scripts and good story ideas out there, and then when we find one, what do we do? We kill the goose that laid the golden egg. Now, I know that this doesn't happen all the time but in the film community the prevalent attitude is that the writer is expendable, replaceable. And if the writer (in the next draft) doesn't give us the script *we want*, then we'll find someone else who will. Can you imagine treating any other artist that way, especially the artist who originated the material?

Curious, isn't it, that more great literature has come out of the theatre in the past 100 years than out of the film industry. The theatre, which is so poorly financed and offers so little return, even on a hit show, continually produces literature worth publishing and studying. Where is the great literature in the film industry? Is it just an ironic circumstance that the art form that treats its writers with such disdain would produce literature of such little significance?

It is my contention that if we showed respect and admiration for writers in the film and television industry as we do in theatre, screenwriters would be delivering better products and we would be producing better films.

As soon as you believe that the artist is expendable and removable from a work of art, then you cheapen the entire process and diminish the potential of that particular work. You cannot remove one from the

DIRECTING FEATURE FILMS / *Travis*

other without damage. This does not mean, of course, that you cannot enhance the project by the *addition* of collaborators and other writers. We add other collaborators all the time (designers, editors, actors), but there is a big difference between adding a writer and replacing a writer.

If you feel that it may be necessary to bring on another writer, you are in a very delicate position. Even though you feel that the original writer is not capable of bringing the script to the level you desire, you want to keep the writer involved in your process.

But before you add a new writer you need to go through a few tough but necessary steps.

1. Tell the writer that you are considering whether he will be able to complete the writing process alone.
2. Be very clear and specific about what your (and the script's) needs are, where the writer is falling short, and why you think the writer won't be able to fulfill those needs.

These steps are crucial. Be honest, up front, and *include* the writer in your process and your decision.

Inclusion vs. Exclusion

Somewhere during the making of your film you are going to find that some collaborator is not carrying her weight and is actually impeding the process. It will probably become obvious to you that you will need to replace this person. It is not so much the action itself that is important here (although the replacement of any artist is disruptive and causes its own ripple effect), but the manner in which it is handled that will set the tone.

As I was entering the process of directing my first feature film, I was told by a fellow director that I should fire someone in the first week or two in order to establish my position on the picture. This is not an uncommon notion or practice. Many directors will establish their authority and control in the early stages of filmmaking by legitimately firing someone, thereby sending a message to the rest of the crew.

This is control by fear. This is control by *exclusion*.

I am suggesting a different way of handling the same problem: Inclusion.

When you are faced with fellow collaborators who are not measuring up, don't excise, making them the enemy, but instead bring them in closer. Include them in your process and even in the problem that they may have created. What you are seeking here is one of two possible solutions: (1) the artist in question will adapt or adjust and by the very nature of being included in the process will be able to fulfill his function to your satisfaction; or (2) the artist in question will come to a clearer understanding of why he is not able to fulfill your needs and will understand the need to be replaced.

Either way the artist has been given every consideration and opportunity to resolve the problem. Now you are sending out a very different message to the rest of the crew. It is still a message of control and power, which is important, but you are also saying you are willing to face these problems head-on and you expect each collaborator to do the same. This is not power through fear and intimidation but rather through responsibility and communication.

In consideration of our writer whom we have just deemed incapable of completing the job, practice inclusion. Bring the writer to the heart of the problem. Approach the writer as a fellow collaborator who will help you face and resolve a problem, even though the problem may be her inability to deliver an acceptable and shootable script.

Be very specific as to where you see the shortcomings. Don't just tell the writer that it's not going to work. the problem may lie with the writer's scriptwriting ability, or the insight, tone, character development, structure, or cinematic vision. Be specific so that the writer can see and address your concerns. There is always a chance that a miscommunication or misunderstanding had occurred and once the problem is identified it can be resolved between the two of you. Seek resolution through collaboration. Admittedly this is not easy, but if you cherish the relationship you have developed with the writer, then this is the only way to maintain that relationship while still honoring your needs in terms of script development.

REVIEW: THE STEPS TO BRINGING ON A NEW WRITER

1. Practice Inclusion vs. Exclusion.
2. Identify the problems.
3. Attempt to resolve the problems.
4. If you both feel they can't be resolved, agree that you are at an impasse.
5. Agree to bring on another writer to collaborate with both of you (unless writer elects to be replaced or steps aside).
6. Continue the collaboration; the writer is still extremely valuable to you.
7. If you have to part ways, come to that mutual agreement and find closure on your process.

WORKING WITH THE NEW WRITER

When you bring on a new writer, remember, this person is <u>not</u> the originator of the project. This new team member needs to respond to the script much as you have. Find a writer who shares your passion for the material, not just someone who you think can "doctor" the script. The new writer can, and hopefully will, work in collaboration with the original writer, interpreting, extending, and expanding on the original concept. If a new writer is brought on a project with the instructions to "fix" a script, then the perception will be that the script is damaged and unworkable. But if the writer is asked to collaborate with you and the original writer in order to further realize the promise of the script, then the perception will be that the script is working, acceptable, and in need of a fresh eye in order to achieve its full potential.

READINGS AS A PART OF THE SCRIPT DEVELOPMENT PROCESS

In the world of theatre we are constantly developing, testing, and refining new works. One of the procedures we use to test the strength and viability of new material is readings.

For some unknown reason the film industry seems reluctant to embrace this approach. From my experience there is no greater tool in the development process than hearing the script read by a cast of professional actors.

There are three types of readings: cold, rehearsed, and staged.

The Cold Readings

These are unrehearsed readings with actors sitting around a table. Cast the roles as best you can from the actors you know, get the scripts to them a week or so prior to the reading and then just let them come together for the reading itself. It is important to allow the actors to study the script and their roles on their own but not be influenced by the other actors. Keep your direction confined to the nature of their character and their objectives and obstacles. What we want is that magic that happens when actors interact for the first time. Let them go into these first readings prepared, but not overly directed. Tell the actors that you want them to bring their own vision to the reading; you want to see how they see the character. This will please the actors and you will be fascinated with the results.

It is important to cast all of your primary roles with actors who will bring a certain quality to each role. In other words, let's say you are doing a reading of *The Fugitive* and you're thinking about casting the Dr. Kimble and Lt. Gerard roles. What are the qualities that you want to explore in these roles? For Dr. Kimble it might be a gentleness and patience. Or you might want to cast an actor who intuitively brings an edge, a suspicious restlessness. Or you might want to cast an actor who is by nature more playful, open, and gregarious. What we are doing here is experimenting with a 'what if'. What if Dr. Kimble is basically this or that kind of personality? How will that affect the story? And the same thing with Lt. Gerard. You could cast an actor who is meek and insecure, or one who is confident but brash, or one who is proud but arrogant, or one who is humble. Whatever choice you make is going to affect the reading, but you have no idea how. You won't know until you hear the script read with this particular mix. That's the nature of the experiment. That's the excitement of the cold readings. The magic of actors.

You need a couple of good actors who will handle all of the significantly smaller roles. If there is something very specific you are looking for in one of these roles, cast one actor just for that character. Also, it is important to have a good storytelling actor read all the stage directions. Find an actor who can bring life to the often dreary descriptions of scenes and locations and who will keep the energy of the story alive. An actor who reads the stage directions with a lackluster quality will infect the rest of the cast and you will find the energy of your story waning.

During the reading let the story wash over you once again. Listen to the voices, sounds, and rhythms. Be aware of when the story grabs you and when you are getting restless, of when scenes seem too long or too short. Hear the relationships, the arcs, the developments, the adjustments. This is like a first reading, only it is a first *hearing* of the script. Notice the mix of personalities you cast. How does this mix affect the story? Does it enhance it, impede it?

The writer's presence at these readings is crucial. You are now beginning to take the writer on *your* journey as the script is slowly being transferred from the writer's domain to the domain of director and actors. If you want the writer to remain with you as a collaborator, then the writer has to be a part of this transformation.

After the reading, express your enthusiasm and appreciation. Before you launch into your analysis of the reading, take a moment to hear from the actors. An actor's response to a script, especially after having just read it out loud and having experienced the interchange with the other actors, is very special, very unique, and an important part of your process. They have a tendency to be more honest and to be more concerned with the credibility of their characters than they are with the overall story. These points of view will keep you grounded and it will give you your first indication of what actors will be dealing with as they attempt to create these roles on film.

Invite a few trusted friends to the reading. Actors, writers, and other directors are always good. You want to hear their reactions to the story — where and when they were interested or became restless and bored. This is their first viewing of the material. They are a first time audience and their responses are invaluable.

The Rehearsed Reading

For these readings you want to begin to shape the characters and their relationships. These rehearsals should not include the writer. You are establishing a new relationship with the writer; the writer is now moving into the "third eye" role.

In the rehearsed reading you are testing the material and your ability to bring this material closer to the levels you imagine. You will begin to see where the actors are struggling, where the material is supporting them and your vision, and where they have to fight the material. (Fighting the material is not necessarily a problem as we will discuss in Chapter 7.)

Note: For rehearsing these readings see Overall Priorities, Chapter 7. A clear comprehension of the story, your vision, and character histories and relationships are all that is needed.

It is best for you and the writer to confer privately after the reading. Although it is the intention of the actors to please both the writer and director, it is not always best for them to hear your in-depth discussions. When talking privately you can be more specific and honest about the script, the direction, the actors, and other matters. Also, you want the actors in the next reading to be focusing on the needs of the characters rather than your needs in the telling of the story. These readings and discussions will bring you and the writer to a better understanding of your story and how it can best be told.

The Staged Reading

A staged reading is a rehearsed reading that is staged in order to bring behavior and activity to the story. It is the story "on its feet."

The staging in a staged reading is actually quite simple. We are not talking about elaborate sets or props or costumes. We are just allowing the actors to get away from the reading table so they can move within an environment that simulates the environment of the film. In other words, if the scene takes place in a living room establish a couch, a few chairs and table, whatever is important, so that you can get a sense of the physical dynamics of the scene. If the scene is in a car, put the actors in a couple of chairs facing front. The scene will play differently when the actors are forced to look through the windshield of the car than it will if they are sitting at a table across from each other. Or if the scene is outdoors in a large field, let the actors walk about the room getting a feeling for the open space. You want to see how the movement and environment affect the scene and the relationship between the characters.

Do as many readings as you need to address the concerns you and your writer may have. It's also a good idea to audiotape these readings because listening to them again will often bring you to a deeper understanding of the strengths and weaknesses in the script.

THE WRITER AS THIRD EYE IN THE REHEARSAL PROCESS

Many directors and producers dismiss writers as soon as they feel they have secured the best possible script from them, but they are overlooking perhaps one of the most important contributions of the writer — the third eye.

During your readings you have been gradually easing your writer into the role of observer of the process. As you move closer and closer to rehearsal and production, you are going to begin to lose some of your objectivity. During the writing and rewriting process you maintained the objective stance, while the writer kept close to the material maintaining a more subjective and intimate position. As you enter the rehearsal process and begin focusing on some of the more intimate aspects of the script and begin working intensely with the actors, the roles are reversing.

It is a good idea to keep the writer away from rehearsals for a period of time. This is your private work with the actors and the material and you don't need someone looking over your shoulder, second-guessing you. Many writers do not have an intimate awareness of the director/actor process and often, when they observe actors and directors in rehearsal, they either become so intrigued with the process or so thrown by the results of experimentation that they lose their objectivity. And you don't want that. Bring the writer into the rehearsal process when you feel you have a scene or two up on its feet ready to be viewed. You want the writer to be able to respond to your work in exactly the same way you responded to her work when she was rewriting. The writer is now allowing the material (rehearsed and performed) to wash over him and that first-time response to the material in its latest form is invaluable to you. At a later time you and the writer can discuss your intentions and her reactions. But it's important to understand how the director/writer relationship is now shifting and how each of you is there to support the other in the telling of the story.

Explain honestly to the writer exactly how you want her to function in the rehearsal process so that she won't be offended when you ask her to leave a rehearsal and she will know what is expected of her when she is asked to attend.

THE WRITER IN PRODUCTION AND POST

In the production process the writer can be a very important ally and collaborator. This is where many directors, out of a desire for complete autonomy and control, will dismiss or even ban the writers. It is the confident, capable, and flexible director that can permit and even encourage the writer to be his collaborator to the end.

If you have established a supportive relationship to this point and been very clear with your writer about areas of responsibility, you can have a healthy collaboration of checks and balances during the production and post-production process. (See Chapters 8 and 9.)

THE WRITER/DIRECTOR

Changing hats is a difficult but necessary process for the writer/director. Read Chapters 1 and 2 again from both points of view. Understand that you have to assume both roles independent of each other. You have to be tough on yourself. Your writer has to be demanding of your director, and your director has to be demanding of your writer.

It is definitely an eye-opening experience when you as a director sit down with your own script and *treat it as if someone else wrote it.*

IN SUMMARY

Below is a brief reminder list for the three stages of your collaboration with the writer.

SCRIPT DISCUSSIONS
1. Express enthusiasm.
2. Identify key relationships.
3. Determine the writer's vision.
4. Establish the genesis of the story.
5. Begin to blend your vision with that of the writer.

THE REWRITE PROCESS
1. Test the rewrite waters.
2. Go back to *point of agreement*.
3. Go from the *general to the specific*.
4. Look out for *black holes*.
5. Stay objective while writer stays subjective.
6. Be aware of the *ripple effect*.
7. Remember, *inclusion* rather than exclusion.
8. Use readings — cold, rehearsed, and staged.

PRODUCTION AND POST
1. Establish writer as "third eye" for rehearsal process.
2. Let the writer be objective while you're subjective.

CHAPTER 4

THE SCRIPT BREAKDOWN

During the script breakdown we are going to look at the script in a very different way than either of the two previous times (the script wash and working with the writer). The script wash was intended to establish a balanced relationship between you and the script. Working with the writer was intended to establish a balanced working relationship between you, the writer, and the script.

The script breakdown is a clinical analysis of the essential elements of the script. Our goal is to specify how each component of our script is integral to the telling of the story.

STEPS TO SCRIPT BREAKDOWN

The steps to the script breakdown will be discussed in the following order but in practice many of these steps are done simultaneously. For our purposes it is more convenient to look at each of them separately.

1. What Is the Story Really About?
2. Director's Objective for Telling The Story
3. Point-to-Point Description
4. Defining the Acts
5. Character Objectives and Obstacles
6. Analysis of the Script Units
7. Asking the Hard Questions
8. Character Arcs
9. Character Analysis
10. Visual and Aural Design Arcs

We will be using *Forrest Gump* as our model.

> You will not get the full value of this process by only reading what is in this book. Take the time to apply the steps to your own script (preferably a script you intend to direct) and you will begin to see how they will support you as you enter the team selection, rehearsal, production, and postproduction process. As with directing itself, it is impossible to learn until you do it.

The first two steps of the script breakdown (What Is the Story Really About and the Director's Objective for Telling the Story) are the same steps we took in our initial work on the script in Chapter 1, but now they are coming at a very different point in the process. You have now completed your work on the script and your work with the writer and it is time to reassess your relationship to this story. These steps are never, ever completed. You are asking these questions and refining the answers from the moment you get your script until the moment the picture is finished. The relationship between you and your script, like any vital growing relationship, is always changing and challenging.

1. WHAT IS THE STORY REALLY ABOUT?

In order to achieve a cohesive and workable script breakdown, we must begin with a reason for the story.

> *Forrest Gump.* We know that it is the life story of a young, simple man, Forrest, and how, through no fault or design of his own, he affects the lives of those around him. He is a man with a simple, yet positive, point of view of life (as instilled in him by his mother), largely unaware of the effect he has on others as he embraces each new event in life with a refreshing openness and integrity.

Fine, but what is this story <u>really</u> about? We know it is more than just the story of a simple man affecting those around him and how the love

78

of his life, Jenny, eventually comes back to him and becomes a part of his life. But what is it that you want to say through this movie?

"Life is just like a box of chocolates. You never know what you're going to get."

For me, *Forrest Gump* is not so much about the character of Forrest Gump and his adventures as it is an examination of how we perceive our world and our experiences. Do we create the world we exist in? Do we have any effect? Can we really make a difference? Or is it as Lt. Dan says at one point, "Anything that happens to us is controlled by natural laws that govern the universe . . . ! We all have a destiny. Nothing just happens . . . it's all part of a plan, a scheme." And how about Jenny and all of her attempts to affect change in the world (peace marches, antiwar rallies, the Black Panthers, etc.)?

If we look at our main characters (Forrest, Lt. Dan, and Jenny) and their individual approaches to life, we discover three specific approaches producing very different results. The core of this story resides somewhere within this triangle. We see three individuals (a simple unassuming man, a die-hard fatalist, and a restless, frightened rebel) affect each other's life as they try to make sense of a very confusing and complex world. What we discover (or what happens) through the course of events is that the simple unassuming man, through embracing life as it comes, has the most fulfilling and nurturing of life experiences and the most significant effect on others.

This is what *Forrest Gump* is really all about:

> *Our approach to life will create the life we have.*
> *Our assumptions will generate our experience.*
> *What we resist will persist.*

Look at Lt. Dan, and Jenny. If we approach life with a sense of futility and powerlessness (Lt. Dan) then that is the life we will experience. If we approach life with anger and resentment attempting to force a change in our surroundings (Jenny), then we will only attract those very things that we are trying to eradicate (violence, hostility, abuse). But if we approach life unassuming, as an open book with blank pages on which we can write (Gump), then we will create a life experience that is open and honest.

Now, look at your script and ask yourself what it is really about. Go beyond the obvious. Don't settle for the quick easy answer. Find the one which goes beyond the events of your story, taps into your passion, and resides in your soul.

2. DIRECTOR'S OBJECTIVE FOR TELLING THE STORY

We also need to clarify our reasons for telling this story. Without a clear definition of our objectives and what the story is really all about we will be venturing rudderless into uncharted waters.

The director's objective is a very personal statement so some of you may disagree with my objective and that is fine. Each director will have a very different reason for telling this story. What's important is that you, as the director, have to have a clear objective for the telling of your story before you proceed with the script breakdown.

My objective in the telling of the *Forrest Gump* story:

> I believe that most of us live lives that are controlled by our past (whether we are willing to admit it or not). I believe that many of us create a future for ourselves based primarily on our past experiences and that we assume (consciously or unconsciously) that we will live a certain kind of life because that is the only kind of life we have known. Lt. Dan knows a life of military service and preordained sacrifice. In the introduction to Lt. Dan's character Forrest Gump tells us that "Lt. Dan came from one of the oldest

families in America. He was from a long, great military tradition . . . .Somebody in his family had fought . . . and died . . . in every single American war. I guess you could say he had a lot to live up to." And Lt. Dan is determined to fulfill his preordained destiny.

Jenny, as a severely abused child (by her father) and with apparently no mother, brothers, or sisters, will create a life of isolation, her only relationships being cruel and abusive. Because this is the life that she knows, it actually feels comfortable (or familiar) to her. She creates a life that is familiar. Any of us can get trapped in a life created out of our past experiences.

But Forrest Gump doesn't do this. Credit it to his simplicity, his mother, or other factors, Forrest takes life as it comes to him, without assumption, without predetermination, without expectations. He is living totally in the present, in the moment. This is what makes him extraordinary. He is a pure soul. He is Christ-like. It is a sad statement that Winston Groom and Eric Roth had to create a simpleton (who many might consider stupid or retarded) in order to portray a character that the audience would accept as so pure, unassuming, and authentic.

My objective in the telling of this story is to encourage my listeners to reassess how they approach their own relationships. There is a lot we can learn from Forrest Gump if we are willing to set aside our own prejudices and assumptions and simply listen and experience. It is my objective to make the world of Forrest Gump so accessible to my audience that the very experience of sitting for two hours with this film may affect change. I want to make a difference with this film, and I want to do it in the same manner as Forrest Gump, unassumingly. It is my objective to create a film that can affect change by the very nature of it's existence.

We have determined what our script is <u>really</u> about and our personal objective for telling the story. Now it is time to begin the script breakdown.

3. POINT-TO-POINT DESCRIPTION

Write a point-to-point description of the events of your story. This is not meant to be an analytical or flowery description of the story and is only for yourself. It is important that you write it out and not just imagine it. You think you know your story. You think you know the structure and flow of your story, but you will be surprised at what you will discover when you go through this simple but revealing process.

Below is a point-to-point description of *Forrest Gump*.

Forrest Gump begins with Forrest sitting on the park bench, narrating his story and soon we cut to the beginning of his story, the day he got the braces on his legs. We learn that he doesn't have a daddy, and he was befriended by a young Elvis. He meets Jenny on the school bus and they become best friends. Forrest learns to run by running from the teasing boys and as his braces come flying off he discovers a new freedom. Jenny confides in Forrest about her abusing father. Forrest and Jenny grow closer. Jenny's father dies in an accident, and we see that Jenny caused it.

Years later Jenny is going to go off to school and will be separated from Forrest. Forrest saves Martin Luther King from the police dogs during a river baptismal and peace rally (cut from the movie). Forrest, still running from the teasing boys, is noticed by a football coach and suddenly he is accepted into college on an athletic scholarship. Mrs. Gump is very proud. While in college Forrest witnesses the forced integration of a local school with the ever resistant George Wallace at the doorway and Forrest innocently assists one of the young black students into the school. It is televised nationally. Forrest visits Jenny at her college, saves her from her passionate date, and ends up in Jenny's room where they have their first sexual encounter (unsuccessful). As a member of the All American Football Team, Forrest meets President Kennedy. Forrest graduates from college and is approached by the local army recruiter. He joins the army to "let someone do my thinking for me." [End Act One.]

In Act Two Forrest meets Bubba Blue in basic training and Bubba tells Forrest about his dream of owning a shrimp boat. They go through basic together, two slow witted men happy together. Forrest sees Jenny's picture in *Playboy* and thinks that she is just beautiful. He goes to see Jenny folksinging in a club only to discover she is singing in the nude. He tries to rescue her from the leering men. Jenny is furious. Jenny confides in Forrest her dream to "fly away" (we hear her suicide urge under this). She asks him to stay away from her and gets him to promise to run if he gets into trouble in Vietnam. Forrest visits his mom before going to Vietnam and tells her of the "pain in his heart."

In Vietnam Forrest and Bubba meet Lt. Dan. Forrest writes to Jenny almost every day. Bubba and Forrest make a pact to work together on a shrimp boat when they get out. It rains all the time. The rain stops and suddenly they're under a severe attack. Forrest runs but then runs back for Bubba, Lt. Dan, and several other soldiers. Bubba dies. Forrest gets wounded in the buttocks. In the Army hospital Forrest is next to Lt. Dan who has lost his legs and is angry at being saved by Forrest. Forrest learns to play Ping-Pong. Forrest is awarded the Congressional Medal of Honor for bravery. He meets President Johnson and shows him his scar (on his buttocks). Later, at the Washington Memorial, Forrest gets mistaken as a protester in an antiwar rally and is asked by Abbie Hoffman to speak to the crowd. Jenny, hearing Forrest speak, comes out of the crowd and they are reunited. Jenny takes Forrest to the Black Panthers headquarters where her boyfriend Wesley is working. Forrest rescues Jenny from being slapped by the resentful Wesley, disrupting the Black Panther meeting. Later, Jenny tells Forrest of her life on communes and drugs and living in Hollywood and San Francisco, and tells him that he has to stop saving her. Forrest gives Jenny his Medal of Honor. Jenny leaves with Wesley.

The army sends Forrest to play Ping-Pong in China. He returns a celebrity and is on the Dick Cavett show with John Lennon. Forrest runs into Lt. Dan (who is drinking heavily) on the streets of New York. He stays with Lt. Dan to celebrate New Year's and tells him of his plan to buy a shrimp boat. Mockingly, Lt. Dan says if Forrest ever gets a boat, he'll be his first mate. Their relationship strengthens and Lt. Dan protects Forrest from verbal abuse by a prostitute. Forrest is invited to the White House (as a member of the Ping-Pong team) and meets President Nixon. He stays in the Watergate Hotel and reports a disturbance (the Watergate break-in). Forrest is discharged from the army (his time is done), and he goes home.

Taking the money he was awarded for a Ping-Pong promotional Forrest keeps his promise to Bubba and buys a shrimp boat which he names *Jenny*. We learn that Jenny, who is on drugs, is prostituting herself and contemplating suicide. Lt. Dan, a man of his word, joins Forrest on the shrimp boat. A hurricane destroys the shrimp boat fleet, except for the *Jenny*. Forrest and Lt. Dan prosper and Lt. Dan comes to terms with his rage. Mrs. Gump is dying and Forrest returns home to see her. Mrs. Gump gives Forrest her final maternal guidance before she dies. "Remember, don't let anybody tell you they're better than you." Forrest decides to stay near home and gets a new job cutting grass at the football stadium. Forrest shares his wealth with Lt. Dan and Bubba's family.

Jenny returns to visit Forrest. She's burned out. She stays with Forrest to rest. They spend a lot of time together and reconnect. She tries to destroy her past by throwing rocks at her father's house. Forrest asks Jenny to marry him. She says no, that they're just friends. But that night Jenny slips into Forrest's bed and they make love. The next morning she leaves. Forrest is alone again, devastated. The next day "for no particular reason" he starts running, beginning the running sequence that covers 3 1/2 years zigzagging across the country. He is running and thinking about Bubba and Lt. Dan and his momma, but mostly about Jenny. He gathers a following, and then one day he just stops running and goes home. Totally alone. [End Act Two.]

Forrest gets an invitation to come visit Jenny and that brings us to Forrest on the bench, waiting for the bus that will take him to Jenny. He learns that Jenny's house is only a few blocks away and he races there. Jenny is at home and Forrest meets their son, named Forrest. Forrest is shocked but relieved to learn that little Forrest is indeed not slow or retarded. Later Jenny tells Forrest that she is sick and dying. She asks him to marry her. At their wedding Lt. Dan shows up with his fiancée and new legs. As Jenny is dying Forrest tells her about all of his adventures and how she was with him all the time. Jenny dies. Forrest has Jenny's father's house bulldozed to the ground. Forrest says good-bye to Jenny for the last time at her grave. We last see Forrest as he is sitting with his son at the school bus stop. Little Forrest gets on the bus proudly announcing "I'm Forrest Gump." [The End.]

4. DEFINING THE ACTS

The act breaks are my own, indicating where I feel the primary movements of the story are delineated. Let's look at these acts and begin to define their structure and integrity.

An act by act analysis of *Forrest Gump*.

The first act begins with Forrest acquiring the braces and ends with Forrest joining the army. From one support system to another. From one "family" to another. At the beginning he is being supported by his mother saying to others, "Haven't you ever seen anyone in braces before?" and by the end he has a new family, the structure of the army. This is not coincidental. We are beginning with a very strong image of a young boy who not only is limited in intelligence but can barely support himself and is already the object of ridicule. He has no father, he has no friends, he only has his mom. He meets Jenny, who has no mom and a father who abuses her. She is his only friend. She teaches him to run to save himself. When Jenny goes off to college, abandoning Forrest, where does he go? To another family structure, another college doing the only thing he knows how to do — run. Forrest does try to reconnect with Jenny (disrupting her lovemaking with a date) with disastrous results. When Forrest finishes college, an athletic hero with no future and still no friends (except the distant Jenny), he joins yet another structured family, the army.

That is our first act. A young man adrift. Alone. Lonely. Without skills. Without a goal. Searching for security and friendship. And he makes a choice — "to let other people do my thinking for me" — to put his life in the hands of others.

In Act Two Forrest's world changes dramatically. He is now in a male-dominated world (the army) as opposed to the female-dominated world (Mrs. Gump and Jenny). During the first half of the act Forrest is under the control of the U.S. Army. He meets the two most significant men in his life, Lt. Dan and Bubba. He discovers a sense of loyalty, honor, and commitment he had not known before. He finds a real friend in Bubba and they form a bond. His relationship with Lt. Dan is one of admiration and respect (Forrest to Lt. Dan) and irritation and impatience (Lt. Dan to Forrest). Forrest loses Bubba but he saves Lt. Dan. He is bonded to both. Even the story of Jenny takes on a male-dominated tone: Jenny singing nude and being ridiculed by men, Jenny being abused by Wesley. Forrest discovers Ping-Pong, reaching celebrity status again (as he did as a football player), but this appears to have no significance for him. It's reconnecting with Lt. Dan in New York that has Forrest excited. Lt. Dan, for the first time, protects Forrest. Forrest is discharged and it's time to go home.

In the middle of Act Two Forrest is at another crossroad. He has lost his support, the army, and is now on his own. He has to make new choices.

> Note: As I do this breakdown I am finding the celebrity moments (meeting Kennedy, Nixon, Johnson, Dick Cavett, John Lennon, Martin Luther King, George Wallace, Ping-Pong in China) as being some of the least significant moments in Forrest Gump's journey. Perhaps this is because Forrest doesn't

find them particularly significant or perhaps it is because they have so little to do with Forrest's overall objective. Isn't this in part what this story is about? Aren't we saying that the truly important relationships in our lives are not necessarily with people of stature or fame?

My analysis of *Forrest Gump* is not important. (You may disagree with me, and that is fine. I have no investment in convincing you of my point of view). What *is* important here is that this discovery came *during the process* of this script breakdown. I am in effect discovering my own personal connection as I realize that I keep skipping over the celebrity moments, not finding them particularly significant and not wanting to give them significance. Without taking myself through this process I could have very easily approached these moments from a different point of view. The more free-floating dialogue you have with the script, the more you are going to clarify your own personal vision of your film.

An Exercise: Take any scene in your screenplay and just start writing about it. Don't think about what you are going to write. Don't plan it out. Just start writing. Write about the characters, their relationships, the arcs in the scene. Write about the beginning of the scene and what you see and about the end of the scene and what you see. Let your thoughts flow. Don't worry about being right or accurate or profound. Just write. You will see that there will be thoughts emerging that you had never before considered.

In the second half of Act Two Forrest purchases a shrimp boat (keeping his commitment to Bubba) which he names *Jenny*. Lt. Dan, true to his word, joins Forrest. Jenny is spinning out of control. Lt. Dan and Forrest cement their relationship. Mrs. Gump dies. Forrest is now without a family, without structure. He shares his wealth with his best friends and returns home. Jenny comes back to Forrest to heal. He nurses her back to health and asks her to marry him. She says they are only friends. That night she steals into his bed and they make love. The next morning she slips out of the house leaving him again.

Forrest is devastated. He feels as if he has lost everything. He starts to run. [End Act Two.]

Forrest runs for 3 1/2 years, until he can run no longer. Jenny contacts Forrest and he learns he has a son — a family. Jenny tells him she is dying and asks him to marry her. They marry and the family is complete. Jenny dies and Forrest is left alone with his son, young Forrest Gump. He is exactly where his mother was when the story started. He has come full circle. The third act begins with Forrest totally alone, as far away from his objective as he has ever been. He runs but can't run away from himself. He learns to accept himself and goes home, and the family he had been pursuing comes to him.

Now we are beginning to get a feeling for the arcs of each act and can see that each act has it's own integrity and sense of completeness while at the same time thrusting us into the next act.

We'll continue this process by looking at each act in terms of character objectives and character arcs.

5. CHARACTER OBJECTIVES AND OBSTACLES

Each character has an overall objective, that one thing that he/she is attempting to achieve during the entire course of the story (or during the period of time that the character appears in the story).

FORREST GUMP

Question: what does Forrest want throughout the entire film? What single objective drives him throughout this story? Now, it is easy to see Forrest's objectives within specific scenes or sequences, but it is necessary for us at this time to determine his overall objective. And remember, the overall objective is usually general but profound in nature.

One note before we proceed: Because Forrest is actually telling the story that we see (remember he is sitting on the bus stop bench throughout the movie relating his life story to whoever sits beside him), we have to look at the character of Forrest from two perspectives. First there is Forrest the storyteller and then there is the Forrest character (at various ages) in the tale that Forrest is telling. The overall objectives for these two aspects of Forrest's character have to work in sync with each other. We cannot have two overall objectives for the same character. There has to be consistency within the character.

From my perspective Forrest's overall objective is *to connect, to have fulfillment and meaning in his life*. Forrest is always working very hard to make sense of the world around him, not in an analytical way, but in a simple visceral way. Forrest is on a constant search for clarity, comprehension, and connection. In every scene and in every moment of this story, Forrest is seeking a connection, family, and structure.

Note: One trap, or difficulty, in this story in particular (and there are many other stories and characters that fall into this same situation) is that the character of Forrest Gump could be seen as a man who just drifts through life, going wherever the tides take him. And in many ways that is his character. But if we interpret this character (or any character) in this manner then we run the risk of the audience losing interest in the character. As we have stated earlier, it is the strong objectives of the characters (and their apparent inability to achieve these objectives) that keeps our interest. An unmotivated character will become a boring character. So for us to stay interested in a character like Forrest Gump we need to identify very clearly his objectives so that we can always see him as a character with a purpose.

JENNY

Jenny's overall objective may appear easier to define, but you do need to be careful not to get trapped by the obvious.

One note on objectives at this point: There are actually two objectives for each character at any one time. Whether it's an overall objective or merely an objective for a particular scene these objectives exist on two levels, the conscious level and the subconscious level. There are objectives that the characters are aware of (conscious) and then there are objectives of which the characters are not aware (subconscious) (see Chapter 2).

Looking at Jenny's character we can clearly see that she is intent upon making a change — in the world, in her life, wherever possible. So you could easily say that her overall objective is to make a change. She might even agree with you because that is her conscious objective. But what about her unconscious objective? What is it that is really driving her? Is she really trying to make a change or is there some greater ulterior motive? Why is she such a loner? Why is she such a rebel? Why are almost all of her relationships abusive? Why the drugs? Why the suicide attempt? What does she really want?

If we examine her character more deeply we will recognize that Jenny is a wounded soul who is really searching for some kind of identity, or validation, something that will return the self-esteem that was burned out of her by her abusive father. Here is an overall objective that is definitely unconscious and would understandably motivate Jenny's behavior — *the search for validation.*

LT. DAN

Again, as with Jenny, it would be easy to settle for the obvious overall objective with Lt. Dan. We could easily say that this is a guy whose sole purpose in life is to fulfill his destiny, his legacy. He is dedicated to service and sacrifice for his country just like all the men in his family before him. But is that really his overall objective? It appears to be what he is *consciously* trying to achieve but isn't there perhaps a stronger overriding internal objective?

Like Forrest and Jenny, Lt. Dan is a loner searching for significance in his life. Despite Lt. Dan's best intentions to follow in the footsteps of the men in his family who came before him, his deeper intention is to do just the opposite. To survive. To not follow in their footsteps. To make a difference by surviving rather than sacrificing. To break the cycle.

It appears that we have an internal objective (to survive) that is in conflict with an external objective (to sacrifice). This happens frequently and when it does happen we are usually left with a character like Lt. Dan in tremendous conflict.

> Note: If you want to create a character that is highly conflicted or you want to add more conflict to a character, just make sure that the external objective and internal objective are in conflict.

Now, there are two ways of dealing with Lt. Dan's situation. We can either work to bring these two seemingly conflicting objectives under a cohesive overall objective (thereby removing the internal conflict), or we can recognize the dramatic potential of this conflict and allow the apparent contradiction to exist.

Maybe he wants to sacrifice but just *thinks* that his sacrifice is to die in Vietnam. He doesn't realize that he needs to make another kind of sacrifice, to <u>break</u> the tradition of his family and make a difference. In many ways he is right; there is a legacy, a preordained destiny, but it just may not be what he had imagined. His sacrifice seems to come in a very different form. Losing his legs. Losing his ego (working <u>for</u> Gump rather that being the boss). Learning humility and compassion. There is also the feeling that he <u>can't</u> be killed, whether in Vietnam or on the shrimp boat during the storm. Maybe part of his sacrifice is simply to live.

Let's look at a couple of secondary characters and their overall objectives:

Mrs. Gump

Even though she appears in only a few scenes in this story she is definitely a significant character and we have to recognize that her overall objective (to instill a sense of pride and independence in her son, Forrest) is going to have a great deal of impact on the character of Forrest. It is actually the philosophy of Mrs. Gump that instills in Forrest his sense of balance in a world that views him as being stupid or ignorant.

Bubba

Bubba appears in only one sequence of the film (Vietnam) yet his character has a lasting influence. We don't actually get to know Bubba that well, but we do know a few important things about him. He is also simple, like Forrest, and like Forrest he has a dream. He has a dream of one day owning a shrimp boat. His overall objective (and remember the overall objective covers only the amount of time the character is in the story) is to finish his time in Vietnam and then get his shrimp boat. Bubba needs a place where he can feel important, in charge, useful and intelligent, and the shrimp boat is such a place. Here is a simple man who can say, "I know what to do with my life. I have it all worked out. I know how I can make a difference."

Identify the overall objectives for <u>all</u> of the characters in your script. Remember, each character does have an objective, no matter how small the part. And as you go through this process you will begin to recognize that your story is really a result of the intermixing of all these characters and their overall objectives. This is a slow and difficult process but the rewards are enormous.

OBJECTIVES IN ACTS, SEQUENCES AND SCENES

As we continue the script breakdown we need to look at the script in smaller sections (acts, sequences, and finally scenes) and identify the objectives for all the characters involved. We need to determine that the objectives for the smaller units of the story do indeed support the overall objectives of the characters.

For instance, Forrest's character in the first act of the movie.

In the first scene he is sitting on the bench, alone at first. He discovers the feather and places it in his briefcase with his other possessions. The black woman sits down next to him, he offers chocolates, comments on her shoes, and then begins to tell her about his first pair of shoes.

What is Forrest's objective in this scene and how does it support his overall objective? It seems clear that Forrest simply wants to talk and he makes the assumption that others will be willing to listen. Even if the black woman doesn't respond, he will tell his story. This desire to connect obviously supports the overall objective.

In the next scene (flashback) we see young Forrest getting his leg braces fitted and even though he says nothing in the scene (and for the next few scenes) we can sense a determination in him. Part of this determination is reflected in his mother's attitude. There is a determination to make it work, to be normal, to be accepted, to overcome. He's trying to make a connection, to fit in with his world. And what of Mrs. Gump? What is her objective in this scene? Even though she is having Forrest fitted with these awkward braces she is still attempting to achieve her overall objective: make life as normal as possible for Forrest, instill in him pride and self-assurance.

In the next series of scenes we see Forrest adjusting patiently to the world around him. Silently attempting to fit in, find his place. Then he meets Jenny and even in that scene on the bus he is trying to find his place. Jenny tells him where he fits in — next to her. "Like peas and carrots," he says later. And what of Jenny's overall objective? Her search for her own identity, for a sense of belonging. She is sitting on the bus, alone, isolated, and she offers Forrest a seat. Even at this young age she recognizes a like soul and reaches out to someone with whom she feels safe, who makes her feel worthy.

Look at every scene in your script and make sure that the objectives of each character are there to support their overall objectives. If they don't then you need to reconsider the scene and/or your interpretation of it.

You may feel that this work is tedious (it is) and unnecessary (it is not, it is vital). I ask you, how can you begin to direct a scene in your movie if you are not fully aware of how that scene supports the larger movement of the story (for instance the act of which it is a part) and how it supports the overall movement of the entire story?

> Too often I have seen wonderful scenes that have been rehearsed, shot and edited, but when they were cut into the movie they suddenly didn't work. They seemed superfluous, unwieldy. The problem was, they were directed without the clear understanding of how the scenes were intended to support the story.

Have you ever been sitting in a film and suddenly you find that you are losing interest during a particular scene? (We discussed this in the last chapter regarding the running sequence in *Forrest Gump*.) Don't blame the writing, don't blame the acting. Take a look at the scene and ask yourself, "Why is this scene in this movie?" If it's not clear then you have your answer as to why you are losing interest. In the final analysis it is the director's job to make sure that every scene works to support the overall story. If the writing is not supporting the story, then deal with the writer. If the performances aren't supporting the story, then deal with the actors. The bottom line: it's the director's responsibility.

OBSTACLES

Without obstacles there is no drama, no story. Without obstacles our characters would have already reached their objectives. So, as we do the script breakdown, it is important that we define the overall obstacles that each character faces as well as the obstacles in each act, sequence, and scene.

FORREST GUMP

So, if Forrest Gump's overall objective is to connect with others on some significant level, then what are his obstacles? Remember, obstacles come in three categories (with other characters, with the environment, and with the self).

Other Characters

It is very easy to see from the first moment of this story that Forrest is going to face severe obstacles with other characters. Even our own snap judgment of this man brings us to the realization that others are going to make similar quick assessments. With every step Forrest is going to encounter other characters who are going to impede his progress toward his objective. There is the laughter, the ridicule, and the prejudice that keep others distant. There are very few characters (Mrs. Gump, Jenny, Bubba) who immediately accept Forrest as a person. Then there's Jenny's attitude (low self-esteem) and Lt. Dan's attitude (arrogance) that also are obstacles to Forrest.

The Environment

The environment plays an enormous role in this story, whether it is the jungles of Vietnam and New York City, the shrimp boat with the ocean and its elements, the distance across the country (when he's running), or the physical distance between Jenny and Forrest. On a more subtle level we have the rain, Jenny's room, Forrest's own house, and Lt. Dan's apartment. As we continue our breakdown of this script, we will see that the physical environment plays a significant role in Forrest's journey.

There is another environmental level in this story — the political and social environment — that is very important. As we examine these obstacles we could easily say that they are really character obstacles but in reality it is the political and social environment. There are powerful forces (opinions and attitudes) that are in opposition to

Forrest's objectives: racism, prejudice, war, competition, jealousy, sexism, abuse, distrust.

The Self

These internal obstacles give this story its deepest resonance. As we look at Lt. Dan and Jenny we will indeed find that it is their internal obstacles that are responsible for the greatest amount of conflict in their lives. But what about the character of Forrest? It is highly unusual to have a character who appears to have so little internal conflict, but let's not assume that there is no internal conflict or obstacles. We know for certain that one potentially significant internal obstacle is Forrest's awareness of his own limited intelligence. He knows that he is not as smart as the average person yet he seems to overcome this obstacle with relative ease and grace. Another internal obstacle (and this may seem contradictory) is his undying love of Jenny. It is often the case that objectives (Gump's determination to have Jenny in his life) become obstacles to other objectives. In one significant sequence Jenny comes back to be with Forrest, he nurses her back to health, and for the first time they actually sleep together. But the next morning she is gone again leaving Forrest devastated. For the next 3 1/2 years Forrest does nothing but run and run and run. He runs across the country several times in apparent contradiction to his overall objective. He seems no longer intent upon connecting with anyone, but he is connecting with himself. He had become his own internal obstacle and he needs to deal with that before he can proceed.

As I stated earlier, this process for Lt. Dan and Jenny might be a bit easier. With Lt. Dan we can readily see the rage and determination to become a significant soldier as internal obstacles. We can see the family legacy has placed such a cloud over him that it will take extraordinary effort to overcome these obstacles. And Jenny is obviously battling severe internal obstacles: lack of self worth, abandonment, low self-esteem, and fear of commitments.

What becomes apparent relatively quickly as we begin this breakdown is that the most important obstacles that our main characters are battling are internal. The major conflicts in this story are within the characters themselves. We will discuss in Chapter 7 ("The Rehearsal Process") how the creation and adjustment of obstacles is a very powerful directorial tool. Recognize that when we are dealing with a story wherein the major obstacles are internal, then we know we are going to be facing a very delicate directorial process.

6. ANALYSIS OF THE SCRIPT UNITS

We will now look at the sequences and individual scenes. Now that we have established what the entire story is really all about, done our point-to-point description, act definition, and defined the objectives and obstacles of our characters, it's time to look at these smaller units and determine how they function in the telling of the story.

Consider this: You have a story (such as *Forrest Gump*) which in real time is a thirty-year story (it starts in 1951 and ends in 1981). But we have only two hours in which to tell this story. We can't take thirty years; that would be ridiculous. Since we only have two hours, we have to be sure that each component of this story (every episode, scene, sequence, or event) is absolutely necessary and functions to move the story forward. If it's not an integral part of the story, then it shouldn't be in it. We have very little time to tell a very big story, and every moment has to count.

Look at some of the units in *Forrest Gump* and see how they function in the telling of our story.

The opening sequence of *Forrest Gump*.

Sequence of scenes (with scene numbers from final draft dated 12/9/93):

A1. The feather falling from the sky and landing, by chance, at Gump's feet.

1. Gump sitting on the bench begins his story, the shoes of the woman next to him reminding him of his first pair of shoes.

2. 1951 — Doctor's office. Forrest getting his leg braces.

3. Street. Forrest walking with his mom. Voice-over (v.o.) tells us where he got his name.

4. Flashback (f.b.) showing Forrest's namesake as KKK member and getting hung by mistake.

5. 1951 - Forrest and his mom walking home. Mrs. Gump admonishing townsfolk who gawk at Forrest's braces. We hear her "don't ever let anybody tell you they're better than you, Forrest . . . if God intended everybody to be the same, he'd have given us all braces on our legs . . ."

6. Mailbox corner. Forrest and Mrs. Gump turn into a small dirt road.

A7. Boarding house. Forrest and Mrs. Gump arrive at their home as Forrest (v.o.) explains that this boarding house has been in the family for years.

7. 1954 - Principal's office. Principal is explaining to Mrs. Gump that Forrest is different from everybody else, that his I.Q. is only 75. Says he has to go to a special school. Mrs. Gump refuses. Principal asks pointedly if there is a Mr. Gump ("he's on vacation") and states that they might be able to work something out.

8. Boarding house. Night. Forrest sitting outside listening to principal's orgasm. Principal comes out, makes condescending remark to Forrest. Forrest mocks his orgasmic groans.

9. Forrest's bedroom. Mrs. Gump reads to him from *Curious George*. Forrest asks what "vacation" means. "When you go some-where and don't ever come back," she replies. Forrest (v.o.) tells us how his daddy left when he learned that Forrest was slow.

10. 1948 - Boarding house (f.b.). Forrest's father leaving in the middle of the night as Mrs. Gump, with baby Forrest, watches from window.

11. 1948 - Interior of boarding house (f.b.). Mrs. Gump tenderly tucking little Forrest in. Forrest (v.o.) tells us his daddy joined the merchant marines and was buried at sea.

12. 1955 - Freighter. a crane drops a load of bananas on one of the men, Forrest's Dad, burying him.

13. 1954 - Boarding house. Another day. Boarders in rocking chairs as Forrest (v.o.) tells us he didn't notice his daddy missing because people were always "coming and going in our house."

14. Boarding house, another day. Busy with boarders. Mrs. Gump is calling for Forrest and discovers him in his room with one of the boarders, a young singer named Elvis.

15. As Elvis plays his guitar Forrest is swinging his hips furiously, the braces restricting his leg movements. Elvis is impressed.

16. Greenbow Street. Day. Mrs. Gump and Forrest walking, see Elvis on a television in a store window:

17. TV screen. Elvis performing, gyrating just like Forrest was doing. Mrs. Gump is shocked. Forrest (v.o.) tells us how years later Elvis had "sung too many songs and had himself a heart attack or something . . ."

18. A showroom. The aging Elvis is straining in performance. Forrest (v.o.) says, "It must be hard being a king . . ."

These eighteen scenes (about twelve pages) comprise the first major sequence in our movie. (The next sequence establishes Forrest going to school, being teased by the kids, and meeting Jenny.)

A quick note about sequences: There are a variety of opinions and attitudes about the definition of sequences in screenplays. For the sake of this book I am using sequences as a collection of individual scenes that are being used to convey a unified theme or idea. A sequence usually has a beginning, middle, and end. But a sequence does work as a unit with a singular story telling purpose or objective. A sequence may contain as few as two scenes or many scenes (as the opening sequence defined above). I really do not think that it is at all important that any of us agree on the definition of sequences. What is important is that you recognize the power and importance of employing a series of scenes in order to convey specific information in the telling of your story.

Let's look at this first sequence as we continue our script breakdown. First the sequence and then the scenes.

What is the purpose of this sequence? It begins with the feather falling to Forrest's feet, he begins his story, and the sequence ends with him seeing his impact on Elvis. This is an establishing sequence. We establish: Forrest telling the story; his leg braces (Forrest needing support); his mother's powerful protection of him and positive influence on him (he has no father); where they're living (in the South in the 1950s); the fact that Forrest has a low I.Q. We also establish: to what degree his mother will go to give Forrest everything he needs (sleeping with the school principal); that his father was killed in a freak accident; and the innocence of Forrest's first celebrity encounter.

What we have here is mostly back story, the information we need in order to start our story (which begins with the next sequence where he meets Jenny). We can now look at each of the scenes (or even smaller sequences within this larger sequence) and determine how *they* function to support the larger sequence.

Scenes A1 and 1 actually form a small sequence. They comprise one scene, our opening scene. I think it is safe to assume that because the first scene is labeled A1 it was not in the original draft. It's an extraordinary scene (achieved digitally I believe) that sets the tone for the entire movie. The drifting feather, caught on the breeze, brushing up against a shoulder here and a car there and just by coincidence landing at the foot of Forrest Gump. Question: If it had landed at the foot of another person would we have heard a different story? Perhaps. And isn't that the point of the shot (and of our movie) that life is merely a series of coincidental encounters with no apparent or discernible design? As we look at this scene we have to ask ourselves (as we will with <u>every</u> scene in our movie) these four very important questions:

1. Why is this scene here?
2. What would happen if I removed this scene?
3. How is this scene crucial to the telling of my story?
4. What do I need to achieve with this scene in order to insure that it will support my story?

These questions are at the core of our script breakdown. If you are not clear on the importance and necessity of each and every scene (and sequence) in your movie, then you are not ready to direct those scenes. How can you approach rehearsing, designing, storyboarding, staging, shooting, covering, editing, and composing a scene if you are not clear on the function of the scene within your movie? Can you imagine an engineer being asked to design a valve for the space shuttle without being informed of the specific requirements and function of that valve? That would be unheard of. Well, that is what is at the core of our script breakdown, the identification of the specific needs and objective of each and every scene (and element) in our movie.

Note: If we cannot determine a rational reason for a scene we have only two options. Either remove the scene or reconsider (and perhaps reconstruct) the scene in such a way that it will now become an integral part of the story.

Our opening scene — the floating feather. Why is it here? What is its purpose? What would happen to our movie if we took it out? And what do we need to achieve with this scene in order for it to support our story?

If we took it out our movie would begin with Forrest on the bench about to talk to the woman who just sat down. That could work. Our movie could certainly start that way. So, what have we lost? What is it about this feather shot that is so important?

The first shot of any movie, the first beat of any story, will immediately begin to set a mood, a tone, for the entire story. If we start with Forrest on the bench about to tell his story to whoever sits down we have an abrupt and rather jarring opening. We need an opening moment that will draw us into our main character and into our story. The question becomes, what is the nature and tone of that moment and can that be achieved with this feather shot? In other words, don't get caught up in the idea of what a beautiful shot this will be; don't get seduced by a beautifully written scene or sequence. You must think first of what <u>you</u> need to achieve at this moment in your story and ask yourself whether or not that can be achieved with this scene.

So, what do we need to achieve with this opening moment? We want to introduce our audience to the world of Forrest Gump. We want to invite our audience into the world where "life is like a box of chocolates, you never know what you're going to get". Can we achieve that with this feather shot? Now we begin to see the potential of this shot. This is a shot of whimsy. This is a shot of an object floating on the wind, an object that has no control over its own course. This feather could go anywhere, land anywhere. We can easily set the tone for our movie with this shot. We can create the whimsy, the unpredictability and now it becomes apparent that we need to create the feeling that we (the camera) are following the feather and not that the feather is following us. We need to create the feeling that we (the audience) are being drawn into this world and are willing to go wherever this little feather takes us. Perhaps we should start on a blue sky (suggesting that we are starting with a blank slate) and allow the course of the feather to determine the location of our story. And wouldn't it be nice to have a moment or two within this shot that looks like we might end up following another story (other than Forrest Gump's)? Now we have a clear idea of what we need to <u>achieve</u> with this shot in order to make this scene work for our story.

SCENE 1

Now let's take a look at the next scene. Scene 1. The second scene and final scene in this opening sequence. Forrest sitting on the bench. There is a long detailed description of Forrest, his clothes (suit, dilapidated running shoes) and his demeanor (somewhere between slow and retarded with the eyes of a boy). He picks up the feather, puts it in his knapsack between the pages of his book, *Curious George*. He turns to the black woman sitting on the bench next to him and says, "Hello. I'm Forrest. I'm Forrest Gump." He offers her a chocolate which she refuses. He sees her shoes, comments on them and right away we hear two of Mrs. Gump's wisdoms: "Life is like a box of chocolates . . . you never know what you're going to get. . ." and "You can tell an awful lot about a person by her shoes. Where she's been, and where she's going. . ." Then Forrest works real hard to remember his first pair of shoes and how his mama said they could take him anywhere because they were magic shoes. Then we cut to 1951 and Forrest getting the braces fitted on his legs.

> Note: Before we go any further with the breakdown of this sequence we need to recognize that these two scenes are actually part of a much larger sequence (all of the park bench scenes) and that this sequence needs to be considered as a whole. It is the thread that is holding our entire movie together. In fact, it is the present of our movie, and everything else (except of course for the scenes that directly follow the park bench scenes in Act Three) is in the past — flashbacks. It is a mistake to look at these park bench scenes as a mere theatrical device allowing us to cut to any scene or sequence we desire. These park bench scenes are the heart of our story.

Contained within this sequence of scenes (and beginning with this opening scene) is the impetus for our story: Forrest's need to communicate, to connect.

Equally important, Forrest on the park bench is our access to his story. Remember, we are *listening* to his story and then visualizing the events. Forrest is our tour guide and our connection to him needs to be strong, confident, and secure.

We know that we need this scene in our story at this point in order to establish our narrator, Forrest Gump, and to allow him to lead us into *his* story. But, what do we need to achieve with this scene in order to have it support *our* story?

Just as the feather scene drew us into the world of Forrest Gump, this scene needs to draw us into Forrest himself. In this one page we need to discover Forrest, get a sense of who he is, and become attached to him as our guide. This scene needs to seduce us.

> Look at the opening sequence of your movie. Are you clear as to why you are opening your movie with a particular scene or shot? Do you know why that scene or shot must be there? What would happen if you removed it? And what do you need to achieve with that scene in order to insure that it will support your story?

Let's move on to the next scene in *Forrest Gump*.

SCENE 2

1951 Interior of doctor's office. Forrest is being fitted with his new leg braces (intended to straighten his spine). This is the beginning of another sequence (scenes 2 through 19) which basically introduces us to the life of Forrest in 1951. We need to look at each scene in the sequence to ascertain its function and importance for the sequence as well as the story as a whole.

Why is this scene in our story and what is the significance of the braces? And why the curvature of the spine (which is not in the novel)?

What do we want to say with this scene? We have an opportunity to establish a specific tone and attitude about our lead character. It could be pathetic, sad, or morose. But, handled properly, it could be light and cheerful and we could see the spirit of little Forrest Gump and the constant optimism of his mother. We are not only establishing an attitude toward our lead character but we are also establishing how Forrest sees himself, since he is the one telling this story. This is crucial. Forrest, the storyteller, is telling us how he sees himself and how he wants us to see him. And the first thing that he is choosing to tell about himself is the day that he got the braces, the "magical shoes" that could take him anywhere.

SCENES 3 AND 4

This is followed by the sequence wherein we learn how Forrest got his name - from some Ku Klux Klan, Civil War General who was mistakenly hung by his own Klan members. Why do we need this sequence? What would happen if we took it out? Now, quite honestly, this is a sequence that could be cut from the film, but we are being introduced to Forrest's world of innocence and naiveté. The fact that he got his name from some racist Civil War general may not be as important as the fact that Forrest isn't aware of the significance of any of these events. He deals only with the facts, and not with any interpretation of the facts. This is the way Forrest Gump sees the world. With that in mind, this part of this sequence is very important because we get to know more about Forrest.

Let's look at one more scene from *Forrest Gump*.

SCENE 5

Forrest and his mom walking home. Some of the residents of Greenbow stare at Forrest's braces and his Mom admonishes them with "what's the matter, you've never seen anybody in braces before?" Then she tells Forrest "don't let anybody tell you they're better than you . . . etc." Why do we need this scene, what would happen if we lost this scene, and what must we achieve with this scene in order to insure that it will support our story? This is a key scene in our story because it establishes the relationship between Forrest and his mom and it is the first time we see how young Forrest is treated in public. Remember that all of this is being told to us by the adult Forrest; he is relating *his* experience. We see very clearly how his mother protected him and constantly nurtured his belief in himself. It seems clear to me that we need to establish three attitudes in this scene: (1) the judgment of the public, (2) the staunch determination of Mrs. Gump to protect and educate her son, and (3) young Forrest apparently undaunted by the stares, feeling totally supported by his mother. We have also set up three very important relationships in this brief scene: (1) the relationship between Mrs. Gump and the world, (2) the relationship between Forrest and the world, and (3) the relationship between Forrest and Mrs. Gump. This is needed before the next sequence which introduces Forrest's home life (which is then followed by the sequence where Mrs. Gump insures that Forrest will remain in public school).

We begin to see how each and every scene is crucial to the telling of our story and what we must achieve with each scene. This is what will keep us on track as we enter the rehearsal, production, and postproduction stages of our movie.

> Note: What needs to be <u>achieved</u> with a scene will be different for each director. This is not a matter of right or wrong; it is a matter of interpretation. Two directors may disagree (and most likely will) on what is needed from a particular scene and this is because these two directors would make two very different (and perhaps equally valid) films from the same script.

Go through your entire script in this manner. Take each scene and each sequence and ask yourself those crucial questions. Answer them as best you can. Don't get discouraged if you can't come up with what seems a logical or significant answer. If you get stuck just pass over the scene and go on to the next. Once you have finished the entire script you will begin to see a subtextual structure in the script. Those scenes that eluded you may now seem very apparent as they fit into this structure. If you cannot substantiate why a particular scene is in your story and it appears that the story would work just as well without it, consider whether or not you need it.

7. ASKING THE HARD QUESTIONS

Once we have established the function of each scene we need to apply the acid test — the hard questions. This is a misnomer, actually. The questions aren't hard, the answers are. The main question to be asked is "*Why?*" Why are we starting out with this shot? Why does it have to be this location? Why is this character in this scene, and why isn't another character in this scene? Why do we have this scene? Why is this character behaving this way, dressed this way, talking this way?

Read each scene slowly, one detail at a time. And with each detail ask why. For a little variety let's look at the first couple of pages from Barry Levinson's *Diner*.

<u>DINER</u>

FADE-IN:
The SCREEN IS BLACK. We hear MUFFLED ROCK and ROLL MUSIC.
Then we read:

BALTIMORE
1959

FADE-OUT.
FADE-IN:

INT. DANCE HALL BASEMENT — NIGHT

FENWICK walks along the dimly lit basement. Heavy winter coats hang from hooks on the wall. In the background there is constant traffic of people coming and going from the rest rooms. From above we hear the MUFFLED SOUND OF THE ROCK AND ROLL BAND.

Fenwick is in his early twenties and dressed in the Joe College style of the late fifties. sports jacket, button-down shirt, chino pants, and Bass Weejuns. We sense that he is a little lost in himself, confused. He looks out one of the windows that views the parking lot. Then without any outward anger, he punches his fist through a window pane. Seconds later he breaks another window with his fist.

Fenwick, picking up the music beat from above, struts to the sound as he approaches another bank of windows. He calmly breaks another window pane with his fist.

A GUY coming out of the bathroom in the background sees Fenwick's actions and then heads up the steps.

CUT TO:

INT. DANCE HALL — NIGHT

The crowd is gathered around the bandstand listening to the local group, the SHAKERS, playing their popular hit "Hot Nuts." The song is played

toward the end of the evening because of its
risqué lyrics.

> BAND LEADER
> Hot nuts, hot nuts, get from the
> peanut man.
> Hot nuts, not nuts, get me any way
> you can.

As the crowd swings the verse back to the Band
Leader, the Guy who spotted Fenwick breaking windows approaches BOOGIE. Boogie is something of a
dandy, flashier in dress than others in his crowd.
Although he isn't particularly good looking there
is something about his attitude that is very
appealing to girls. Boogie, after hearing the
Guy, heads downstairs.

INT. BASEMENT — NIGHT

Fenwick casually breaks another window with his
fist. His hand is bleeding. Boogie approaches.

> BOOGIE
> What's up, Fen?

> FENWICK
> Just breaking windows, Boog.

> BOOGIE
> What for?

> FENWICK
> It's a smile.

He breaks another window with his fist.

> BOOGIE
> C'mon, don't be a smuck.

> FENWICK
> I know that glass is made from
> sand, but how come you can see
> through it?

He breaks another window. Boogie grabs him.

> BOOGIE
> Leave the windows alone. What's
> the matter with you?

> FENWICK
> It's a smile, that's all.

> BOOGIE
> I'm cracking up.

Fenwick struggles to get free.

> BOOGIE
> (continuing)
> I'm warning you, Fen, break
> another window and you're
> gonna get a fat lip.

He lets Fenwick go.

> END OF SCENE

Here are the hard questions.

For the opening FADE-IN we have a black screen, we hear the muffled rock and roll music, and then a legend comes on the screen: Baltimore 1959. Why do we open on a black screen? Why not another color? Why not an image? A picture? Why are we beginning with no visual information other than the legend? Do we really need the legend? If so, is this the best place for it? And why the rock and roll music? Why is it muffled? What is this particular piece of music going to be? What messages are we giving out right away with a black screen, a legend, and muffled rock and roll music?

Then our second FADE-IN is the basement of the dance hall. Why is our first visual in a dance hall, and in the basement? What kind of dance hall and what is the nature of this basement? Why is it dimly lit? Does this mean that there is a depressing look, a sense of isolation, or does it have a comforting and soothing quality in its dimness? Why are there heavy winter coats hanging from the wall? How many coats? Men's coats, women's coats? What do these coats say about their owners? And why wouldn't they be hung somewhere else, like upstairs? Why do we see people coming and going from the rest rooms in the background? Why is that important? Are these the owners of the coats? And is it important that we know that they are traveling back and forth to the rest rooms rather than somewhere else, and that we still hear the muffled rock and roll music? Is it the same music? Has it changed? In character? In perspective?

Now, I know these seem like a of lot picky questions, and many of Mr. Levinson's choices may seem obvious and clear to you. But, until you have questioned each of them and satisfied yourself as to their purpose and placement, you will not have made them your own. And you need to make them your own, to make this <u>your</u> story, to know in your <u>gut</u> the reason for every choice, every detail.

Another way to look at this is by asking "what if?". Let's look at the next descriptive paragraph which describes Fenwick: early twenties, dressed in Joe College style of the fifties. Questions: Why is he dressed this way, or what if he were dressed differently? What would that do to our story, our character? Why is he "a little lost in himself, confused"? What if he weren't? What if he appeared confident, cool, in control? What would that do? And why is he punching out the window panes? What if he didn't? What would he do then? What is it that we are trying to communicate through Fenwick's attitude and behavior? And why should we begin the film on this moment? What if we started with the dance upstairs and then cut to Fenwick? What then? How does that affect the beginning of our story? And why start with Fenwick? What if we started with Boogie? What would that say?

These hard questions are not presented with an eye toward change, but toward comprehension.

You must be very clear in your mind and heart as to why each element, each character, each speech, each detail is in this film. Each element has a function, makes an impression, and affects the telling of the story. Each element is a necessary piece of an elaborate puzzle. But if it isn't assisting in the telling of the story, then it doesn't belong there. If it's not helping, it's hurting and the audience will feel it. They will know intuitively that there is something wrong and it will jar their suspension of disbelief. It is our job as directors to make sure that every element of our film is part of an integrated whole so that the audience never questions and is never thrown out of the picture, out of the story.

> For example: The winter coats hanging in the basement hallway in the opening sequence of *Diner* make a statement. It's winter. It's cold outside. There are many people here who have shed their coats for this particular activity (the dance). The coats can be seen as a warm and comforting contrast to Fenwick's dress (a sports jacket , no winter coat) and his emotional state (lost in

himself, confused). We can get the feeling that Fenwick's state is in direct contrast to the other participants in the dance. He is in the basement. The owners of the warm coats are very active in a group in the background. Fenwick is alone in the dimly lit basement. The rock and roll music to which the other participants are dancing is muffled, in the distance, unavailable to Fenwick.

If you have satisfactorily answered these questions (to be quite honest, you will never answer them all since there will always be some elusive details) and in production you are faced with decisions concerning changes (such as a change in location, costume, prop, color, or set), you will now be able to make new selections based on the *function* of the original element in the scene, not on the element itself.

If, for instance, for some reason you are not able to have the warm winter coats in the opening scene of *Diner* you will know you need something in that hallway or that basement that will give you (and therefore the audience) the awareness of the other participants in the dance, something that will be warm and comforting, and in contrast to and unavailable to Fenwick. But you've just been told you can't have the coats, and you are aware that an element will be missing from your scene. So maybe you elect to place some of the members of the dance in the hallway themselves, moving in a direction opposite to Fenwick, dressed in contrast to Fenwick, with attitudes (happy, secure, festive) opposite to Fenwick. You make this choice, or something similar, because you know what you need in this scene to make the scene work appropriately for you. The coats were not mere decoration or set pieces. They were not so much about winter as they were indicative of a group of people who were unlike our protagonist. And if you can't have the coats then you need to include this element in the scene in another manner. You could easily have Fenwick walking through the dancers in the opening and then move downstairs to the basement. You could show the dancers upstairs first and then move downstairs and find Fenwick in the basement. There are a variety of ways in which you could achieve this. The point is: you have decided, based on your initial work on the script and your hard questions that the coats are a <u>necessary</u> element in the opening scene; they make a statement that is important to you and the loss of the coats will affect the scene.

Now, I am using my interpretation for the coats in this opening sequence. You, in your own analysis, may see it very differently. That's fine. It really doesn't matter. What is important at this point is that <u>you</u> know why <u>you</u> want each element in your scene (and which ones you are willing to lose) so that when you are faced with having to make changes and alterations you are basing your decisions on your own sense of the importance and function of every element in the scene.

8. CHARACTER ARCS

A character arc is the journey of that character through the story. We say that a character has an arc when there is discernible and significant change in that character. All primary and secondary characters will have an arc; otherwise their involvement with other characters and with our story will lose significance.

The tracking of a character arc is similar to the point-to-point description we did earlier except that we are focusing on one character.

> Example: The character arc for Jenny. Jenny meets Forrest on the bus and invites him to sit beside her. Jenny goes on long walks with Forrest and teaches him how to run. Jenny confides in Forrest about her abusing father; she hides in the field and Forrest hides with her. Jenny kills her father. Years later Jenny goes off to school and is separated from her best friend. Jenny is visited at college by Forrest, who interrupts her lovemaking in the back seat of a car. In his first sexual encounter, Forrest shares an intimate moment with Jenny in her room. Jenny sees Forrest in a whole new way. (End Act One.)

While Forrest is in the army Jenny poses nude for *Playboy* and also has a job singing in the nude is some sleazy nightclub. Forrest discovers her there and rescues her, but Jenny is furious and pleads with Forrest to stay away from her. She also gets him to promise to run if he gets into trouble in Vietnam. Jenny gets involved with Wesley of the Black Panthers. At a peace rally in Washington, D.C., she runs into Forrest again. Forrest is a war hero and she's thrilled to see him but when she introduces him to the abusive Wesley, Forrest once again protects her and she is angry and embarrassed. Alone, she tells Forrest of her life in the communes, and about taking drugs while living in San Francisco and Hollywood. She tells Forrest that he has to stop saving her. Forrest gives Jenny his Medal of Honor. Jenny leaves with Wesley. (End Act Two.)

Jenny is prostituting herself, heavy into drugs and contemplating suicide. On her own she goes to visit Forrest, burned out and in need of rest. She spends a lot of time talking to Forrest like she used to. She tries to destroy her past by throwing rocks at her father's house. Forrest asks Jenny to marry him. She says no, that they are just friends. But that night she slips into his bed, and they make love for the first time. The next morning, Jenny leaves. Jenny is pregnant and gives birth to a son whom she names Forrest. She learns that she has a terminal disease. Years later she gets a message to Forrest that she wants to see him. Forrest comes to her. She introduces him to their son and assures Forrest that little Forrest is completely normal. She tells Forrest that she is sick and dying and now she asks him to marry her. At the wedding she meets Forrest's friend, Lt. Dan. As Jenny is dying Forrest tells her of all his adventures and she says, "I wish I had been with you." He replies, "You were with me all the time." Jenny dies.

As you plot a character arc you begin to feel the ebb and flow of that character's experience. Define for yourself the significant moments or the turning points in the journey. For Jenny they might be: Meeting

Forrest, confiding in Forrest, killing her father, realizing her sexual attraction to Forrest, feeling shame when Forrest sees her nude or abused, attempting suicide, returning to Forrest for the first time for his comfort and his love, having a baby, contracting a disease, her final bonding with Forrest, and finally Forrest easing her into death.

Track each character arc and define the key moments in that arc. Viewing your story in this manner will give you greater insight into each character's journey and will assist you enormously in the casting and rehearsal processes.

9. CHARACTER ANALYSIS

A very important aspect of the script breakdown is the character analysis. This will be your first step in the intricate and extremely vital casting process (to be discussed in Chapter 6).

The character analysis is different from the character arc, since we are now considering the basic nature of each character.

What I do at this point is just to begin writing about each character. I sit at my computer and without preconceived ideas I free-associate. These thoughts are not intended to be restrictions in terms of types of actors but rather insights into my own personal identification with each character as I see it at this point.

For example, here are thoughts on some of the characters from *Forrest Gump* and *The Fugitive*.

Forrest Gump

FORREST GUMP:

He is a simple man but must not appear simple to everyone. There seems to be a tendency on everyone's part in this movie to merely accept Forrest as he is, without severe judgment. He must not appear retarded, just simple. Perhaps the most important part of Forrest is his natural tendency to exude trust and compassion, and this must seem effortless, without ulterior motive. Forrest is basically a good man, with good intentions, who can only see the good in others. Even though the novel suggests that Forrest is a rather large man (larger than average), I feel it is very important that Forrest be of average size. There should appear to be nothing unusual about him, either physically, emotionally, or even mentally. It is curious that very few people refer to Forrest as slow, retarded, or stupid. Most of the remarks in this vein are made by Forrest himself. Forrest is more keenly aware of his own limitations than most people around him. I am going to need someone of enormous patience and compassion.

LT. DAN:

This man is such a mixture of anger, rage, suspicion, passion and purpose that he is unpredictable, mercurial. Right away I feel that it is important to find someone with whom the audience does not have a specific identification. It is going to be important to balance the constant rage and sense of fatalism with a quick and genuine sense of humor. Lt. Dan needs to be athletic. He is constantly doing battle, with Vietnam, his past, his legacy, and eventually with his infirmity and with God. We need to feel that this is a man who could and would take on the world. Like the other main characters who surround Forrest, Lt. Dan should appear to be just slightly off center. There are no characters around Forrest that seem to be totally normal, whatever that means.

Note: A thought as I write this. As a central concept for this movie I want Forrest, despite his limited mental capacity, to appear as the most normal, balanced, or sane person around. Forrest, regardless of his limited mental capacity, is no more handicapped than anyone else around him, and this includes the celebrities and politicians.

The Fugitive

DR. KIMBLE:

He is a man whom we have to accept as a renowned physician and surgeon. A man of intelligence. We also need to see him immediately as a man of integrity and compassion (as opposed to Lt. Gerard). Dr. Kimble is an everyman, a common man, and should not appear to be extraordinary. Yet at the same time we must accept him as being capable of the numerous physical feats he has to accomplish in this story. Because it is what drives him during the entire story, the most important attribute of Dr. Kimble is his sense of fairness, integrity, and loyalty.

LT. GERARD:

In contrast to Dr. Kimble (and basically because we have a story pitting two men against each other), Lt. Gerard has to be a mystery at first. Is he trustworthy? Is he honest? Who is he? Because of the arc of this character (from a single-minded ruthless lieutenant to a compassionate and caring man), it is important that he be mercurial. Just as we feel that everyone knows and understands Dr. Kimble, we must feel that nobody knows or understands Lt. Gerard. The arc of the relationship between the audience and Dr. Kimble depends on us knowing him from the beginning. We will not get to know Lt. Gerard until the very end.

Start this process with your script. Do not think too much as you write these descriptions. Let your basic, primal gut feelings come through. These impressions, along with the character arcs, will lead us into the casting process in Chapter 6.

10. VISUAL AND AURAL DESIGN ARCS

Film is a medium of sights and sounds. As you break down the script it's time to begin visualizing your movie, to think in terms of impressions, colors, movements, and designs.

How do you want to tell the story visually? It is very seductive when you begin to think of all the visual and aural possibilities, but once again we must make sure that the look of your film is generated by the script, by the needs of the story.

Production Design And Locations

When you realize you actually have the entire world (real and imagined) in which to shoot your movie and whatever choices you make will either support or undermine your story, the task of considering production design and locations is at once daunting and thrilling.

What is the look of *Forrest Gump* as described in the script? And how can we create a visual logic in our movie that will support our telling of the story? We'll look at the first few scenes of *Forrest Gump* to give you an idea of the possibilities.

Scene A1. The feather scene. We've already discussed the importance of this scene so now the question becomes, what are we looking for visually? What should we see from the beginning? Trees? Stars? Clouds? How about blue sky? Just blue sky. A blank slate. We could be anywhere and, as the feather appears against the blue sky and we begin to follow it, we have a sense that we could end up anywhere.

119

And then what should we see? Trees. We could still be anywhere. Eventually we will have to see buildings and a sense of the town of Savannah, Georgia. But again, what do we want it to look like? We know that later we will land at the feet of Forrest Gump who is sitting at a bus stop, but in what part of town? What do we want the look of this opening picture to be? What do we want it to say? All it says is that we are at a bus bench in Savannah, Georgia. That's it. Do we want it to be in an upscale part of town? On the outskirts? Poor district? There are a lot of choices here and each choice is going to make a slightly different statement. Let's say for the moment that we want this first shot to make as little a statement as possible, that we don't even want the audience to know right away that we're in the southern part of the United States. Perhaps it will just say "Anytown, USA." We could certainly achieve that. Another blank slate of sorts. And what kind of activity do we see going on in the background and foreground? Is it orderly or disorderly? Peaceful or chaotic? And what do we want Forrest wearing, and what is the black woman (who is a nurse) wearing?

As we look at all these visual elements we realize that every choice we make impacts our story.

Sound Design

What about sound? Even though ambient and atmospheric sound won't be added to your film until the postproduction stage, what kind of sounds do you hear? With this opening shot do you hear birds, cars, traffic, people talking, distant sirens, or city sounds? Perhaps it's quiet, uncommonly quiet. Perhaps it is as peaceful, quiet, orderly, and simple as Forrest himself.

Production design (both visual and aural) can be used to support the characters and events or they can be used to offset (by contrast) the characters and events. You may elect to have Forrest's home at Greenbow be peaceful, quiet, and serene. And you may elect to have the worlds of Vietnam, New York, and Washington be chaotic, unsettling, and disturbing. These are all directorial choices and the beginning of creating a visual and aural design for your movie.

Think of it this way. Imagine your movie without the dialogue tracks. Just characters moving in an environment of sights and sounds. Imagine watching the entire movie that way and being able to discern the story of your movie only through watching your characters against a visual and aural backdrop.

Think of the visual and sound design of your movie (including effects tracks and music) as characters. These characters take us on a very specific journey through the story. Consider how the look and sound of your film are going to support your story.

Let's look at a couple more scenes.

Scene 2. The doctor's office where Forrest is getting his braces and Scene 3. The streets of Greenbow, Alabama.

This is the first look we get at Forrest as a child and at Greenbow, Alabama. How different do we want it to look from Savannah, Georgia? How different were Forrest's experiences in Savannah, Georgia, in 1981 and in Greenbow, Alabama, in 1951? Thirty years apart and quite possibly worlds apart in terms of experience. In 1981 Forrest is a pretty secure man. In 1951 Forrest is an uncertain naive boy. How can we support this in the look of our film? If the opening shot in Savannah shows a world at ease, uncomplicated, gentle, and inviting, what do we want the world of 1951 Greenbow to look like? Forrest is isolated, alone, and getting fitted with encumbering braces. This world could be claustrophobic, limiting, harsh. Or perhaps it is a more expansive environment within which little Forrest feels lost and unprotected.

What about the sound? What kind of effect do we want as we try to create the world of young Forrest? Is it a different world in the doctor's office than it is in Forrest's home?

And what about the music? What do you hear? Do you want music from the period? Contemporary music? Original or classic? Listen to music as you read the script. Start now to incorporate the rhythms, tones, and moods of music. You'll know when you've found what will work for you.

When you are making a movie you are a painter with a blank canvas. You pick the colors. You pick the size of the brushes. Just because a tree has green leaves in reality doesn't mean you have to paint your tree with green leaves. They can be blue or yellow or purple or black. Whatever suits you in the expression you want to make.

Considering the visual and aural design of your movie will open your mind to limitless possibilities. Your palette is full of colors. Allow yourself expression without limitation.

Go through each scene and sequence and ask yourself:
1. Where does this scene take place?
2. What could it look like?
3. What could it sound like?
4. What music could underscore it?
5. How can these looks and sounds support my story?

The visualization and auralization of your film are constantly under consideration and development. It doesn't end until you have locked the film. Keep your mind open. Watch and listen to a lot of movies. Be aware of the effect of a camera move, a production design, a sound, a musical note. See and hear the details. Be bold, be courageous, but most of all be true to your vision.

SUMMARY

The script breakdown, as promised, is a lot of work, and at times it will seem terribly technical or too analytical, taking us far away from the immediacy of the storytelling process. But it needs to be done. And once it is done it can be put aside. Yes, that's right. Once you're done with your script breakdown, put it away. You don't need to read it, and, most definitely, *do not* bring it to rehearsal. No one wants to see it or even know that it exists. This is your private work. If your breakdown has been honest and thorough then whatever information you need will come to you when you need it.

Remember the fireside storyteller. Trust the process, it will support you. Concentrate on the story and the listener. You, as a filmmaker, can be as fluid, versatile, imaginative and daring as the ancient storyteller when you spin your story.

You are now ready to select your creative team.

CHAPTER 5

THE CREATIVE TEAM

Cinematographer, Production Designer, Casting Director, Actors, Editor, Composer

You are now ready to begin assembling your creative team. Unfortunately many directors will begin this process long before they are ready, before they have a clear vision of the film they want to make.

> I just came from a consultation with a director today. We were exploring the look that he wanted for his film and he said, "I think I have the wrong cinematographer." I am sure that the cinematographer that he had hired was very competent and talented, but as the director told me, "We don't see the same movie and I'm going to have to convince him (persuade him) to see the movie I see." This is an unfortunate situation that could have been avoided with the proper preparation. But this director was working the way many directors do: select a script, hire your team, and then begin the preparation process.

Up to this point, except for your work with the writer (and producer), you have been working alone. It has been you and the script and you have been able to envision the movie without limitation. In your mind's eye it has played out exactly the way you see it.

Now comes one of your most important tasks: selecting those artists that will actually collaborate in the making of your movie. Your key function is to inspire other artists to contribute to the making of your movie in such a fashion that the project maintains a cohesiveness along the lines of your vision. If you don't cast the appropriate artists for your movie, then the collaboration process is going to be a trying uphill battle.

The single most important requirement for any member of your creative team is that he is making the same movie as you are. It's amazing how many different movies creative artists can envision from the same script. Personal identification with a written piece of material means that very likely each person will see the story quite differently. Like a team of horses pulling a stage coach each horse has its position and a slightly different function, but they are all pulling in the same direction and all in response to the driver. Otherwise there would be chaos.

THE INTERVIEW PROCESS

Select team members that share and support your vision. This is obvious. The questions become: How do you determine whether or not this person you are interviewing shares your vision? Does this artist have the same passion for the project as you do (or is it just a potential job)? Will this artist merely support you or is she confident enough to challenge you in an effort to make you be your best? Will this artist go beyond what is expected and deliver that extra touch that will raise this project beyond the ordinary?

All artists are talented. Almost any cinematographer can light and shoot your movie. Any production designer can design and build the sets, dress the locations, and any editor can cut the film together into a logical and serviceable assemblage of your story. But you don't want just anybody. You want those very special artists who are going to hone their disciplines into specifically unique contributions to your film.

The process of selecting the members of your creative team is part intuition and part science. To an extent you can interview, question, probe, discuss, query, communicate, and test your applicants to determine their suitability for you and your project. Beyond that you have to rely on your gut, your intuition, your inner voice. Let's look first at what you can do in a practical interview and selection process. Then we'll take a moment to discuss that crucial, elusive, compelling, and oh-so-powerful inner voice.

YOUR COLLABORATORS AS STORYTELLERS

We are now entering into that phase which can become either maddening or exhilarating: the process of telling the story <u>through</u> other artists. This is a unique collaboration wherein you rely heavily on other artists to interpret <u>your</u> vision and deliver various elements of the story <u>to you</u>. Their ability to tell a story is as important as their individual talents. You want each member of the team to be a good storyteller in his own right and to be passionate about the telling of this particular story. This of course does not mean that the members of your team have to be a Garrison Keillor or Mark Twain, but you do want them to be adept at the telling of your story *through their craft*.

How to explore each applicant's ability as a storyteller:

> There is an acting exercise that is frequently used to help an actor focus on the story from the *character's* point of view. For example, let's say we have an actor who is playing the role of Biff in *Death of a Salesman* and we ask him what the play is about. Most likely he will say it is about a man, Willy Loman, who has been a salesman all his life and who is now finding that not only is he losing his business but also the is losing the respect he thought he once had as well as his grasp on reality. Now, if we stop the actor at this point and say, "Fine, but what is the story about from Biff's point of view?" the actor might say that *Death of a Salesman* is about a young man who has returned home after banging around the country for several years (in and out of jobs, in and out of jail), to try to find out where it all went wrong and recapture that feeling

127

of success and worthiness that he had when he was in high school. It's the same script but it sounds like a very different story only because we have shifted our point of view.

Use a similar exercise when putting together your creative team. There are three steps to this process.

Step One: See your vision as expressed through each discipline;
Step Two: Allow each potential team member to tell the story through her craft; and
Step Three: Consider the compatibility of this vision with your own.

Step One.

Prior to your meeting with potential members of your team you need to have a pretty clear idea of how <u>you</u> see the story being told from their perspective. This is not an easy task, but if taken seriously it will pay off handsomely. For example, think for a moment about your film and how you could tell the story from the point of view of the cinematographer. Let's look at *The Fugitive* from the point of view of the cinematographer. It's the story of two men trapped in a city, trapped in a system (feels like long lenses, much compression). Two men in constant movement in the midst of a chaotic environment (fluid, moving, restless camera). The story starts out simply, elegantly (the reception for Dr. Kimble) and quickly turns chaotic, violent (the murder of his wife) and then becomes tight, claustrophobic, breathless (as the chase begins). Already we can begin to see how this story will be impacted by the vision of the cinematographer.

Or the costume designer's point of view of the story: How can the costumes tell the story? Dr. Kimble goes from tuxedo to bloody tuxedo to prison uniform and then through various disguises. As he searches for the identity of the man with one arm he continually conceals his own identity. Even Lt. Gerard's costumes can help tell the story. This is a man who is who he is. He cannot hide behind a costume because he is visible. He represents the public. He is in suits and uniforms; he has badges and the identification of police on his back.

Or the production design: From the elegance of the reception and the tastefulness of Dr. Kimble's home, to the starkness of the courtroom and the bus, and eventually the confusing, frightening, and uninviting city of Chicago. Even the hospital itself which used to bring such comfort is now a potentially dangerous environment. The environment is an enormous obstacle in this story (to both Dr. Kimble and Lt. Gerard), and through the nature and design of that obstacle you can tell this story.

Once you have a fairly clear idea of how you see your movie through these various disciplines, you are ready to begin your interviewing process.

Step Two.

Ask your potential team members to tell you the story through their craft.

Since this may appear as an unusual request to some, I suggest that you give applicants an opportunity to prepare their response. As you are setting up the interviews, let them know verbally or through a letter what you are requesting.

You may have to help them a bit. Try putting it this way: "Look, here's what I want you to do for me. Tell me the story of the script, as you see it, through (cinematography, costumes, makeup, production design, editing, or whatever). Use your craft as the main defining element of the story. Tell the story as if your craft were the main tool of communication." It's always a good idea to throw in an apology such as "I know this may sound strange, but humor me. . ." That apology will take the edge off this unusual request.

Help them get started. To a production designer you may say, "Describe the story as a series of sets and locations, such as (for *The*

Fugitive) our story begins in the lush and lavish ballroom of Chicago's most elegant hotel. The room and decor comfort the inhabitants as they toast our guest of honor. We then shift to the comfortable and secure rooms of the guest of honor's home as his wife comes home early. The rooms and tones seem perfectly suited for the night of lovemaking that they both anticipate. . . ." This should be enough to get them started. Listen to their story. Allow their telling of the story to stimulate pictures, moods, and tones in your imagination. You will now begin to sense the power of this particular tool and see the potential of this artist's contribution.

Step Three.

The compatibility of this vision with yours: Does their vision of your film work with yours? Do you see their imagery, their imagination supporting your passion, or do they have a different movie in mind? If their vision of the film does not match yours, this does not necessarily mean they won't be an able collaborator. Perhaps they're bringing something new that you hadn't imagined. Perhaps they are challenging your vision and that challenge might inspire you. Consider all possibilities.

Freedom of expression comes most easily when the boundaries are well defined. Artistic expression will flow with ease when the objective is clear and the collaboration is consistent. When all the artists are pulling toward the same goal and are otherwise unrestricted, you will see boundless creative energy and imagination.

It is your job at this point to insure that each member of your creative team will indeed be pulling toward the same goal with equal enthusiasm.

CINEMATOGRAPHER

The cinematographer's craft is light, composition, lenses, framing, and camera movement.

The cinematographer is one of the most important members of your creative team. As head of your production team, he is going to be in charge of the entire look of the film, not so much the production design but definitely how the physical elements (sets, locations, actors, etc.) are going to be lit and recorded. You can have the most spectacular sets and locations, costumes, props, and even the most terrific performances, but if they are poorly recorded or inappropriately lit they will be diminished. All your meticulous work with design and performance can be enhanced or diminished by the work of the cinematographer.

Forrest Gump through a cinematographer's eyes:

This is a story of simple colors and simple hues, a story of innocent magic, the wondrous made simple and the simple made wondrous. I want to tell this story unobtrusively. The camera style and techniques should be reminiscent of the thirties, forties, and fifties — simple, flowing, and unpretentious. The look must reflect a time of uncomplicated innocence, like Forrest himself.

Once upon a time there was a simple man who lived in a complex world, but saw it simply. His was a world of balance, openness, and honesty. Every time we see Forrest we see him straight on, simple, direct. But quite often the world around him will be complicated and complex and at times even a bit confusing. I always see Forrest himself at eye level — eye to eye. The same is true of his home in Greenbow — uncomplicated and solid. But when we move out of the South and away from Greenbow the world takes on a mysterious and, at times, disturbing look. The college stadium is huge with high energy. The boot camp is dark and foreboding. Vietnam is concurrently lush and disorienting. The ocean and the shrimp boat are at times peaceful and serene and, during the storm, ferocious but never frightening. And when Jenny comes into Forrest's life again, the world glows. By the end we have returned to the solidity and simplicity of Greenbow. Forrest is stronger and more confident and his world finally feels complete.

You also want a cinematographer who has a good sense of story structure and scene structure. One who will merely light and photograph your work is not enough. You want an ally who is not just thinking about her work but is constantly thinking about the story.

PRODUCTION DESIGNER

The production designer oversees the creation and/or selection and dressing of the environment within which your events will occur.

Forrest Gump through the eyes of a production designer:

> Once upon a time there was a simple man in a complex world. We first meet him in a world that is balanced and unthreatening while at the same time being a bit distant and removed (the bus bench). As Forrest takes us (through his narration) back to his childhood we see that his childhood was confusing and at times overwhelming. It was not a particularly friendly environment. It created struggle and isolation. Then he meets Jenny and his world begins to change. We start to feel that there is more room, more light, more possibility, more promise. As he faces intolerance (the teasing boys) Forrest discovers that he can escape — the environment opens up and all seems possible. As his running leads to fame and acceptance, the environment (stadiums and school) seem to embrace him rather than ridicule him.

You need a production designer who has a clear vision and can see how the environment will support your story (and not become a story in itself).

Obviously the working relationship between the cinematographer and the production designer is an intricate and intimate one and as you are considering these positions you need to keep in mind their potential collaboration.

EDITOR

Your editor is your final storyteller, the person who will help you find the movie in all the elements you have created. You need someone who has that unique ability to see and feel the story existing within the material you supply. Selecting editors (and composers as we will discuss) is a great leap of faith. The editor has no clear indication of the material you will deliver and you have no clear idea of how this editor might assemble that material. So the question becomes, how will you work with the editor in preproduction and production in order to insure a smooth and satisfying post? Involve your editor as collaborator and guide in your storytelling process long before you hit postproduction. Dream together about the looks, rhythms, and designs of each scene.

Let each potential editor tell you the story of your film as he sees it visually. Have him speak in emotional rhythms, pacing, and patterns. Go inside the visual imaginings of each editor and see the movie that he sees.

Editing is more than just cutting your picture. It's overseeing the assemblage of your entire movie which includes the music and sound effects. As your cinematographer is head of your production team, your editor is head of your postproduction team. You want an editor who understands and appreciates the power and significance of music and who has an ear for sound effects, both realistic and nonrealistic.

Also, this is a person with whom you are going to spend a lot of time in a little dark room. Many hours, the two of you will be laboring over the finest and most frustrating details of your movie. Of your entire creative team you will probably have the most intimate and intense relationship with your editor. You are looking for someone with whom you can share your most intense creative concerns, ideas, and impulses. You want an editor who will be a listener, a supporter, and a healthy challenger.

COMPOSER

The composer is responsible for the creation and selection of the musical score for your film. It is the final comment in your movie, the last flavor added. As many directors will attest to, this is one of the most exhilarating and frightening aspects of the process. Rarely do you get to hear a note of music until you have locked the picture, and most likely you are running out of money and out of time. There is a great element of trust here. This is not like working with actors where you can shoot various takes on a performance and make a final decision in post, nor is it like working with production designers where you can see drawing after drawing until you settle on the one of your choice. As you meet potential composers for your film remember, like the editor, they can only respond to your input. They are eventually going to have to write and select music for the material that you deliver. How they respond to your vision is very much how they will respond to your film.

SHARING YOUR VISION

The next step is to share your vision and listen to their response. Some applicants may strongly disagree with your vision (be careful), many will enthusiastically accept your vision (be careful), and then there will be those who will just listen and absorb and ask questions and offer support and then listen some more (this is collaboration). Collaboration is *not* unquestioning support and certainly *not* dig-your-heels-in resistance. Collaboration is a journey wherein the team members share a vision, but are willing to challenge and be challenged with the keen awareness that the end result can far exceed the efforts of any one individual.

As you listen to a potential team member's response to your vision, you are experiencing the first stages of your collaboration with this artist. How does it feel to be discussing this movie with this person?

Who is leading? Who is following? Do you feel that this person's support of you is genuine? Are her questions reasonable, informed? Is she stimulating you to think beyond your initial vision? Or is she challenging you in such a way that you feel blocked, stymied, defensive? Your response to this person is very important. You want team members that excite you, stimulate you, make you laugh, make you think, make you a better director.

ADDITIONAL SCREENING METHODS

Once you have a potential team member who you feel is going to be a healthy collaborator it's time to determine whether or not that team member is going to be able to deliver what he envisions. Enthusiasm and clarity of vision are one thing, the ability to deliver is another. They have to be able to walk the walk.

There are several methods you can use in order to determine the ability of each artist.

1. Looking At Their Past Work

With most artists you can look at their past work and get an indication of the depth and range of their talent. But just looking at (or listening to) their work is not enough. You need to understand the project they were working on, the requirements of the script, the vision of the director and the conditions under which they were working.

Sit with a cinematographer as you watch his reel. Tell him which pieces of his work interest you (whether they are appropriate for your project or not). Let him explain to you the conditions, the needs, and the requirements for each project and how he resolved certain problems or limitations. What you want to know is how he translated the specific needs of another director (and script) into a visual solution. Many cinematographers can light and shoot beautiful pictures. You're looking for the extraordinary one who can tell stories with light, composition, and movement.

As you look at a production designer's portfolio (or reel) follow the same process. You are not just looking for how imaginative or creative the design is, but how it interpreted the story, fulfilled the needs of a directorial vision, and worked within the constraints of a budget. How did this artist translate story need into environment? This is the key. If the solutions differ from your own taste or sensibility, this may not be the designer for you. But if you find the solutions do indeed reflect your own taste and sensibility, then this may be the one for you.

Same with an editor. Look at her work. How can you judge if the editing is good or not? You have no idea of the conditions, available footage, range of performance, or influence of the director or producers. How do you judge the quality? In this case you definitely need to sit with the editor and discuss each project she is showing you. Let her explain how she arrived at these final solutions. Realize that what you are listening to is not only her solutions but also her process. Unlike a production designer, cinematographer, writer, composer, or casting director, the editor can only work with the materials she is given. It is always a limited palette. Consequently, it is difficult to judge an editor's work until you know the nature of the palette.

Go through the same process with the composer. As you listen to the music, realize that it was created for a particular project with particular requirements. How much more satisfying to view the composer's work by seeing the films themselves so that you can see how the music supports the story. Music alone, apart from the project for which it was intended, may or may not give you a clear indication of the talent of the composer. You need to know the requirements of both story and director before you can judge the composer's ability to translate story need to music.

The casting director (we will discuss the process of selecting the casting director in Chapter 6).

The above is a painstaking process which admittedly many directors don't go through. But when you realize that you are picking the team to whom you are going to entrust your film, then you'd better be sure that each and every member is working in a "translation" process that is in sync with yours.

2. Checking References And Referrals

References and referrals are vital. There is nothing like getting an assessment from someone (especially another director or producer) who has worked with the prospective team member.

When you talk to the references be very clear about what you need to know. Give them an idea of the nature of your project (style, genre, budget conditions, etc.) and then let them know what you require from the person you are discussing (i.e., for a cinematographer it might be speed, communication, imagination, innovative camera work, or style of photography; for a production designer — economy, imagination, creating a specific look; for an editor — sense of comedy/drama, ability to work with the director and producers; and for the casting director — how they work with actors, with the director, access to talent, flexibility, etc.).

Presenting your specific needs to each reference will insure that you get the most from this exploration.

3. Having Them Produce Something Specifically for Your Project

This can be a touchy part of the process but I find it enormously valuable.

Of course this can't work for all team members (such as casting directors, cinematographers, and editors), but it can work very well with production designers, costume designers, and composers.

> David Michael Frank, the composer I used on my first film, was reluctant to make any kind of demo tape for me demonstrating some of his ideas for my movie. At the time I was leaning toward one composer, but I had four of them create short tapes demonstrating different themes for the movie. As soon as I heard David's I knew immediately that he was the one for my movie.

Having a production designer produce even the simplest of drawings or renderings depicting sets and locations and the look of the film is your assurance that you are both indeed making the same movie. Yet there are many film artists who will refuse such a request feeling that their work and reputation should speak for itself. When the director is uncertain as to which artist will be the most appropriate for his project quite often it will prove to be the artist who is willing to go the extra distance and give the director something concrete by which to judge.

When you ask for a sample be specific. For a production designer ask for a particular set or location. For a costume designer pick out that particular costume that you feel will give you an idea of their approach. For a composer suggest certain themes for specific characters or specific moments in the story. Give them all the full benefit of your input.

> I am always suspicious of any artist (including actors) who are not willing to demonstrate to the director the nature of their potential contribution. I had one actress who was unwilling to audition for me because she felt that I, as a theatre director, should be fully aware of her work (which was mostly in theatre). But I wasn't. I had only seen her in two projects and I felt it was imperative for me to see her interpretation of the project I was doing. She refused. I eliminated her from consideration. She was angry but I felt I had no choice.

4. Communicating Through A Third Source, i.e., Other Films And Works Of Art

With cinematographers, editors, casting directors as well as other artists, it is sometimes best to communicate through other works of art. View, examine and discuss the cinematography in other films that you and/or your potential cinematographer feel represent the possible look of your film. Discuss paintings, photographers, styles, composition. Go to museums and galleries.

> For example: Let's say you are looking at the works of Edwin Hopper. Listen to the cinematographer's reaction. How does he respond to the composition, the lighting, the framing? Does he feel this is an appropriate look for your film? If so, why? If not, why not? You are now discussing the look of your film in concrete terms — color, framing, lighting, composition.

You can use a similar process with editors except now you really need to view film, and not necessarily a film this particular editor cut. Look at other films for rhythms, pacing, techniques, and styles of editing. Show the editor works that have impressed you and that you feel might be appropriate to your film. Let the editor suggest or show you works that she might think appropriate for your discussion and consideration.

With production designers you can review architecture, interior design as well as paintings and photography. Find buildings or spaces or environments that give you the appropriate feeling for your film. View the production design of other films to find the color, tone, lighting and scale that you both feel are appropriate.

You can go through a similar process with all the various designers and editors and even the casting director.

5. The Balance Of The Creative Team

Unlike the casting process (Chapter 6) you will not be able to bring prospective members of your creative team together and mix and match them until you find the most appropriate and desirable combination. So you need to rely on the most important tool in this selection process, your instincts. Regardless of all the preparations, screenings, story telling, referrals and references and long discussions, eventually it is going to come down to your instinct and gut reaction. You do know which members will work best together, which will be the leaders and which will count on the leadership of others.

Essentially, if each member of your creative team is a person you really want to work with and whom you feel will selflessly support your vision of the film then you can feel assured that they will form a cohesive and productive creative unit.

6. The Working Personality Of The Artist

Artists bring with them their own attitudes about the process and those attitudes will become part of your process. Some artists find every job difficult and any difficult condition adverse. Others will accept the challenges and continually make the best of whatever conditions arise.

We create the world in which we live. If we believe that every job is difficult, that no one appreciates our contribution, that there is never enough money or time and that there is always someone else at fault -- then that will be our experience. But if we believe that regardless of the conditions, personnel or talent we will be able to create a meaningful and joyful experience out of which will emerge a significant film, then that will be our experience.

Hire people who will create the experience you want.

TEAM MEMBERS WHO HAVE BEEN PRESELECTED

You may find that you have to work with creative team members who have been hired before you, were selected by the producer or are attached to the project for some reason. You need to go through the same process to determine the compatibility of your visions and your ability to work together.

If you feel that they are not right for you and the project then you have to approach them in a different way. You need to infuse them with your passion, bring them into your process and find the aspects of their vision that are compatible with yours. Let them know that there is a difference of opinion and that it is your intention to establish a healthy and productive working relationship. Practice inclusion and they will be there to support you.

PREPRODUCTION WITH THE CREATIVE TEAM

As you enter the preproduction phase of your film you will have most of your creative team together. (Sometimes the composer, the editor, and members of the editorial team are not hired until later). It is in these initial stages of preproduction that you will begin to set the tone for the whole movie.

1. Allowing Each Artist Individual Freedom While Demanding Compliance To Your Vision

This may sound contradictory but this is an essential element in your working process. As you work with each individual artist (and as you work with the creative team as a whole) you must encourage them to challenge you, to present you with new ideas, new insights, and new inspirations. If you are concerned about being thrown from your original vision by the strength of these new ideas, then you are not clear on your vision. It is not the strength of the new ideas that could be the problem, but the weakness of your vision or your commitment to it.

It is your ability to listen to and sort through the input from others (selecting what is useful and appropriate and passing on those ideas that are not) that will create the strength of your team.

2. Communicating With Each Artist On A Regular Basis

One vital aspect of the creative team is communication. As we have discussed earlier, all a director does is talk or communicate. It is through this communication that the film is achieved and your vision maintained. What I suggest is a weekly (at minimum) written communication with each and every member of your team. Even though you will most likely be talking with each member every day it is a good idea (for them and for yourself) to put your discussions, decisions, and agreements in written form.

On the next page is a weekly communiqué for *Interlude*, a project that I am currently preparing. This project is an improvised film (developed by myself and the actors) intended to be shot on one location.

Date	Notes	Team Member
Monday 4-22	Per our discussion we need a house that will serve as a bed and breakfast with enough open landscape around it (with preferably a mountain range in distance) to double as Taos, New Mexico. Because of the fluidity of cinematography that we plan to achieve and the documentary feel of the film, I see little likelihood that we will be able to have interior of the B&B and exterior of B&B in two locations. Interior bedrooms need to be individually dressed to suit each couple that is staying there. I'm open to suggestions on this.	Location Manager Cinematographer Production Designer Set Dresser
Tuesday 4-23	We need to set meetings with the individual actors to discuss appropriate wardrobe. Because these characters are based on and created by the actors it is important that each actor have input, but not final say over wardrobe. I want to see specific character arcs reflected in each character's wardrobe as discussed. We need to look at edited version of rehearsal tapes with Paul and Victor to discuss shooting and editing style. Prelighting of main areas of house: need areas to hide lights, create natural light, make use of natural light.	Cinematographer Editor Production Designer Set Dressing Key Grip
Wednesday 4-24	Rehearsals will resume next week with everyone except Paul and Ellen. I'll need two standby actors (as discussed) to fill in for them. Rehearsals will be recorded on hand-held video (Hi-8). Need to set meeting with David to review his initial music ideas and for him to hear more of my "rehearsal music" selections.	Casting Director 1st AD Cinematographer Camera Operator Composer
Thursday 4-25	Digital video blow-up from Sony will be ready in a few days. We need to look at this ASAP with ALL production team members, esp. Victor, Paul, Richard and Ken.	Cinematographer Editor Production Designer Key Grip Producer
Friday 4-26	"Script" will be ready in about three days (in time for rehearsal next week) Robin still working on "script within script." Copies will be circulated to ALL when ready and I need notes from all creative team members ASAP.	All

This is a condensed version which can sometimes go on for pages.

This kind of communication will keep everyone informed of the developments and progress of your project. As the film gets larger and the crew gets more extensive, you will find that this update, along with regular production meetings, will keep everyone on track.

3. Letting Each Artist Find His Own Answer (even though you already have the answer)

As you work with members of your creative team (and with actors as well) even though you may have a solution to the question at hand, often it is best to allow the artist to work through the problem on his own. There is nothing quite like seeing an artist arrive at his own solution (even if it's exactly what you had already envisioned). It's called letting the artist own the choice. Choices that are imposed upon an artist are never embraced with such enthusiasm as those discovered by the artist.

4. Using The Script As The Source Of All Inspiration And As A Grounding Point

As you go through the preproduction process with your creative team remember that the source of all information and the grounding point for your film is the script. You spent a lot of time on this script (and with the writer) in order to have a solid base for this project. It is your guide and the foundation of your vision.

We talked in Chapter 3 ("Working with Writers") about going back to the point of agreement whenever there's been a disagreement or differing points of view. Use the same process here. The point of agreement is the script itself. If you and the cinematographer disagree on how a particular scene should be shot, go back to the script, look at the scene. find the point of agreement. Remind yourselves what the scene is really about, why it's in the script and what you need to achieve with this scene in order to make the film work. These are the points you must agree upon before you can proceed. Then you can discuss how the scene needs to be staged, lit, and shot. It is very easy to get carried away with exciting, provocative, and imaginative solutions, but if these solutions are not directly related to the needs of your story, they can (and will) undermine your efforts. Be assured that the very best solution is the one that supports the story.

5. Inclusion vs. Exclusion

I have often wondered, when either watching or being involved in a production, why things go wrong. Of course there is stress, there are money problems and personality problems, there is fear and anxiety. These problems occur on every project. So what is the difference between a cohesive and collaborative team and a fractious, competitive one? From my experience I can see only one difference: the way the director (or producer or department head) handles disagreement, dissension, and disparity. As you encourage individuality among your team members (and they do so within their departments) you have to be aware that you are also courting disagreements and possibly dissension. This is not a problem. The problem is in how the disparities are handled. It needs to be done with inclusion rather than exclusion. If you embrace the differing opinions, if you accept a new point of view as valid (this doesn't mean you have to include it in your film), and if you encourage each and every team member to continue to express his/her varying points of view and ideas, then your team will remain cohesive and collaborative. But if, even once, you allow disagreement or dissension to cause a rift between crew members, to cause even one member of your crew or staff to feel or appear to be excluded from the process, then your cohesion will begin to erode. Distrust and fear will replace the confidence and joy that used to exist. It takes no more effort to be gracious and appreciative than it does to be critical and judgmental. This does not mean that you have to acquiesce to every whim, thought, or idea or that you are not firm and decisive. It just means that you are open and will continue to maintain an environment that encourages individual thinking.

Now it is time to consider the casting of actors for your movie, the final members of your creative team.

Chapter 6

The Casting Process

"With a good script, a clear vision, and a good cast
you'll have a good movie."

We are now entering into the most exciting and perhaps most treacherous phase of the directorial process — selecting and working with actors. It is often said that casting is 70 or 80 percent of the directing process. Most directors agree that without the proper cast and a well-balanced ensemble of actors, even the finest script will be courting disaster. With a film well cast the director can and will rely heavily upon the talent and sensibility of the actors to bring the story to life.

How do we prepare ourselves for casting? How do we make the best use of a casting director, and is every casting director suitable for every picture? What do we do during the casting process? What about cold readings, prepared readings, rehearsed readings, solo readings vs. paired readings? How do we determine which ones to call back, and what do we do with them once we have them back? How do we determine their range of abilities and how directable they will be on the set? Do we know how any actor will work with another actor? And what about stars, personalities, and actors that refuse to read?

These are the questions that plague many directors; yet there is a way to approach this process with confidence, precision, and a clear vision.

SELECTING THE CASTING DIRECTOR

First of all you have to understand that the casting director, as a member of your creative team, is working as an extension of you. The casting director *does not* cast the film. It is the casting director's primary job to make actors available to you that could fulfill your vision of each of the characters (and the ensemble). It is *your* job to cast the film.

The casting director is the one member of the creative team who is directly involved in helping you select other members of the creative team — the actors. When the casting is completed, the casting director's job is essentially done.

When selecting a casting director, there are several attributes to be taken into consideration:

1. Storytelling ability (through cast)
2. Response to your vision
3. Attitude about actors
4. Access to talent and agents
5. Ability to negotiate

1. Storytelling

"Tell me the story of the film by just describing the actors." Some interviewees may be confused by this or balk at the question. Help them with an example.

> For example: *Death of a Salesman* as told through the eyes of a casting director. Willy Loman, a small wiry, feisty yet fragile man in his mid–sixties is attempting to show his wife, who he believes to be more fragile than himself, that he can still make it in the world of salesmen. His wife, Linda, a woman of tremendous tenacity and resilience who harbors secrets that would have

destroyed a lesser being, protects this man from the real world. Biff, their eldest son, a boy of great talent but little self-esteem, has returned home to try to reconnect with the power and admiration he had as a high school athlete. On the surface Biff is all confidence and determination; underneath he is a frightened child. His brother, Happy, is anything but happy. Although he is pleased that his brother is home, Happy, taking after his mother, is painfully aware of the severity of his father's illness. Happy's burden is that he sees reality and hasn't the elaborate masks of the rest of his family.

Forrest Gump from the point of view of the casting director: Forrest Gump, a simple, unassuming, and usually unnoticed man is telling his life story to complete strangers as he waits for a bus. He tells of his childhood with his adoring, strong, and willful mother. He tells how she gave him simple yet profound outlooks on life. Forrest tells how as a child he was ridiculed and teased because he was slow and a bit stupid. But then there was one young girl, Jenny, a sweet child who took a liking to him, and they became best friends "like peas and carrots." Jenny and Forrest couldn't be more unlike; he's gangly, awkward, and slow while she's beautiful, gracious, and smart. But together they make a team. Forrest does not make a lot of friends, but the ones he makes are significant and lasting. Bubba is just like Forrest — slow, lovable, and simple. He has a heart as big as all outdoors. Lt. Dan, who has no intention of being an acquaintance let alone a friend of Forrest's, is pure military stock — muscular, tight, single-minded, and driven. Lt. Dan is as humorless as Forrest and Bubba are open and vulnerable. Jenny has perhaps too many "friends" which really means no friends at all, except for Forrest. As she grows older and more bitter she loses her softness and her beauty develops an edge. Only in the presence of Forrest do we see her angelic glow.

As you can see, we are getting the beginning of the story but most importantly we are getting the characters in rich detail. Now, some may read the above descriptions and disagree; they may see these characters differently than I have described them. That's fine. This is not about being right or wrong. It is about having a vision, about seeing very distinct characters and being able to tell the story through those characters.

As they describe each character and their role in the story, listen and visualize. Are they in sync with you? Are they sharing a similar vision, triggering new ideas, new thoughts? Or are they way off on another track?

See if their vision of the film and their passion for the characters is compatible with yours. As with the other artists, concurrent visions and passions are not a necessity. Contrary visions and passions can often complement and stimulate your own. You may want a casting director who will challenge your vision of the cast. If we look only for artists who see everything exactly as we do, then we may end up with a film of limited vision. But if we are willing to employ artists who will challenge our vision, then we have a greater chance of excelling.

2. Conveying Your Vision

Listen to the response to your vision. Is the enthusiasm genuine? Is their skepticism well founded? Are they able to see the movie you see? If they don't have the ability to connect with your passion, then it is quite possible that they will always operate separately from you.

3. The Casting Director's Attitude About Actors

Acting is a very noble profession and deserves to be treated as such. If you assemble a creative team that respects actors and their profession, you will automatically get a higher level of performance from the actors. This attitude begins with the casting director.

Talk with casting directors about actors and how they like to work with them in the casting process. Find a casting director who shares your feelings for actors and respects your way of working.

4. Access To Talent

You want a casting director who has access to actors in a variety of arenas.

> Because my background is primarily theatre, I want a casting director who not only respects the theatre but one who frequents theaters. I want a casting director who is aware of all the new talent.

It's important that your casting director have access to the reputable agencies; otherwise you will have a limited selection. Some casting directors are reluctant to work with many of the smaller agencies. Again this is limiting your selection. Many of the finest actors are with the smaller agencies and many have no agent at all.

Find a casting director who is willing to explore all avenues such as theatre, clubs, performance spaces, high schools, and even the streets. There is nothing quite like discovering new talent in unexpected places.

5. Ability To Negotiate

A good casting director is a good negotiator. Not being one who has been deeply involved in the world of negotiation, I only know that an affable, creative, and tenacious casting director can often create casting possibilities where others can't, and they can do this without losing the respect of agents, actors, producers, and directors. When considering a casting director, call the agents, directors, and producers that you know who have worked with this particular casting director and get their feedback. It's vital.

PREPARATION FOR THE AUDITION PROCESS

The preparation for the audition process starts long before hiring the casting director.

The Character Profiles

One of the most important aspects of the casting process is your ability to previsualize each character, not only in physical type, age, and sex, but also in terms of temperament, attitude, sensibility, and rhythm.

If someone says to you, "Wouldn't Harrison Ford be great for your leading man," think about it before you quickly say yes just because Harrison Ford is a fine actor and with him your movie will get made. As fine an actor as he is, he may not be right for your project. What does Harrison Ford bring to a role? What are his energies, rhythms, sensibilities? Harrison Ford is an everyman. He is the guy next door. He's not a superhero. He's quiet, unassuming, pleasant, and professional. Probably a family man. It would be hard to imagine him harming anyone, except in self-defense.

He was perfect for *The Fugitive* because we needed a man that we could all identify with. We did not want Dr. Kimble to be extraordinary (Stallone) or inaccessible (DeNiro) or hard-edged (Pacino). And Tommy Lee Jones was a perfect choice for Lt. Gerard because he is mysterious and seemingly unapproachable. If you had switched Ford and Jones in these roles, it would not have worked as well.

What about *Forrest Gump*? (When the casting is so accurate, it is difficult to imagine another actor in the role.) But what would have happened if Harrison Ford had played Gump? Harrison Ford carries a certain level of intelligence with him that is difficult to discard whereas Tom Hanks always maintains an aspect of wonderment and naiveté. Tommy Lee Jones would not have been able to achieve Gump at all because of his seeming lack of vulnerability and innocence. Tom Hanks would not have made the Dr. Kimble that Harrison Ford did. Remember, none of this has anything to do with talent or ability. It has to do with *how we perceive* these actors and the levels of expression we are willing to accept from them.

Before you begin thinking about specific casting, write a character description for each character. (See Chapter Four, "Script Breakdown".) These profiles should be in depth, thorough, and go well beyond the physical, age, and sex attributes. You want to get into the very core of the character and define what you are going to need from the actor in order to realize this character.

> For instance: Let's consider Bubba from *Forrest Gump*. Bubba is like a big, lumbering four year old. This is a man who never grew up and maybe never wanted to. Physically, he is not an attractive man. The parts just don't come together in the most appealing way, but beneath this man's off-putting outward appearance is a heart as big as all of Louisiana. This man would lay his life down for a child — or a bird. He can see the balance of life so profoundly that he is fearless. Bubba has the ability to memorize the most complex information (the variety of ways to prepare shrimp), but only if he sees a good reason. He is a man devoid of prejudice; he sees good everywhere.

The Actor Profiles

Once you have an in-depth description of each character, write a description of the <u>actor</u> you are seeking to fill this role. These two descriptions (character and actor) may not end up being identical, but this is okay because what you need from the actor is not the same as the character. The sensibilities of the actor will not be the same as the character.

For instance, you may want an actor who has a greater sensitivity to a certain aspect of the story than the character does, because this will create a tension within the character when the actor has to repress that sensitivity. Or an actor who is less knowledgeable than the character, who has to work hard to comprehend what the character knows, again creating tension within the character. You could have an actor who is more athletic than the character so that there is an ease in the movements, or on the other hand an actor who is less athletic than the character will create a struggle to perform. All of these attributes (the similarities and the contrasts between the character and the actor) have to be taken into account. Each actor, just because of who and what he is, will create a slightly different character.

Example: I was casting the role of Stanley in a production of *A Streetcar Named Desire* and I was interested in exploring the role in a new way. Rather than look for an actor who had the animal magnetism and primitive brutality that we attribute to this role, I wanted someone who had to make an effort, who was trying to prove himself. Richard, the actor I cast, was tall and lanky, moved like a leopard, but you could always feel the animalistic urge rumbling underneath.

In these actor profiles (which you will be giving to the casting director), give yourself latitude and flexibility. For example:

I need an actor with a great sense of humor for this role. At the present that seems very important to me. But then of course if we cast someone who is humorless, droll, and terribly serious, that might just bring an appropriate tension to the relationship. All I know is the sense of humor is important; let's look at it from both sides. Surprise me.

This level of flexibility and openness is very important for both you and the casting director.

TYPECASTING

I have often said that I cast by type and as soon as the words are out
of my mouth I get a guaranteed groan from many actors. They are
horrified. But when they understand what I mean and the basic
wisdom of casting by type they have a different response.

Let's say you are casting two roles: Anthony and Gilda. Anthony is a
young street-wise Italian gangster and Gilda is a gentle unassuming
New Jersey grandmother. Now, if you say, "I only want to see tall,
good-looking Italian men for the Anthony role, and bring me only
Jewish grandmothers for the Gilda role," you are practicing an aspect
of casting by type that is very injurious and limiting. You are doing no
one any favors, least of all yourself. But if you look at casting by type
from a different perspective, you will begin to realize the wisdom of
this process.

If, for instance, you say:

> For the role of Anthony I need actors who have a strong affinity
> for life on the streets, who feel comfortable with the language,
> behavior, and morals. Yet, because of the nature of this character,
> they need to be at ease with their own vulnerability and not afraid
> to show their soft side.

> For the role of Gilda I want actresses who have a strong sense of
> family and family obligation. Preferably I would like actresses
> who have children and grandchildren, and a strong identity with
> an eastern (New Jersey) life style. Because of the strong religious
> beliefs of the character, I would prefer actresses who come to this
> conviction easily while not being afraid of their own strengths
> and anger.

This is typecasting. It's not casting by look, age, ethnicity, acting ability,
or experience. It's casting by life experience. You are taking into

155

consideration what the actor or actress is naturally going to bring to the role. Look at the character and ask yourself what sensibilities and experiences you need from the actor in order to bring the character to life.

There are dozens of actors who could portray any character well. But you want authenticity, that extra edge, taste, or flavor that will give each of your characters dimension.

At times you may want to cast *against* type for the very same reason. Often I will cast a role with an actor who has to work in order to accomplish certain attributes of the character, creating a new dimension. For instance:

> The role of Anthony:
> I want an actor who appears to be from the streets, very urban and at home with street life, but who in reality (as the actor) has had a suburban or rural background. I am looking for an actor who has to struggle a bit to maintain himself within the street world, one who always feels like an outsider.

> The role of Gilda:
> Ideally I would like an actress who does not have her own family but has a strong maternal pull. An actress who still wants that family she never had would be great. I want to feel that pull so that the envy and desire for children will be a predominant essence.

When you add the above ingredient to the casting process you are automatically adding a new dimension to the character, one that may or may not have been written. How wonderful to find an actor who automatically brings that quality and doesn't have to <u>act</u> it.

THE ACTOR/CHARACTER MELD

As we begin to approach the task of selecting actors to play our characters we need to consider two specific aspects of the acting process: the actor/character meld and the actor/character split.

One of an actor's main objectives is to bring herself as close to the character as possible — to actually align herself with the feelings, experiences, moods, objectives, and desires of the character so that at any given moment she can and will react just as the character does. She will move out of the actor's head and into the head, heart, and soul of the character. When this happens, the behavior, sensibilities, and process of the actor are left behind. This is the meld.

THE ACTOR/CHARACTER SPLIT

When at first you cast an actor in a role, there is a total split between the actor and that character. They are very distant from each other. During the course of rehearsals, development, and creation, the two move closer and closer together until finally at the time of performance you hit the meld. Even though the two may have merged there is always a significant degree of separation. Think of it this way — the actor, as he develops a deeper understanding for the character, the character's needs, desires, fears, and internal conflicts, actually gets to a point of knowing more about the character than the character does himself.

> For example: In *Rainman*, Charlie's (Tom Cruise) overall objective is to get the inheritance money that has been awarded to his brother Raymond (Dustin Hoffman). Charlie didn't even know that he had a brother until his father died and left all the money to Raymond, who happens to be autistic. But Tom Cruise knows that deep underneath his character's glib facade is a sense of loss that has always been eating at him; he wants to reconnect with

157

Raymond. *That* is his unconscious overall objective. There is a conscious overall objective (get the money) and a subconscious overall objective (reconnect with Raymond). The actor is aware of both objectives, but the character, Charlie, is aware *only* of the conscious objective, yet he is *driven* by the subconscious objective. As Tom Cruise aligns himself with the character he has to do two things: infuse the character with the internal desire or struggle and then, as the character, be unaware of it but driven by it. In this way the actor knows more about the character than the character does.

Another example: In *Forrest Gump*, Jenny is determined to change the world. She sees the world as brutal, unfair, abusive, and violent. She joins every peace movement and antiestablishment organization imaginable. She rebels against authority at every turn, yet she is never satisfied or appeased because the demon she is fighting is not outside herself but within herself. She is fighting against her father whom she already killed once but who will not die inside her. The actress, Robin Wright, playing this part knows all this. She knows that Jenny is fighting a losing battle. She knows that Jenny is actually destroying herself as she takes on every authority figure around her. And even though the fear and hatred of her father is what is driving her, she has to play Jenny without that specific awareness. She has to allow the rage against her father (who destroyed her childhood) to drive the character *without* the character being aware of it.

As you enter the casting process you need to be aware of what the *actor* is going to bring to the role of the *character*. If there are internal aspects of the character that are driving the character, then often it is advantageous and economical to seek an actor who brings those qualities with her so that they become a natural part of the package.

For example, suppose you are casting a role of a woman who, regardless of how caring and compassionate she is, has an angry, desperate, and destructive element that pulses way under the surface. The question becomes, do you cast someone who is naturally compassionate and caring and can create this destructive element, or do you cast someone who naturally has that desperate angry edge and can attempt to cover it up with a caring and compassionate veneer? The role will probably work either way, but there will be a discernible difference. In the first we will have an actress who is infusing her own nature with a dark and destructive quality. In the second we will have an actress who is trying to mask her dark and destructive tendencies with a veneer of compassion and gentleness. The question is: which is the *character* doing? If she is genuinely infusing herself with these darker qualities (for some reason), then cast the first actress, but if the character is trying to mask her darkness with this cover of gentility, then cast the second. You want the actor/character meld to occur as easily as possible. *This* is typecasting.

SELECTION OF SCENES

Once you have determined the arc of each character (see Chapter 4, "Script Breakdown") you will have a clear idea of what scenes you need for the audition process. Select scenes that represent turning points, different attitudes, relationships, struggles, and experiences of the character.

For instance: Here are some potential audition scenes for Lt. Dan from *Forrest Gump*:

Scene AA88. (page 55A). This is where Forrest and Bubba meet Lt. Dan. What is key about this scene? What is Lt. Dan's objective and what are we looking for in terms of our audition? Lt. Dan needs to impress upon his new recruits that he indeed is in charge, and that everything is going to go his way. It's more than just informing them of the risks and dangers in the Mekong Delta; Lt. Dan is intent upon maintaining control in an environment that is way out of his control. So what we are looking for in the audition is the authority, intimidation, and ability to take control of a situation immediately.

Scene A116 (page 74). Lt. Dan and Gump in the hospital ward. Lt. Dan is explaining to Forrest how Forrest cheated him from his destiny. We need to see the sense of anger and rage and disappointment in Lt. Dan for being saved from his "destiny." This is a key element in the character, his inner demon and major obstacle. In the audition you want to insure that the actor has the ability to connect with that rage since that is what drives the character for much of the rest of the movie.

Scenes A147-150 (page 97). Lt. Dan and Forrest in Lt. Dan's room off Times Square. This is a key scene for Lt. Dan. Still in his rage (and drinking deeply), he is slowly destroying himself. Forrest's openness, simplicity, and humanity begin to work on him. From rage (about the government abandoning him) to amusement (about Forrest's dream of owning a shrimp boat) to compassionate protection (when the prostitute Lenore calls Forrest stupid), it's an extraordinary sequence. All aspects of Lt. Dan are contained in these scenes.

There are several other scenes you could select (such as Lt. Dan railing against God in the storm on the boat or the scene where Lt. Dan finally thanks Forrest for saving his life), but the three scenes above contain most of the qualities you are looking for. Note: It's always a good idea to have the actors look at all of the scenes you might consider so at the last minute you can ask them to read an additional scene.

PREPARING THE ACTORS FOR THE READINGS

Uninformed and unprepared actors will give limited auditions. It is your job to see that every actor has the opportunity to be fully informed and prepared. Cold readings are of no value; they only tell you how well an actor can read the material cold, guessing at the intentions and context. You want to know how well an actor can handle the material knowing the context, objectives, and background of the character.

Consider the point of view of the actor:

> You're called to audition or read for a specific role. All you are given are the sides (the scenes to be read). You know nothing of the script, the director's vision, the background of the character, or what the director may be looking for in this particular character. You will have to rely on assumptions, intuition, and instinct to get you through.

In this scenario the actor is not able to bring all of his talent to the audition. An actor's talent is not just his ability to read a part or bring an emotional truth to a scene. It is also his ability to create a richly textured portrayal based on his understanding of the character and of the director's vision. Don't limit your actors; show them the respect for their craft as you show other artists.

Supply the actors with the following:

1. A paragraph on the project.
This is a short paragraph outlining the basic story line of your project and how you see the film. You don't need to go into great detail about your vision, but allow your passion for the project to be evident so the actors can get a sense of the movie as you see it. This will stir their own passions even if they have not read the script. Too many directors sit back and remain aloof when it comes to personal expression about the project. That is only going to cause others (actors included) to remain cautious and uncommitted. A committed director creates an environment of trust and safety and will stimulate the commitment of others.

Example: *Forrest Gump*.

This is a very simple yet profound story about an unassuming man whose only objective in life is to have a good life. He is not interested in wealth, accomplishments, career, or acclaim. He simply wants what each and every one of us wants, a life filled with love, growth, and happiness in the company of those individuals he cares for. He is an extraordinary man in his simplicity and an admirable man in his integrity and humanity. I genuinely believe that this project can, and will, change lives.

2. A paragraph on the character the actor will be reading.

First, tell the actor how the character is an essential element in the telling of the story (see Chapter 4, "Script Breakdown"), and then how you see the character.

Example: Jenny in *Forrest Gump*.

Jenny was never given the opportunity to have a childhood. Through brutality and abuse, she was thrust into a protective adult mode. With no mother and an abusive (physically and sexually) father, Jenny is alone and angry. She trusts no one except the simple and unassuming Forrest Gump. Jenny's life is spent searching for the person, organization, or substance that will turn her world right-side-up and destroy her demons. Even though she finds solace in the presence of Forrest, it is almost impossible for her to accept his genuine care and concern. She is so unaccustomed to unconditional love that she distrusts it and has to push it away.

It is important to me for Jenny always to come from a good place, and for her intentions always to be honorable (even though her actions may be objectionable). She means no harm to anyone. It is just that her demons are bigger than herself, and she fears that she will be destroyed if she can't destroy them.

3. The script.

An actor who is about to read for a project, no matter the size of the role, should have access to the entire script. This does not mean that you have to send a copy to every actor, but at least have a script available (at your office or casting director's office) that the actors can read. Give them the opportunity to study the work and bring their own sensibilities and interpretations to the role.

4. A letter from you to the actor

This informal greeting is intended to demystify and personalize the process. It is your first contact with the actors, and you want to take this opportunity to establish a level of communication that is personal and inviting. The letter might go something like this:

Dear _____ ,

First, I want to thank you for agreeing to read for this project. I am very excited about the potential of this film and I look forward to your audition.

I know that the audition process can often be rushed and impersonal. I will make every effort to give you the opportunity to show us your best work. I have enclosed some of my thoughts on the project and on the role you will be reading. I trust that these will be helpful as you prepare for our meeting.

Please feel free, when we meet, to ask me to clarify any aspects of this project, your character, or our audition process that may not be clear to you.

I look forward to meeting you.

Sincerely,

Fred Johntz, who recently completed a short film entitled *Toast*, sent me the following note after having read this chapter:

> Just a note to say that I followed the above suggestions in contacting actors to audition for *Toast* and many of them expressed extreme gratitude for being illuminated as to what was going on in the story, and just for being treated with respect.

5. The scenes to be read.
Along with this packet will be copies of the scenes that you want the actors to be reading (see Selection of Scenes).

Now the actors will be sufficiently prepared for the auditions. You will be seeing actors who are enthused, prepared, and passionately connected. The entire casting process therefore will run much more smoothly.

CASTING NAME ACTORS

Which brings us to the question of actors who won't read, or don't need to read, for whatever reason.

The process of casting well-known actors and personalities has to be viewed from a very different perspective. First you have to understand how and why a certain actor becomes well known and what that actor has to do in order to maintain that status.

Two considerations when casting name actors:

1. What are the character attributes that the actor brings with her?
2. What is the audience's expectation of this actor as based on the actor's previous work?

Actors have earned their "star" status because they have been able to consistently deliver certain qualities through the characters they portray.

For the purposes of our discussion I am dividing "name" actors into two categories, "persona" and "character". Please remember that actors have a way of surprising us. Just when we thought we knew them and their talent they go ahead and break the mold. The following discussion is not an attempt to categorize specific actors but rather an exercise to help you see the potential strengths and weaknesses of casting name actors in your film.

"PERSONA" ACTORS

Some actors are best known for their persona. These actors work in a limited range within which they are able to dynamically portray certain characters. Having carved out a very specific niche for themselves (Stallone, Eastwood, Sharon Stone, Goldie Hawn, Schwarzenegger) they will often refuse to consider roles outside their range. The more entrenched one of these actors is in his own niche (i.e., Sylvester Stallone as the macho rebel) the more the audience wants and expects him to play that role again. That's his bankability, his guarantee. This is not to say that you can't defy the odds and cast him in a lighthearted comedy where he may deliver a fine performance. But be aware of your audience's expectations and consider that you may have an uphill battle convincing them that their macho hero could be otherwise. In these cases, the audience's loyalty is actually to the persona the actor keeps portraying more than it is to the actor himself. Quite often they see no difference between the persona and the actor.

"CHARACTER" ACTORS

Other star actors have a wider range and have established their status primarily by their ability to portray an eclectic array of characters (Dustin Hoffman, Meryl Streep, Bill Pullman, Kathy Bates, Gary Senise, Tom Hanks). These actors have earned a very different audience expectation. In the case of, say, Meryl Streep the audience will have a loyalty to the actress and not any particular persona because each time they see her, it's a new persona. In this case we are anticipating that we will witness this actress lose herself into her character, and perhaps so totally that the actress will be lost to us. As a matter of fact we want her to lose herself, we want her to take us deep into yet another complex character.

With the persona actor we are not expecting the actor to lose himself into another persona at all. The actor is the persona. Quite often these films are structured around this central, predictable performance.

With the character actor we don't want or expect her persona on the screen. Often we don't even know what the persona is. In some cases we remember the characters so well that we have forgotten who portrayed them.

I have presented these as two extreme examples to make a point: name actors have a legacy and an audience expectation. Obviously, the less well known the actor, the smaller the legacy and the more undefined the audience expectation.

Steps that need to be taken when casting stars or name actors:

1. Consider the story and the particular character within the story
2. What will casting a name actor in that role do to the balance of the story (will it require you to cast names in any other roles)?
3. How will their perceived persona affect a particular role?

Note: For the moment I am putting aside all commercial concerns so we can look at casting name actors from a purely storytelling perspective. Having a well-known actor in your film will of course give it more commercial clout, but if the actor is miscast or does a disservice to your telling of the story, then the additional value may be minimal. (It could even work against you.) Often a lesser known actor or less commercially influential actor, well cast in the same role, may be a wiser and more beneficial decision — artistically and financially.

If you have a role where the persona of the actor and the predictability of the character are an asset, then you should cast an actor who brings that history and generates that audience expectation. But if you want the audience to discover the character as a new and unique person, then you want an actor who will be absorbed by the character.

THE AUDITION PROCESS

Before setting up your audition and casting schedule, you need to make sure you are very clear about your objectives during this critical process. This is more than just casting actors, it is a delicate and multifaceted process of interviews, readings, meetings, and private consultations. Here are some of the key aspects of the audition and casting process that you need to consider:

1. The Environment: where you will have the auditions
2. The Audition: getting to know the actors professionally
3. The Callbacks: testing the actor/director relationship
4. The Interviews: getting to know the actors personally
5. Mixing and Matching: checking for the chemistry
6. Creating the Ensemble: the "family" of the film
7. Directing the Actor in the Audition: when, how, and why
8. Screen Tests: when, how, and why
9. Viewing Past Work of the Actors
10. Contacting References

It is your responsibility to create an acting unit for your film that will individually and collectively bring emotional power and truthfulness to every role and to the film as a whole.

By the time you enter the casting process you are probably deep into preproduction, every department head wants and needs your attention, and you are lucky if you can devote half of each day to the casting process. You must be prepared.

167

1. The Environment

You want every actor to be at ease and to be able to give you his best. If you're in an office or a living room (not the ideal locations but frequently used) move the furniture back to create a space for the actors. Show them that you have made an effort on their behalf. And think about who's going to be in the room and where you want them to be in relationship to each other. In my casting sessions, besides myself, my assistant, the casting director, one or two producers, the writer, and the reader are usually in attendance. (We'll talk about the reader in a moment.) Once you have created a space for the actor, consider where you want the reader. Realize that the auditioning actor is going to play the scene primarily to the reader, so place the reader in a prominent central location. Then think about where *you* want to be in relationship to the actor and the reader. Remember, the actor is auditioning for you. You want the actor to feel that you can see his work easily, that there are no obstructions. Don't put yourself behind a table or a desk. Be accessible. Place everyone else (producers, writer, casting director) behind you and the reader since they are observers in the process, not participants. There are only three participants: you, the actor, and the reader.

THE READER

When you bring actors in to read one at a time, which is the ideal way in the first reading, you need someone to read with them. No matter how much you may want to and no matter how much someone may try to convince you, don't use the casting director, the writer, or one of the producers to read with the actors. Even if they are fairly decent actors, don't use them. It is their job to assess the auditions, and they can't do that fairly if they are in a performance relationship with the auditioning actors. Also, it is unfair to the actor to have her reading with someone who is judging the performance. Hire an actor (preferably a friend of yours that you have worked with) as your reader. There are three important reasons for this.

1. Since you want your auditioning actors to be working under optimum conditions, giving them a professional actor to read with will only enhance their performance.
2. The reader is a constant in the process. Every auditioning actor gets to read with the same actor.
3. Your reader's feedback is also an important part of your assessment. If the reader you have chosen is an accomplished actor and one whose insight you trust, you can get invaluable information from "inside" the actual audition. Actors sense and feel things while they are reading with other actors, and your reader's experience may give you understanding of the potential strengths and weaknesses of that actor.

You have your reader in place, you have everyone else located in the room and the room is to your liking. Now you are ready to begin the process of the first readings.

2. The Audition

Note: Since the bottom line is acting and performance ability, your primary litmus test must be the audition itself, saving the interview and other areas of exploration for phase two.

The Audition Sequence.

The first reading is about an actor's interpretation and imagination. It is not important that the actors come anywhere near your interpretation. You are looking for actors of imagination, courage, and conviction, and you need to create an environment that is conducive and supportive of that work.

The first readings.
1. Give actors enough time (schedule 10 to 15 minutes each) to be able to present their work.

2. Take a moment before each reading to allow the actor to adjust to the room and the surroundings.
3. Introduce *everyone* in the room. And *you* do it. You are the director. Guide the actor (and everyone else) through the process.
4. Let the actors take control of the session, when and how they'd like to start, whether they want to talk a bit first, or just get straight to the reading. You will have plenty of time in later sessions and eventually in production for taking control.

What to watch for when the actor is reading.
1. Script comprehension:
   Does the actor have a clear comprehension of the dynamics and flow of the script. Is there intelligence in this reading? Does the actor have a good sense of storytelling and does he bring clarity and shape to the material?
2. Courage:
   Is the actor simply delivering what seems obvious in the material (especially in terms of character choices) or is she making bold choices and courageous adjustments, thereby bringing unpredictability and freshness to the material.
3. Originality:
   Is there anything about this actor and his choices that is totally original and unique or is he playing everything very safe. Look for actors who make unpredictable choices and yet can make them believable within the context of the material.
4. Clarity of objectives, character arc:
   It is not enough just to be courageous and original. The actor also has to bring clarity to each choice. Vagueness causes confusion. Look for those actors who can make you feel that their choices for action and for character are so clear that they seem to be the only logical choices.
5. Selflessness:
   You want giving actors. Be aware of actors who require high maintenance, who feel that the whole event is about them, who can literally suck the energy out of everyone, including you.

6. Honesty:

    And beneath all there must be integrity. No matter the nature or genre of the material, all choices have to be based in some form of reality and therefore appear to generate from some sense of truth. This is the actors' job. If you don't believe in the characters, you won't get involved in their journey.

Don't forget to express enthusiasm (honest enthusiasm) after each reading. Remember, the actor is working hard, doing the best she can and that hard work deserves recognition, regardless of the quality of the work. The effort itself is admirable.

If you are interested in an actor and you want to explore further you can:

1. Have him read the scene again with a slight (but significant) adjustment.
2. Have him read a different scene.
3. Take a few moments to discuss the character, the project, acting, or whatever (the beginning of an interview).

If you are genuinely *not* interested in the actor who has just read: Do a short interview. See if there is something within the actor herself that may renew your interest. Often good actors read badly, especially on the first reading. You may discover in a brief interview that there is something within this actor that could serve the character very well and that it is worth giving her another audition. More times than not, if you are not pleased or interested in the actor based on the first reading, you will not find something in the interview to change your mind, but it's worth a shot.

Note: Be honest with the actors. They deal with hope and rejection all the time as a part of their life experience, they can handle it. But they don't deserve to be lied to. Tell them you appreciate their talent and effort. If they're not right for the role, don't lead them on unnecessarily.

Keeping A Record.

After each actor leaves either write or dictate your reactions: what you liked, didn't like; areas of strength and weakness, and whether or not you would like to call this particular actor back. If there is a callback, note the areas you'd like to work on, test, or explore.

Do this immediately after each audition. After hours of casting you will be hard pressed to remember individual actors, let alone your specific reactions to their work. This record will become helpful for this audition as well as future projects. Don't trust your memory and be specific. See the chart below as a suggestion.

ACTOR'S AUDITION RECORD - PROJECT NAME _____

Date: _____

Actor's Name: _____ Role: _____

Agent or Manager: _____

Phone Numbers: Agent: _____ Actor: _____

First reading: _____ Call back #: _____ Call back again: Y ___ N ___

Strengths: _____

_____

Weaknesses: _____

_____

Next Callback look for: _____

_____

Other roles to consider for: _____ None: _____

Notes: _____

_____

I prefer to have my assistant record my comments because it is much easier for me to verbalize my feelings than to have to write them down myself, and it saves a lot of time.

At the end of the day's session review your notes with your assistant and the casting director to determine potential callbacks.

3. The Callbacks

Before you begin callbacks think about what you want to achieve:
1. Pairing of actors
2. Further exploration of original material
3. Exploring new material
4. Directing the actors

Note: When actors go in for their first reading they are aware that, with so many called in for each role, the odds are not in the favor of any single actor. In the callbacks they know they are being seriously considered for the role. Then there is an attitude change; there is a vote of confidence, the odds are shifting. The stakes are higher. As the confidence rises, so does the apprehension. Then there are the interviews and the screen tests. As the odds get better the tension gets greater and the actor slides deeper into a protective posture. Not being called back after the first reading has little impact on most actors, but the rejection at the point of final callbacks or screen tests can leave one reeling.

You need to be sensitive to the stages that actors go through during this process. Be aware of the fact that as the competition becomes more fierce the actors will tend to be more isolated, removed, cautious, and protective. They will be moving further away from the attitudes and behavior that they will exhibit in the rehearsal or production process.

This is one reason why it is important that you as the director begin to take more control of the process. The more disciplined, supportive, and controlled the process is, the more likely it will be that you will elicit genuine and secure auditions from your actors.

During the callbacks and final stages of the auditioning process, you want to explore the range and compatibility of the actors in their potential roles and how each actor is going to respond to you and your direction. If I think that I might have to push an actor in order to achieve a certain performance level, then I very well might test that actor's ability and willingness to collaborate with me in the callbacks. If I find an actor is particularly resistant to my way of working, I may consider that sufficient reason to go with another actor.

If you sense that an actor is going to be difficult or resistant to your way of working, make note of it. Don't overlook any signs or gut feelings that you might have. Use the improvisations and rehearsals in casting to test the working relationship. Bring up your concerns (see Interviews) when you talk to the actor privately. Ask other directors and producers (see References) what their experiences have been. And then, always trust your gut instinct. One resistant or difficult actor can severely damage the balance of your acting ensemble.

4. The Interviews - Getting To Know Your Actors Personally

Note: We are only interviewing actors who are under strong consideration.

There is often a great difference between the actor and the way he will present himself through the character. As we discussed earlier it is often the struggle and tension between the actor and the character that creates that subtle yet profound tension in the character. So, you need to have an idea of who this person is when he is not acting.

You also want to know how she works as an actress. What is her approach, her process; who is she currently studying with? You want to know how she sees this character and this film. Remember, you might be spending many hours with her in rehearsal and production, possibly under great stress. She could be a member of your creative team, and you need to have a good sense of how she is going to participate.

This interview could be as important as the audition. You could find an actor who gives a great rendition of the role but who in the interview displays an approach or attitude that seems counterproductive and could cause distress during rehearsal and production. On the other hand you might find an actor who gives a good reading of the character and yet in the interview there is an energy, approach, and attitude that could be an enormous asset to your production. Go with the second actor. He could easily surpass the first just through sheer enthusiasm.

Prepare yourself for these interviews. Here is an example:

Here are some of the questions we might be asking for the role of Lt. Dan in *Forrest Gump*:

1. Do you have a feeling of destiny in your life? Do you ever feel that you are here to fulfill a certain obligation or objective (even though you might not know what it is)?

2. What is your feeling about war? Do each of us have an obligation to protect and serve? Under what conditions is self-defense or attack justified in your opinion?
3. Is there someone in your life that you feel obligated to? That you would give your life for?
4. Do you have someone in your life who has changed your opinion about yourself and your relationship to others?
5. What are your thoughts about Lt. Dan? His commitments? His attitudes about war and obligation? His attitudes about Gump and Bubba?
6. Have you ever felt that life wasn't worth living anymore?
7. What's your relationship with God, a higher power, or destiny?

You have to understand that we are <u>not</u> trying to replicate Lt. Dan. We are exploring the similarities and differences between the actors and Lt. Dan. Remember what we said earlier about the conflict between actor and character (and how that tension can help create the energy of the character). We are merely getting an indication of the potential energy that will be generated when we begin the actor/character meld.

5. Mixing And Matching

Acting is a highly collaborative art form and actors have the tendency to either bring out the best in each other or hamper each other's work. You will never know (but you can guess) how two actors are going to work together until you put them together. I have made the mistake of assuming that two actors, whom I have worked with in one production, will produce the same chemistry in another production. It is not necessarily so. The mix is not the same. In a new production there are new characters who will affect the actors in very specific ways and suddenly they may not be working as well together as they did previously. The only way to test potential working relationships is to put the actors together and work with them. How you mix and match the actors in these callbacks is very important.

For instance: you may find one actor is having difficulty finding the strength in a particular character but when matched with another actor he is suddenly able to find that strength. Or maybe it is vulnerability (always a tough attribute to play) that seems to be lacking, but when you match that actor with another actor who has a certain gentleness or compassion you may find the vulnerability is suddenly present.

In another situation you may find that when a particular actor is forced to deal with the strong presence of another actor, the resistance or friction that is created actually lends a credibility and genuine tension that was lacking before.

This is not to say that we are trying to cure actors' shortcomings by the magic of pairing, but rather that we as directors have to be aware that there are certain attributes in our characters that are difficult to play in solo and that may never appear if the actor is inappropriately paired. We cannot (and must not) make assumptions about the effects and affects of pairing. Use this time in the casting process to test your suppositions. Experiment, be daring, and be willing to be surprised and proven wrong.

6. Creating The Ensemble

Casting is creating a family and each member of the family has a specific function. During the entire casting process you have to be cognizant of how a potential cast member might affect the family balance. A talented actor who gives a great reading is not necessarily the best actor for the ensemble.

It is usually impossible to assemble the entire potential cast to see how they are all going to work together, but do make every effort to bring together as many of the key characters as possible so that you can experience the dynamics that will be created between them. Don't wait until you're on the set or in rehearsal to find that you have a dynamic occurring between some of your actors that may be counterproductive to your film.

7. Directing The Actor In The Audition

For both the actor and the director the audition process bears little resemblance to the rehearsal or production process. The audition process is nothing more than a testing process — a result process.

Think for a moment about how an actor approaches the audition process. He gets a script, a certain amount of information on the role, the scene, and some idea of what the director is looking for. Then it is his job to arrive at the appointed time and deliver a performance. He has to go for results. There is no time to develop and create a multifaceted character. This is not about his training or willingness to work with other actors or the director. This is about performance, and he knows that this is what the director wants and needs to see. The audition is not a time for exploration or experimentation; it is a time for results.

> Likewise, directing in the audition process bears little resemblance to directing in rehearsal and production. From the uninitiated or uneducated observer they may all seem the same but there are subtle yet profound differences that are felt and experienced by both the director and the actors. All actors intuitively know that the actor-director relationship is going to be different during the auditions because the needs of all are different. The actor knows that she is there to be tested, to be pushed and stretched, and she is willing and eager for that testing to happen. Using the same techniques in the rehearsal or production process would very likely produce very different results as we shall see.

As you watch the actor in audition ask yourself the following questions:
    1. What would happen if he were to play it the opposite way?

2. What other objective could I give him to play? How about the opposite objective?
3. How about a new obstacle? A bigger obstacle? A smaller obstacle?
4. What qualities of the character am I not seeing?
5. What aspects of the relationship am I not seeing?
6. What tones, rhythms, or qualities of the scene am I not seeing?
7. What subtle adjustments could I give him?
8. What drastic (and even outrageous) adjustments could I give him?

Then, after his reading, it's time to start directing.

I like to open this phase of the process with "Forgive me for going for results, but I just want to try a few things. I have this idea that . . ." This disclaimer is very important (and it is a great directorial tool as we shall see later) in that it states your acknowledgment that you are about to go for results and it implies that you don't customarily work this way. It will immediately put the actor at ease (which is what you want) and focus his attention on the "few things" you want to try.

Now you can shamelessly go for those results, you and the actress together. "Let's try it again this way — I want more subtlety, brashness, anger, resentment, joy, (whatever)." Or, "let's start with this objective or with a different obstacle, etc."

By giving the actress very specific goals, obstacles or objectives you will immediately see how quickly and successfully she can respond to input without questioning the rationality or taking the time to develop these choices.

You may elect to use improvisations, staging, rehearsal exercises, personal explorations, or even theatre games to further explore the range and depth of this particular actor. (In the next chapter we will discuss these rehearsal techniques and how they can be employed in the casting, rehearsal, and production processes.)

Regardless of your assessment, offer a compliment after each audition. The actor is working hard and doing the best that he can and deserves your acknowledgment.

8. Screen Tests

Directors use screen tests for a variety of reasons. The most obvious is to see how the actor comes across on film. The camera truly does capture different aspects of each person, and you never know how a particular actor is going to appear on the screen until you test her, or how she will come across vocally. If you have any concerns about either the image or the sound quality of an actor, do a screen test. The cost of the test can be one of the best investments you make.

Other reasons include: colors, textures, and tones of sets; actors in costume; the actors' ability to work in front of the camera; and even testing the chemistry between actors on the screen.

There are directors who insist on a screen test for all actors in major roles but there are others who find screen tests a total waste of time, relying on their instincts and intuitions about the actor. Then there are some directors who don't even read their actors, but just meet with them and cast on the basis of those interviews.

It's important that you be aware of all the various aspects of the casting process and their pros and cons. Screen tests can be very useful and can even be used to convince an uncertain producer or executive of the value of a particular actor. Be clear what are you testing for and design the test so you get the answers you need. Why are you testing this particular actor? What's the scene to be used? Why that scene? Who are the other actors? What potential relationship are you looking for between these actors? How much rehearsal do you want to do? What type of rehearsal? What kind of environment do you want to establish? All of these factors will affect the nature of the screen test because they will all affect the performance of the actor in question.

9. Viewing Past Work Of The Actors

One of the sheer joys of this business is the existence of videotapes and laser discs. At our finger tips is immediate access to the work of thousands of actors. When considering actors, look at their work, no matter how small or seemingly insignificant.

10. Contacting References

Directors, producers, writers, and other actors with whom the actor has worked are an important source of information. Very rarely has the information I have received from another director or producer totally swayed me from either hiring or not hiring a particular actor, but I have always gained further insight into the nature and working habits of the actor. I am always impressed by the willingness of most directors and producers to share this very valuable information. The times that I have been burned have been the times that I have not made the calls, when I have assumed that there was no need. Make the calls!

And finally . . .

As I stated above, actors are never the same in the casting process as they are once they have been cast. An actor vying for a job is a very different person than an actor who has the job. Once you have offered an actor the role, you often will find that you are dealing with a different person than the one you were dealing with in the casting process. This is not a problem, just something you need to be aware of. Accept it as one of the joys and surprises of the process. And remember, *you* change too. You're not the same director in the casting process as you will be in the rehearsal and production process.

CHAPTER 7

THE REHEARSAL PROCESS

One way of looking at the filming process (or, more specifically, the storytelling process via film) is this: We *create* an event, we *record* the event, then (in postproduction) we *recreate* the event. But no matter how you look at it there does have to be that *initial event*. Through the magical mix of script, director, and the actors the event is created and it becomes the heart and soul of our story. Without an event there is nothing to record.

The question becomes: How do we create this event? We have the script, we've done our breakdown, we've selected our actors. Welcome to the rehearsal process.

THE NINE BASIC STEPS

As you enter into the rehearsal process you must keep in mind the nine basic steps of film directing. They are:
1. What is the story really about?
2. What is this scene about?
3. Why is this scene in the movie?
4. What must I as director achieve with this scene so that it will function properly within the movie?
5. What are the character objectives, obstacles, arcs, means, actions, activities, adjustments, windows of true nature, risks, stakes, etc?
6. How can I direct and stage the scene in order to clarify and underline the essential dynamics within the scene?
7. How can I capture (record) this scene in order to enhance the essential dynamics of the scene?

8. How do I rediscover the story that is contained within the material I have created?
9. How do I reassemble this material in order to create the most dynamic version of my story?

We have already covered steps 1 to 4 and are now, in the rehearsal process, addressing steps 5 and 6.

With any luck, and usually with a lot of persistence, you will have scheduled a rehearsal period for your film. It will vary anywhere from a few days to a few weeks. Regardless, the approach will be the same.

The rehearsal process has two time periods: preproduction and production. Much of what will be established in the preproduction rehearsal will be the basis for rehearsals during production.

THE REHEARSAL PLAN

First you must develop a plan that will maximize your rehearsal time. On one hand you need to be realistic about what you can accomplish in the time you have (both in preproduction and in production), while on the other hand you need to be ambitious and bold.

Let's look at a typical preproduction rehearsal plan. Imagine that you have two weeks of rehearsal (this is about average), five days a week. In reality this will probably end up being half days as you will need the other half days for your other preproduction concerns. If you can hold on to these ten half days for rehearsal and rehearsal only, you will be doing very well.

This comes to four hours a day for ten days over two weeks. Forty hours. That's a lot of rehearsal time. What do you do with it?

The real question is: What are your priorities and what are the specific needs of the script?

Overall Priorities:
1. Give the cast a comprehensive feeling of the whole story and a sense of your vision of the film.
2. Establish rhythm, pace, tone, attitude, and style for the story and the characters, etc.
3. Develop specific relationships between the characters and between the actors.
4. Develop a history of the characters.
5. Explore specific working relationships between the actors and the director.
6. Explore working relationships between the actors.

Note that all of the above have nothing to do with working on specific scenes or events. We are developing significant relationships which will inform those scenes and how you will work on them.

Specific Priorities:
1. Those scenes that have specific problems or challenges that have to be addressed and resolved.
2. Scenes that mark significant changes or turning points in characters or relationships.
3. An understanding of the structure and arc of each sequence (a series of scenes with its own unity of beginning, middle, and end)
4. The unwritten scenes and events. This includes all significant scenes and events that are *not* written in the script but which are either alluded to or have helped shape or inspire the events in the script.

Having completed your script breakdown and character analysis you should have a pretty clear idea of where your priorities lie in terms of rehearsal time. But let me suggest that no matter how much or how little rehearsal time you have, you cover the six overall priorities listed above. You need these in order to establish certain attitudes and working relationships; even if you have only a couple of days of rehearsal you can easily address all six.

Here's how a typical two-week rehearsal schedule might look. We will discuss each aspect in more detail.

DAY	HOURS	REHEARSAL
1. Monday	4 hours	•First read-through of script with all principal actors, producers, writer, staff, and key personnel (3 hours). •Talk-through with actors (1 hour).
2. Tuesday	4 hours	•Ensemble work with the actors. Creating the story.
3. Wednesday	4 hours	•Developing the world of your film.
4. Thursday	4 hours	•Developing character backgrounds and histories.
5. Friday	4 hours	•Read through of the script (with writer present).
6. Monday	4 hours	•Improvise the story (3 hours). •Review any rewrites (1 hour).
7. Tuesday	4 hours	•Working specific scenes and sequences (3 hours). •Improvising the unwritten scenes (1 hour).
8. Wednesday	4 hours	•Working specific scenes and sequences (3 hours). •Improvising the unwritten scenes (1 hour).
9. Thursday	4 hours	•Working specific scenes and sequences (3 hours). •Improvising the unwritten scenes (1 hour).
10. Friday	4 hours	•Final read-through (with writer, producers, key personnel).

DAY ONE (MONDAY)

THE FIRST REHEARSAL AND READ-THROUGH

In this very important first rehearsal you will be setting the tone for the remaining part of your filmmaking journey. That's right. In these crucial three or four hours you are going to establish a way of working not only for you and the actors but for the entire crew as well. Here is how it works.

First, invite everyone. Everyone who has been hired to work on your film must be invited to the first rehearsal. You want them there (or at least you want them to know that they were invited). Especially the actors, producing staff, your creative team, first A.D., second A.D., UPM, and the entire crew. They are all your collaborators and you want them there. Some may not be available to come and that's understandable, but there are certain people who <u>must</u> be there: cinematographer, editor, production designer, all producers, set decorators, makeup artist, hair stylist, casting director, and of course the actors.

Have this first read-through scheduled in a large room — a large rehearsal room would be good — and not in an office or conference room. You want space.

Once you have gathered everyone together your first objective is two-fold: (1) introduce everyone, and (2) create an ensemble. By creating an ensemble I mean creating the experience that everyone is an equal member of this collaborative team and that no one contribution is lesser or greater than another.

There's one simple, painless, and very enjoyable way to achieve these two goals in a matter of 15 - 20 minutes:

First, get everyone in a circle. You'll probably have anywhere from 15 - 40 people so it's going to be a large circle (the reason for the large room). And you'll need a ball — a small beach ball or volley ball. Find one that's easy for everyone to handle. One rule of this exercise, or game, is that <u>everyone</u> in the room must participate. There are no observers. With everyone standing in a circle, start tossing the ball around. Instruct everyone that the ball must be thrown so that it <u>can</u> be caught. This is not a competitive game, it is a collaborative game.

Names

The person throwing the ball must announce the first name of the person he is throwing the ball to. Most of the people will panic because they hardly know anyone, but you can tell them that they can always throw the ball to you. They should know your name by now (and you should know <u>all</u> their names). At first they will be tentative, many will make mistakes, and you'll get the ball a lot. Eventually all the names will have been announced and soon you will see the ball whipping back and forth as everyone gets more confident and secure. Once you feel that sense of security, stop the game and ask for a volunteer to attempt *all* the names. Usually several will volunteer and most will succeed with the encouragement and congratulations of everyone else. Already the family is beginning to form.

Positions

Now we are following the announcement of the names by the position on this project (producer, cinematographer, grip, etc.) and for the actors you have to give the name of the role they are playing. After a tentative start the ball will be whipping around again with everyone gaining confidence. Call for volunteers again to try the whole circle, names, and positions. Several will volunteer and when someone does the entire circle, you will feel the further defining of your creative family as the group celebrates.

That's it. That's all you need to do. There are many more versions of this game that you can play (such as Alphabet, Word Alphabet, Nursery Rhymes, and Story Building), but for the moment let's concentrate on what you have achieved so far.

First, collaboration. These are games without winners or losers and the group's objective is to accomplish a common goal. This is a very important step in the creation of your ensemble: teamwork rather than competition. Filmmaking is collaboration. You could tell this to your cast and crew all day long, and they would agree with you, but it won't be an integral part of their system until they have *experienced* it.

Second, the circle. It puts everyone in an equal position. As soon as you sit at a table, someone has to sit at the head of the table, or some people are at more or less prominent tables and suddenly it doesn't feel so equal anymore. The circle establishes equality — equality in collaboration with *everyone* joining in. There is no separation, no exclusion.

Collaboration, cooperation, familiarity, equality. All accomplished within 15 - 20 minutes. First goal achieved!

Second goal: Input from everyone. Now we want to hear from each person about his/her contribution to this project. Bring everyone to the tables you have had arranged (preferably in a large square or circle so there is no disparity in seating). Let everyone sit where they like. (I like to have all the actors <u>not</u> sit together. For the reading it is much more interesting to have the actors sitting among the other crew and staff members.)

You're going to ask each person to talk about what he is going to bring to the making of this film. Some crew and staff members may balk at this idea insisting that they have nothing to say. Don't let them get away with this. Everyone has to speak. That is the rule. It doesn't have to be much.

I once had a craft service man get up and say, "My contribution to this film is going to be the best coffee, the best donuts, and the freshest bagels possible." And that was sufficient. In fact it got applause.

I was at the first rehearsal of Jeff Boortz's *Tear It Down* and one of the actors (who had a one-day, three-line role) said: "I know you could have found a better actor for this part, but you never could have found someone more passionate about this project. I'm here to give 110 percent." The cinematographer leaned over and said to Jeff, "Boy, that's extraordinary. I sure hope I can live up to that."

You will want certain members to elaborate more than others. Have the designers (production, props, costume, set dressing, etc.) give everyone an idea of the environments and wardrobe they will be creating. The cinematographer can give a more detailed description of the look of the film. It is important that everyone speaks, regardless of their position. Even the actors — even you!

When it's your turn to talk, remember you're not just assuming the position of leader; you're generating enthusiasm and excitement for the project. Your task is to pull all the creative elements together into a cohesive whole. This is perhaps the only opportunity you will have to address such a large gathering of creative personnel.

Impress them with your enthusiasm for the project (it is your enthusiasm more than the project itself that will keep them working at their best when the going gets rough — and it will). Impress them with the beauty of the film, its look, its tone, its rhythms. Let them know that they are each contributing to the creation of a unique work of art. And finally, impress upon them the importance of the collaborative process and how much you are looking forward to working with all of them.

The Read-Through

Take a short break before the reading so that everyone is fresh and alert. There are several points to be considered before you do this first reading:

1. You don't want a full-out performance. The purpose of the reading is for everyone to hear the script and get a feel for the story, the characters, the rhythms, and tone. This reading is not intended to impress anyone but rather to focus everyone.

2. Even though we can assume that everyone has read the script prior to this reading, it is advisable to have someone read the screen directions and descriptions. I like to employ the services of an actor (who may have a small role in the film) who can give the descriptions a special flavor or energy. There is nothing worse than screen directions read in a flat matter-of-fact manner.

3. Watch your audience. This is the first audience with your cast reading the story. Be aware of their responses: when they get restless, bored, excited or amused.

Before you start the reading, announce that one actor will be reading all the screen directions, that you do not expect performances out of the actors and that you just want to hear the text. This will be a great relief to the actors, and everyone will settle in to listen to the story.

As the reading proceeds, sit back and listen. Let the story wash over you. Be aware of the reactions of others but don't judge — just listen.

After the reading, thank the actors. Thank everyone for coming and dismiss everyone except the actors.

Some people may want to make comments about the script or the performances. Make sure they do this with you privately. This is when you need to establish that you are going to protect the actors from outside criticism and comments.

During rehearsal, production, and postproduction it is important that you establish appropriate channels of communication. Let your staff and crew know that they are encouraged to communicate their thoughts and ideas to you. <u>But</u>, they have to do so at an appropriate time and place, and be sensitive to the actors and other members of the creative team. Giving everyone the opportunity to be heard is a major step in the creation of an effective collaborative team. Take the time to listen to the input. You may think that you are sacrificing valuable time, but in actuality you are nurturing the best in each collaborator.

The Talk-Through

With the time you have left you want to reestablish your connection with actors and the story to be told.

The talk-through consists of talking through the story with all the actors present. This is not a reading of the script or telling of the story again, but rather a communal response to the story. Since we have just read the story and the actors have (for the first time) <u>heard</u> it, you want to check in on the individual and collective responses. Avoid critique, analysis, or suggestions for reworking the story. All you want to know is how the story <u>affects</u> each actor. You want to hear their response to the material, the characters, and the journey.

This time you go first. Set the tone by telling the actors how you responded to the reading. This has nothing to do with their performances (you asked them not to perform, remember?) but with the story. My response to a reading of *Forrest Gump* might go something like this:

> You know, when I first read this story I was struck by its simplicity, its honesty, and its sense of integrity. But as I listen to all of you read it today I am moved by the genuine earnestness of each and

every character. I realize how powerful this story really is. This is a story without villains. This is a beautiful story of people simply seeking meaning in their lives, and as I listen to each and every character searching for clarity I am struck by how significant this is to me. As the director of this project I have been seeking my own personal connection with this simple yet profound story, and as I listened today it became clear to me that I don't need to work so hard. What I really need to do is let go and let it affect me the way Forrest affects every single person in the story. And so I thank you. I thank you for bringing this clarity to me.

As you listen to the actors share their experiences with the story, realize that you are building your ensemble. You and the actors are the storytellers. You are the keepers of the vision.

DAY TWO (TUESDAY)

ENSEMBLE WORK WITH THE ACTORS

In each film there is a unique blend of characters that makes up the "family" of the film. It is our goal in these initial rehearsals to develop the acting ensemble into a tightly knit team.

Each film is a world in itself. No matter how biographical, autobiographical, or factual it may be, it is still a work of fiction in a world that does not exist outside itself. Your cast members are the inhabitants of this world and with them you are going to define the behavior, attitudes, codes, and social structure. That is a primary goal of the ensemble — creating the world of the film.

Let's look at *Forrest Gump* and see how we might develop the ensemble.

The original ball game we played with the cast and crew was the first step toward building the *company* ensemble. Now we are going to take it a step or two further and solidify the *acting* ensemble.

Telling A Story

Place the actors in a circle. Tell them that the objective of this exercise is to simply tell the story. One performer goes to the center of the circle and begins a story — any story. Then, after a few moments, that performer will turn the story over to another performer who will in turn add to the story and then turn it over to another.

There are three rules: (1) You cannot deny or ignore what has already been established in the story, (2) You can turn the story over to anyone you chose (no particular order), and (3) You must always turn the story over on a cliff-hanger. In other words, turn the story over in the middle of a thought. Such as: " . . . and then she looked down into the cellar and she saw . . ." and that's when you turn it over. Allow the actors to create any story they want. The stories will wander and may not make a lot of sense, but that's not important. The goal is collaboration in storytelling.

After a couple of stories have the actors tell the story of your film (now referred to as our film). Remind them that they are still storytellers and are not required to play their characters. A new energy and concentration will take over. Suddenly they have an obligation to a specific story. Be aware that each performer, because there is no restriction of character, is performing as herself. You will be witnessing actors at their most expressive. You will see certain qualities (humor, vulnerability, sarcasm, wit, etc.) in the actors that you may want to employ in the development of their characters.

There are other exercises and games you can use to generate unity amongst the cast. The best are those that are designed by you to fit the specific needs of your cast and story. For example: Let each actor in *Forrest Gump* select (or be assigned) a specific aspect of the story for research. For instance, have the actor who is playing Lt. Dan do research on the particular events of the Vietnam War that pertain to your story. Have the actress playing Jenny do research on war protests, the Black Panthers, and the antiwar marches in Washington. The actor playing Bubba can bring in research on the shrimping industry, etc. They can share this information with the rest of the cast through storytelling or a game. Even though these are separate assignments, it is the gathering of the ensemble and the sharing of this information that will again bring a unity to your cast.

DAY THREE (WEDNESDAY)

CREATING THE WORLD OF THE FILM

In *Forrest Gump* we are dealing with a very specific world on many levels. It is the world of the fifties, sixties, seventies, and eighties. America. The South. Rock and Roll. The Beatles. Vietnam. Nixon, Kennedy, Johnson. This is a world that no longer exists, a time when many of us thought we could make a difference, when the whole world was open to us — a land of possibilities, options, innocence, naiveté, and wonder. It was also a world of enormous division and dissension. Many movies have been made about this time period and these events, so what makes the world of *Forrest Gump* special? This is the world as seen through the eyes of Forrest Gump, so it is very specifically his memory, his point of view of these events. The question becomes: How do we begin to create this very special world with the actors we have selected?

Every film and every story is told from one specific point of view, and it is through that singular point of view that we the audience experience this new world. This is your point of view, the director.

But with some films (for example, *Forrest Gump, Little Big Man, Stand by Me*), there is a character, who is also the narrator, telling the story to the audience. In other words we are seeing his version of the story.

195

Reversing The Process

The audience experiences events as filtered through the individual characters (actors) and then through the narrator/storyteller (in this case, Gump) and finally through the director. We need to look at this process in reverse, to explore the world of *Forrest Gump* through the director's eyes first (general), then narrator/Forrest's eyes (more specific), and finally the individual actors/characters (most specific).

Step One. The Director's Point of View of the Story.

This is simply sharing your vision of the story with the cast.

For *Gump* it might go something like this:

> The world of innocence, of simplicity. I see this story unfolding in a simple, direct, and honest manner. I want the experience of *Forrest Gump* to be one of wonderment, no different than Forrest's experience of his world. Regardless of the abuse, pain, violence, and deception that occurs around Forrest, I see his constant determination to do what he feels is right to be a shining light in the darkness. It is his love and respect for his mother, his commitment to Bubba, and his undying belief in Lt. Dan that elevate these relationships above the ordinary. And finally it is his love, respect, commitment, and belief in Jenny that gives us all new insights into the meaning of unconditional love.

> Note: You are actually incorporating the writer's vision with yours in this process. It is important that you do not present the writer's point of view as a separate vision. Disparities between you and the writer need to be handled privately. Unity and cohesion must be presented at this time.

Step Two. The Character/Narrator's Point of View.

This step pertains only to those scripts that have a narrator. This is a delicate area and has to be handled sensitively. We want to explore this particular actor/character's vision of the story he is telling. In other words, how does the actor playing Gump see this story? It is after all his (Gump's) story, and we (the other characters who are portrayed through his vision) can gain great insight into our role in the entire process if we have a clear vision of <u>his</u> view of the story. What is his purpose for telling the story? How does he see each event, each character?

> Note: We all see our own lives and experiences in a very unique way. It is in the telling of stories that we are able to share these special experiences. That is precisely what Gump is doing in this story (and what <u>you</u> are doing as <u>you</u> tell the story through your direction).

Let the actor playing the narrator tell the story from her own point of view. You have to be careful as this actor begins to talk about the other characters. There is a very fine line between one character's experience of another character and one actor telling another actor how to play a character. The first situation is entirely acceptable and important to explore; the second situation is entirely unacceptable and has to be stopped immediately. You need to remind the other actors that this description in no way defines how their character is to be portrayed, but that this is how one characters <u>sees</u> another, *experiences* another.

Step Three. Characters' Points of View of the Events in the Story.

The third and final step is having each actor tell the story from his character's point of view.

For example: Lt. Dan's point of view of the story of *Forrest Gump* might go something like this:

I am proud that I came from a military family. Every man in my family died in a major war. We died protecting our country. And I'll probably do the same thing. And Vietnam comes along and it's perfect. My destiny. But then I get assigned these guys in my platoon. I mean these guys are stupid, really stupid. I was chosen to lead this platoon, 'cause I'm good. I know I'm good and if anyone can lead this platoon, it's me. I'm a military man. But then we get caught in this crossfire trying to take some hill in the middle of nowhere, and it's pretty obvious that this is the end for all of us. And then this guy, Forrest Gump, as slow as molasses and as thick as a brick, starts running. And all these other guys start following him and we're getting blown to bits and then I get hit — both legs — and I know this is my moment. I know I'm going down. But no, Gump's not gonna let me go down. That jerk decides to come back and save me. That jerk hauls my dying ass outta there and he saves me! Pissed me off! Next thing I know I'm in the hospital, next to this jerk. I can't get away from him. I mean this goes on and on. I get stateside and there he is in New York City. Always calling me "Lt. Dan." I mean, all I want to do is drink myself numb and there he is, telling me about some stupid shrimp boat he's gonna have. And all for Bubba, the other retard who was lucky enough to die in Nam. But every time I get away from him I can't seem to get him out of my mind. That stupid smiling face of his. Always being so nice. I told him that if he ever got the shrimp boat I'd be his first mate. And then he does it. Gets the boat. And something tells me I gotta be there. I mean I got no legs now, and I'm gonna be working on some stupid shrimp boat for some mental retard. Except it's Gump. Gump's different. And something happens on that boat. I can't explain it but something happens. And it's not just that we made a lot of money, but Gump changed — I mean, he changed. He's not so stupid. I mean he's stupid and all, but he's kinda smart, too. And then his mamma dies and he gives up the business. So I'm on my own again, alone. Got lots of money now so I guess maybe I should do something. So I get some legs, real wobbly things, I meet a woman, a good woman. And next thing I know Gump calls me and tells me <u>he's</u> getting married. And he's already got a kid! Amazing. The guy's amazing! And I'm at the wedding and I can see that this guy hasn't changed. Not one bit. He's the same guy I met in Nam. But he's different. I don't get it.

You can see in this description the beginnings of an actor's identification with the character, how the actor sees his character, and how he sees the other characters with whom he has contact. And most importantly we are hearing the story from <u>his</u> character's point of view.

Doing this kind of exploration with each and every character is going to take a long time. But it may be your most productive rehearsal time. A bond is being built between these actors as they share their characters' experiences, and the world of *Gump* is being defined.

If you had only one rehearsal prior to production and this was it, you would find that would have created a cohesive working ensemble, and by all standard definitions, you have rehearsed nothing.

Bringing The World Of The Film To The Actors

Many times you will be dealing with events and circumstances that are totally foreign to you and your actors. This is where your research and your personal point of view are highly instrumental. For instance: a significant part of *Gump* takes place during the Vietnam War. Some of your cast members may have served in Vietnam, some may have avoided it, many were probably too young. What is important is how these events in Vietnam serve our story — how they are a part of the world of *Forrest Gump*.

To Forrest Gump the Vietnam War was not about being forced into combat and it was not about politics or protecting freedom in America. It was about loyalty, friendship, admiration, and respect. It was also about commitments and sacrifice.

199

What about the director's point of view? What is it that you want to say with these sequences? You have a different perspective than Forrest or Bubba or Lt. Dan. You are the final filter before this aspect of the story reaches us, the audience.

> From my perspective, these sequences are not about this particular war, but more about war in general and the extraordinary effects a war has on the individual participants. How it inevitably bonds them together, in life and death. It's not about heroism but rather about commitment and responsibility and how under the fires of war we imprint ourselves on each other.

We have already heard Lt. Dan's point of view of the war — his sense of fate, futility, and preordained destiny. And Bubba's on an adventure with his good friend, Forrest; he's seeing this adventure as just a stopping-off place before he gets his shrimp boat.

We are talking about commitment, loyalty, friendship, sacrifice, obligations, responsibility, destiny, and fate. These are the elements that are important — not the war itself. The war is just the environment that allows us to examine these issues.

Bringing the world of *Forrest Gump* to the cast means unfolding each event in a special and specific way so the actors can see and feel these events through a common vision.

DAY FOUR (THURSDAY)

DEVELOPING CHARACTER BACKGROUNDS AND HISTORIES

There are many differing points of view (among actors, directors, and writers) regarding the necessity of developing in-depth backgrounds and histories for the characters. Some say that all the information that is needed is in the script. Others will insist on creating volumes of history and background on each character. Suffice it to say that every artist has his/her own point of view regarding this matter. You, as the director, need to be able to approach this work from three perspectives — writer, director, and actor.

The Writer's Perspective

Be cognizant of the amount of background your writer has done on each character, and how significant this will be to the development of the characters in your story. Select what you want the writer to tell the actors about the genesis of each character. You need to establish an appropriate and respectful working relationship between writer and actor. Asking the writer to share the histories and background of the characters with the actors by no means implies that the writer is suggesting how these characters should be portrayed. That is up to you and the actors.

The Director's Perspective

You have already explored the background of each character with the writer and in your script breakdown; now is the time to share some of your thoughts with the actors. Don't overwhelm or try to impress them with your research; just mention a few of the key elements of the character's background. Allow the actors the time and space for their own discovery. One or two defining facts will usually be enough to set each actor in the right direction.

The Actor's Perspective

Actors will have their own approach to character development and may or may not do extensive research. Honor their way of working. Remember that what matters in the final analysis is the performance. Your job is to stimulate the imagination and creativity of the performers while at the same time allowing them their process.

Note: Some actors will use character history and background as a place to hide (as a crutch) thereby avoiding the truly hard work of developing a living, breathing character. Other actors will resist any and all background and history exploration as a way to avoid looking deeper into their characters. This is where we as directors become quasi–psychologists. We have to be aware of a possible resistance or obsession in an actor's process and help the actors get past it.

Establish an approach to character research that is respectful of all three perspectives. Basically, everyone is going to follow your lead. If you feel the exploration of character backgrounds is important, they will go there. If you feel it is not so necessary, then less work will be done in that area.

PERSONAL HISTORIES AS A MEANS OF CHARACTER DEVELOPMENT

As we discussed in "The Casting Process" (see Actor/Character Meld, Page 157), we have to accept the fact that much of a character will be based on the <u>actor's</u> life experience. This is inevitable, unavoidable, and desirable.

One way to approach character development with an actor is to openly explore the actor's personal experiences as they relate to the experiences of the character. This is a procedure (handled delicately and respectfully) which can bring the actor to an immediate and intimate understanding of the character.

Let's look at Jenny from *Forrest Gump*. There are many significant aspects of this character that the actress will have to assimilate.

1. She befriends a classmate who is an outcast.
2. She feels like an outcast herself.

3. She has been sexually molested by her father.
4. Her new friend becomes very dependent on her (and she on him).
5. She is unable to accept Forrest's deep admiration for her.
6. She has killed her father.
7. She appears to be a loner with no consistent friends, except Forrest.
8. She is, despite her talent and looks, intent on being the rebel.
9. Even as an adult she is unable to embrace Forrest's love of her.
10. She becomes involved in a series of inappropriate and perhaps destructive relationships.
11. She is suicidal.
12. She finally returns, on her own, to Forrest for protection and solace, and to die.

This is a very complex person and most likely our actress who is going to play Jenny has not had such a life — or has she?

Consider these questions:

What is the likelihood that our actress was at one time close to someone who cared a great deal about her even though she never recognized or honored that person's feelings?

— or was betrayed by someone she trusted (or wanted to trust)?

— or out of rage or disappointment found herself allied with persons or groups that were not healthy and did not have her best interests in mind?

— or has considered that not living would be preferable to living?

— or has a yearning in her heart for some one person who was good to her?

Look at it another way. Ask yourself: have you ever been in any of the above situations? Be honest. We all have. None of us are any different from Jenny. Although the specific events may have varied, we have all been in situations and relationships that approximate the events in Jenny's life. We have all experienced loneliness, isolation, betrayal, violation, dependency, fear, rage, destructiveness, rebellion, intimacy, desperation, and comfort. As we begin working with the actress who is to play Jenny, we want to *allow* her to bring those specific parallel events in *her* life to the process.

Let's look at how we can do this, respectfully and appropriately.

As you discuss the events in Jenny's life with the actress, approach her with the following questions (these are merely suggestions but they will give you an idea of how this process can work):

> "Has there ever been someone in your life who was very loyal to you and you didn't totally accept or embrace that loyalty?"
> "Have you ever felt like an outcast?"
> "Have you ever been betrayed by someone you trusted?"
> "Have you ever felt totally alone? No friends, no prospects, no hopes?"
> "Have you ever felt like rebelling against all authority (or perhaps you actually have rebelled)?"
> "Have you ever been involved in an inappropriate or destructive relationship?"
> "Ever felt suicidal?"

This may seem invasive (and if presented harshly it will be), but that is not our intention. We merely want to explore the parallel experiences between the actress and the character. Most actors are more than willing to pursue this process because they know the results can be profound.

The integration of the personal history into the character is the final step of this process. Let's say you have learned that your actress did have an experience of betrayal, but it wasn't her mother or father. It was an old boyfriend. And even though it didn't have the intensity and brutality that Jenny experienced, it was still a betrayal. It still hurt. Our focus needs to be on the emotional impact more than the details. It is the genuine hurt, anger, and rage that we want to bring to our story. As you talk with the actress about her own betrayal you will see the emotions begin to surface. Encourage her to go there and when it begins to get difficult for her, have her talk to the actor playing Forrest. Let her seek and find comfort in him. As they talk quietly to each other, realize that you have just built one aspect of the Forrest-Jenny relationship. They have a bond, a shared experience. And you have established an emotional trigger. If, during rehearsal or performance, you mention the old boyfriend's name you will trigger the related emotions.

This process can be used to deal a wide range of experiences. The key is in establishing trust and respect. The results can be dynamic and profound.

DEVELOPING CHARACTER RELATIONSHIPS WITHIN THE STORY

As we have seen in the script breakdown, there is a substantial amount of information available to us in the script itself to lead us to the development of character relationships. But what we have to remember is that the events in the script are also the *results* of these relationships. In other words, the events in the script occur largely because of the nature of the characters. Gump and Lt. Dan would not have the relationship that they do if either of them had had a different past. So, in the process of developing the relationships that occur within the story we have to look closely at the cause and effect of the past (back story) upon the present (the story).

I am of the school that believes that a lot of analysis and dissecting of the characters will bring the director and the actors to a better <u>understanding</u> of the characters but not necessarily to a better <u>portrayal</u> of the characters. In other words, it is when the actors have actually <u>experienced</u> the characters that the characters become real for them. In the exploration and development process (rehearsal process) the work that is experiential will have the greatest and most lasting effect. For this reason I prefer to explore the relationships and the events of the script in an improvisational and interactive process.

Let's look for a moment at some of the primary relationships in *Forrest Gump* and how they might be explored in our preproduction rehearsal process. One primary relationship is between Gump and his mother. From the very beginning we can see that this is a very protective and loving relationship. We know that Forrest holds his mother in the highest esteem and that Mrs. Gump has instilled a sense of pride and self-worth in her son. All of these are given and established. The question is: How can we go beyond what is obvious in the script and find some of the more subtle and perhaps poignant aspects of this relationship? There are several approaches that are guaranteed to produce results.

IMPROVISATIONS, THEATRE GAMES AND REHEARSAL EXERCISES

Improvisations are most commonly thought of as skit developments, comedy improvisations, Second City type of fare. But we are using improvisations to expand and deepen our awareness and experience of the characters and to explore aspects of relationships that are not revealed in the script.

Reasons to use improvisations in rehearsal:
1. To explore a past event
2. To explore aspects of the relationship
3. To reexamine the written scene

Exploring A Past Event

It is a given in *Forrest Gump* that Forrest is a bit slow, perhaps slightly retarded. We know that Forrest is very aware of his disability, but we don't know how Mrs. Gump and Forrest have handled this issue in the past. Even though this is never addressed (in the script), it is definitely a crucial aspect of the relationship between Forrest and his mother. So, what do we do? We need to establish a scene between Mrs. Gump and Forrest wherein they discuss his infirmity.

For example: Perhaps it happened when Forrest was only four or five years old and it came up because of some specific incident, such as a neighborhood boy picking on him. Determine, between yourself and the actors, what event would most likely catapult Forrest into asking his mother this troubling question and how she would most likely handle this very delicate subject. Give them both clear objectives —

Forrest: *Find out why those boys are teasing you. Are you really stupid?*

Mrs. Gump: *Make Forrest realize that he is special. Give him the courage and strength to be himself.*

— and clear obstacles.

Forrest: *Fear of disappointing your mother. She sees you as special and you're afraid that you're not.*

Mrs. Gump: *Fear that this is all your fault, that Forrest will blame you.*

Once you have the objectives and obstacles established, allow the actors to improvise the scene.

Note: When creating an improvisation you need to consider *your own* objectives as well as those of the characters.

The Objective Of The Director.

You need to be very clear about *your* objectives in the designing of any improvisation. It can't be "oh, I just want to see what happens." You

207

need to know precisely what you are attempting to establish. In the scene suggested above we are exploring a key moment between Forrest and Mrs. Gump. We want to establish how these two individuals handled a delicate issue that resulted in the loving and supportive relationship they have now. We know the *results* of the scene; our objective is to create a moment that will give deeper meaning to this relationship.

> For example: Does Forrest know/believe that Mrs. Gump is lying to him, but to spare her feelings of disappointment he adopts her point of view? And maybe it isn't until years later (supported by the acceptance of Jenny) that he totally adopts this positive point of view.

> Is Mrs. Gump fearful that she is responsible for Forrest's condition? We don't know the circumstances of the conception, pregnancy and birth, but perhaps there was an event that has her concerned and ashamed.

This is when the discoveries from one improvisation can lead you to another.

Specific Objectives For The Characters.

I have seen directors put actors into an improvised scene without giving them specific objectives, hoping that the situation alone will generate some useful experiences. Don't make this mistake or you will end up with a casual and insignificant event. The stronger the objectives (and the obstacles) the more specific the results of the improvisation will be. Make bold choices.

Be aware of when the improvisation goes off track. Sometimes it just gets going in the wrong direction, making it obvious that we are not going to achieve our objectives. Stop the improvisation. You may need to adjust the circumstances, objectives, or obstacles in order to get it back on track.

Each improvisation will become part of the actors' shared experience. As you build a history between these characters, be selective and make every moment count.

Exploring Aspects Of The Relationship

Forrest and Jenny. Forrest (in narration) talks about how close they are, but we get to see little of this. We need to feel this bond every time we see them on the screen. It is going to have to be part of the energy between them.

Improvising scenes of intimacy and sharing (that do not exist in the script) will create the relationship between the two actors that exists between Jenny and Forrest (see Intimacy Exercises below).

Reexamining The Written Scene

Having the actors improvise the dialogue of a written scene allows them to explore more deeply the dynamics. For example, it would be highly beneficial for Forrest and Mrs. Gump to improvise the scene just prior to her death. The written script is very economical and to the point, but through improvisation the two actors could get to explore many of the subtextual and unspoken aspects of the scene. The same with the death of Jenny, which we never see.

DAY FIVE (FRIDAY)

READ-THROUGH OF THE SCRIPT

When you read through the script again it is going to be quite different. The work you have done with the ensemble, character histories and relationships will bring new understanding and dimensions to the events of the story. Sit back and listen. Allow yourself to experience the new event. You'll be pleasantly surprised.

Up to this point we have not discussed how to play any particular scene. We have only developed characters and allowed the effects of that development to inform the events in the story. This is the way it should be. We are aligning ourselves with the course of events and then simply allowing the characters to experience these events without preconceived ideas of how they are going to respond or react.

DAY SIX (MONDAY)

IMPROVISING THE STORY

We are now beginning our second week. Most of the actors will have been spending the weekend absorbing everything that has been covered in the past week and reflecting on the work to be done. Now the question is: How do you refocus the group and reemphasize the collaboration?

There is a very simple exercise: Improvising the story.

> Have the actors sit in a circle, no tables, no scripts. (You need to have with you an outline of your movie with all the scenes, who is in each scene, and what specific story and character points are accomplished in each scene.) Then using the center of the circle as a performance area we improvise the story, one scene at a time. Read off the location of the first scene, who's in the scene, and what is accomplished. The appropriate actors will then improvise the scene in the center of the circle (returning to the circle when they make exits). It is the actors' objective to make all the points in the scene — and they are not allowed to end the scene until this has been done. If they skip over a point or two, make them go back and do the scene again. Once a scene is completed, read the requirements for the next scene.
>
> After a scene or two let the actors provide effects for the scenes that they are not in, such as sound effects (wind, trains, cars, door

slams, gun shots), or they may want to become necessary objects within the scene (a table, a doorway, a tree, a wall) or extras (nonspeaking roles).

This process will obviously take longer than a reading of the screenplay, so plan your time accordingly. As you focus the actors on the collaborative telling of the story, you will see how well the actors have grasped the story.

REWRITES - AND THE CREATIVE TRIANGLE

The strongest geometric form is the triangle. It is also the most powerful dramatic configuration. The creative triangle (writer, director, and actor) contains all the energy of the most forceful storyteller.

The rehearsal process is more than analysis and actor preparation. It is also a reexamination and reworking of the script. Allocate time to deal with whatever rewrites may emerge during the rehearsal process. As each actor finds the voice of his/her character either you and the writer are going to feel the urge or necessity to adapt the script to support these voices. This is the creative triangle at work - actor, writer, and director collaborating in support of the story.

DAYS SEVEN, EIGHT, AND NINE (TUESDAY, WEDNESDAY, THURSDAY)

WORKING WITH SPECIFIC SCENES

It is finally time to rehearse specific scenes. Select these carefully.

Here are some ways to look at scene selection:
1. Key Scenes and Turning Points: Select those scenes that are key scenes and turning points in the story itself.

Forrest meets Jenny. Forrest learns that he can run. Forrest protects Jenny behind her house. Forrest goes to visit Jenny at college. Forrest meets Bubba. Forrest meets Lt. Dan. Death of Bubba. You get the idea.

2. Character Relationship Arcs: Select a specific relationship (i.e., Forrest and Jenny, or Forrest and Bubba, or Forrest and Mrs. Gump, or Forrest and Lt. Dan) and follow that relationship from the beginning of the movie to the end.

Forrest and Bubba: They meet in Boot Camp (establish relationship), they are reunited and sent to Vietnam (rebonding and commitment to each other), they serve together (under Lt. Dan), Bubba gets shot and dies (the final commitment and loss). Forrest meets Bubba's family.

3. Individual Character Arcs: Follow one character in relationship to all other characters and events.

Mrs. Gump. With Forrest as a child, Keeping Forrest in school, Giving Forrest a sense of self-worth, Cheering Forrest through high school, Letting Forrest go to college, Letting Forrest go to Vietnam, Guiding Forrest in his relationship with Jenny, Seeing Forrest become successful (the shrimp business), and Calling Forrest home when she's dying.

REHEARSING THE SCENE

Begin with reading the scene again. Let it wash over you. Don't make assumptions. As you listen to the scene consider the three main questions: What's the overall story, what's the reason for this scene in the story, and what do you need to accomplish with this scene in order to make the story work? And then ask yourself: Is this what I want? If not, what's missing?.

You may think you may want more tension, conflict, vulnerability, or humor in the scene. Whatever it is, you have to realize that you are thinking about results — not the behavior that will elicit these results.

If you talk to the actors about results they will focus on delivering these results and will lose their focus on the objectives of the characters. Modify the scene by focusing the actors on making adjustments in the behavior and attitude of their characters. This is the means to your desired end.

Let's say you're directing a hypothetical scene between a husband and wife. They are arguing about their vacation and whether or not to take the children. The husband wants to go without, the mother wants to take them. As you listen to the scene you realize that even though the characters are present and all the background and historical work you've done is giving the relationship depth, the scene is still not reaching the emotional level you would like. There are many ways you can make significant adjustments in the performances.

Change The Obstacles

The adjustment of obstacles is a powerful directorial tool. By increasing or decreasing the magnitude of an obstacle you can automatically cause a shift in the performance of the character. A character always operates in direct response to the obstacles presented, so rather than request that an actor play something bigger or smaller or with more intensity or calmer, just adjust the obstacle and you will automatically get the change in performance you are seeking. And, most importantly, it will be an organic adjustment.

> If you want more urgency from the husband you could simply tell him, "You have five minutes to convince her or else you are going to lose the baby sitter who has agreed to watch the children." You could tell the wife, "You have already promised the children that they are going with you," and there will be a significant change in her performance. And, obviously, you can soften a performance by reducing the intensity of an obstacle.

Change 'The Moment Before' For One Or Both Characters

The attitude with which a character enters a scene will affect the nature of the scene. If the wife enters the scene delighted because she just made it possible to take the children . . . If the husband enters the scene delighted because he just learned of a great golf course where he intends to play several rounds now that they are no longer encumbered with the children . . . If the wife enters the scene having just read a sad story about a mother who recently lost her children and she's realizing how lucky she is . . . If the husband enters the scene having just had an argument with his son . . . etc.

Alter The Means Of One Or Both Of The Characters

You can create significant changes in performance by adjusting the means by which either one or both characters are attempting to achieve their objectives.

> Telling the husband "You can convince her by being more compassionate or impatient, forceful, demanding," etc. Or telling the wife, "You'll be able to convince him if you're more seductive, illusive, determined, vulnerable," etc.

Raise The Stakes For One Or Both Characters

Raising the stakes has an effect similar to increasing the obstacles, but now you are dealing with the potential aftermath of the scene. Ask each character: "What will happen to you if you don't get what you want?" The more severe you make the consequences, the higher the stakes.

> If the wife decides that she would be upset if they don't take the children, then you will get a performance on one level. But if she decides that she just couldn't live with herself, would feel as if she let her children down one more time and that they might never be able to trust her again, then you'll get a performance on a

different level. The husband's stakes could be anything ranging from general irritation that he lost the argument to rage and a feeling of impotency, deep embarrassment, and humiliation.

Adjust The Subtext

The subtext is the internal monologue that runs constantly within each character as the scene is progressing. As you either deepen or soften that monologue, you affect the behavior of the character. If you actually have the character speak the subtext (in a rehearsal or off camera), you will see the immediate results in that adjustment (see Subtext exercises, page 217).

Adjust The Physical Behavior

Since our physical behavior is often a response to our emotional state we know we can adjust the emotional state by changing the physical behavior. If you have the husband play the entire scene sitting deep into the couch, you will get a very different scene than if he is up and packing. Giving the wife the independent activity of neatly sorting clothes will create a different dynamic than if she spends the entire scene looking for a lost article.

Improvise The Scene

One of the most effective rehearsal tools is improvising the scene. This is simply recreating the scene *in their own words*. This forces the actors deeper into the characters, to think and respond like the characters and not lean on the written text. When they come back to the written text there will be more vitality, integrity, and a sense of freshness (see page 263).

Improvise The Scene Before

Improvising the scene prior to the scene you are rehearsing will add extra depth, dimension, and intensity. If the scene prior does not exist in the screenplay, you can develop it with the actors. Determine the arc of the scene, select strong objectives for each character, and make the obstacles significant. Your objective is the emotional residue, because it will be that residue that launches you into the new scene. Improvise the scene until you have hit the intensity, dynamics, and story points you need, and then go right into the scripted scene. You will see the effect immediately.

Add Or Adjust An Activity

Giving a character an activity can suddenly change the entire dynamics within the scene. The new activity may give the character new strength or definition or a place to hide and it will usually become an obstacle to the other character. Making an adjustment in an existing activity can also affect the dynamics of the scene.

> Let's say the husband is relaxing on the couch in front of the TV and the wife is folding laundry. If the husband suddenly starts channel surfing the wife will have a more difficult obstacle. If the wife stops folding and focuses on her husband, the dynamics will change. The husband could find the program he was looking for, look it up in the TV guide, or turn off the television. The wife could return to her folding, put the laundry away, or join her husband in watching TV, or turn it off.

To truly appreciate the effectiveness of activities, you need to experiment. There are no set rules because each activity is different, the manner in which the activity is engaged is important, and each character will have a different reaction to each activity and change in activity. Experiment in trial and error fashion.

OTHER REHEARSAL EXERCISES

Most rehearsal exercises are actually created, developed, or adapted by the director to fit a specific situation. I am aware that I am constantly modifying old exercises or creating new ones to fit the situation at hand. The point being, you have to keep in mind your needs (within the scene or script) as you consider the use of rehearsal exercises, and you have to select and adapt your exercises to fulfill that need.

Here are a few examples:

Subtext

Exploring the subtext in a scene brings the internal life and energy of the characters to the surface. It makes the feelings that are driving the scene more operative and influential, intensifying the internal dynamics of the scene.

Subtext 1.

Have each actor select a single line that his character would like to say to the other character but can't "because the repercussions would be disastrous." The "repercussions being disastrous" is critical to the selection of the subtext line. If the actor comes up with a line that has little or no repercussions, then it isn't subtext. It could just as well be text.

When both actors have selected their subtext lines, then they are ready to do the exercise. Have them read the scene again, but this time add the subtext line at the end of each scripted speech. The subtext is to be spoken, out loud. Read the entire scene this way, each character expressing her subtext openly and passionately to the other character. You will experience a significant shift in the scene because the subtext is now influencing every moment in the scene. If you read the scene again, without the added subtext

217

lines, the scene will retain this new dimension. The subtext will still be operating.

Subtext 2. This is a variation on the first subtext exercise.

Have the two actors tell you what their characters would like to say to each other *just prior to the beginning of the scene.* Again you are looking for those thoughts and feelings that can't be expressed without disastrous repercussions.

The two actors sit across from each other, knees touching, and speak to each other simultaneously. (We are not reading the scene here, just expressing subtext.) They express these feelings with no attempt to enter into a dialogue. Let this run for about 30 seconds (a long time as you will see) and then say "stop!"; then call "action!" and have them read the scene. Again, you will see that the scene will take on a new energy and focus in relationship to the nature and intensity of the expressed subtext.

The beauty of these experiential exercises is that the actors don't have to think about the new elements that are being added to the scene. The subtext automatically becomes part of their experience, and they cannot help but react accordingly. The actors will be behaving as the characters, attempting to control their emotions rather than create them. They won't be acting.

Remember: *Acting* is creating emotion. *Behavior* is controlling emotion.

Intimacy

Intimacy between two actors (whether they know each other or not) is always a difficult matter. The best of friends, even husbands and wives, will suddenly feel shy and awkward when required to be intimate. Talking about intimacy will actually create more tension and discomfort.

It has to be achieved experientially. These intimacy exercises can do more than just put the actors at ease; they can actually create a level of familiarity and trust that would normally take weeks to achieve.

Exploration Touch

Touching is one of the most intimate of activities. Let's say we have an actor and actress who have to play a love scene. They have never met before and they have to do the scene today.

They sit across from each other, knees touching. They both close their eyes. The actress takes the hands of the actor and places them on her own face (giving the actor permission to touch) and then the actress places her hands on her lap. The actor gently explores her face with his hands (both of their eyes are closed throughout this exercise) describing what he feels. The key to this exercise is that he is describing to her how her face (and eventually neck, shoulders, arms and hands) feel to him. When he finishes describing her hands he lifts them to his face (giving her permission to touch), and she repeats the process. When she is done let them relax for a moment, with their eyes still closed, and watch what happens when you ask them to open their eyes and look at each other. You will see the looks of intimacy and closeness of two people in a very intense relationship. It is genuine. It was experienced.

Whispering Intimacies

Another simple and effective way to establish a deep level of intimacy between two actors is to have them share secrets, and I mean the most intimate secrets. Have the two actors assume a relaxed and close position (on a couch, sitting on the floor against a wall, or even lying down) and ask them to think about the most embarrassing, exciting, or stimulating moment in their lives. They'll think a moment, maybe laugh or blush, but then they'll be ready. Have them whisper these stories to each other with as much detail as possible. You don't want anyone else in the room, including yourself, to hear these stories. Watch as they whisper to each other. It can become a dialogue, one whispering a story, the other whispering back questions or requests for more detail. What you are looking for is the responses. The giggling, the laughter, the moments of shock or surprise, or even sadness. The stories are not important, but the bonding and sharing are. They now share secrets. You can repeat this exercise with stories from childhood, sad stories, happy stories, dreams, fantasies — whatever you feel will help establish the intimate relationship you are seeking.

You can take this exercise to deeper, more profound, and more intimate levels. If I am working with two actors whose characters are supposed to have had an intense sexual relationship and I feel that a visceral awareness of this relationship is crucial, I will have them do the above exercises first. Then I will have them tell each other what they like about each other (still whispering); is it the hair, the smile, the clothing, the smell? Again watch the actors' reactions because the reactions tell all. Then I'll have them tell each other about their (the characters') love life, their sexual relationship. They can go into as much detail as they like. If you lower the lights in the room and put on some soft romantic music, you'll be amazed where the actors will go. You may even feel as if you should leave the room — the intimacy will be that intense. Once it is over, treat it with respect. Don't intrude. You don't need to know any of the details and you don't need to know their reactions and responses unless they want to tell you.

As you read through your script, consider what aspects of each relationship you would like to explore in this manner. Then ask yourself, "What kind of improvisation or exercise could I design that would give my actors a more immediate experience of the characters?" Acquiring the skills of using improvisations and exercises effectively takes time and a lot of trial and error. Be patient. Be courageous.

STAGING AS A DIRECTING TOOL

Staging is perhaps the most powerful, noninvasive, nonimprovisational directing tool available. Unfortunately it is one of the least understood and most frequently misused tools. Before we get into staging methods we need to take a moment to consider its definition and function.

Definition And Function Of Staging.

Staging (or blocking as some refer to it) is simply the movement and placement of characters within the appropriate setting during a scene. In everyday life we move through our world in relationship to each other, our environment, and ourselves according to our needs physically, emotionally, and spiritually. We also move *in response* to our environment, other characters, and ourselves. In short, we "stage" ourselves according to our needs.

We make assumptions about people's attitudes and feelings as we observe their movements in relationship to each other and the environment.

> For instance: As I am writing this I am sitting in a waiting room in the Detroit, Michigan, airport (not a pastime that I recommend), and I am noticing the variety of ways that people have arranged themselves. Assuming that any individual will seek maximum comfort (both physically and emotionally), I know that I can make pretty accurate assumptions about the dynamics of many relationships.

> One woman on the phone has her body turned out toward the room and is casually glancing over the crowd with a light smile on her face, while the man in the booth next to her has his forehead leaning against the wall as he speaks intimately into the phone.

> The couple directly across from me are about as close as allowed in this room. His hand is on her inner thigh, his other hand is playing with the hair on the back of her neck. He is looking

221

directly into her eyes and seems unaware of the rest of the room. She, on the other hand, is splitting her attention between him and the rest of the room. Her body is faced out to the room (his is faced toward her) and her legs are crossed away from him.

Another couple, across the room, are actually sitting on either side of a pillar which forces their seats apart by a foot or so. They are talking to each other but rarely look at one another.

Most likely we all make the same assumptions about these individuals based on their physical behavior. And we can assume that an audience would see these relationships in very much the same way.

Our physical behavior directly reflects our emotional state, and the reverse is also true. Physical behavior and body language can trigger specific emotional responses.

This is staging — reflecting and triggering the emotional life of the scene. We allow the emotional dynamics of the scene to suggest specific staging, then create staging that will stimulate and support the interplay in the scene.

Note: Appropriate staging will support the dramatic elements within a scene. Improper or inappropriate staging can damage, undermine, or even completely sabotage the scene.

I have seen scenes in rehearsal that have completely collapsed when they got on their feet. All the good work was lost because the actors were staged in such a manner that the conflict in the scene was diminished. Consequently, the actors had only one choice — they had to start acting in order to create the necessary conflict. They were focused on making the scene work rather than on the objectives of the characters.

Every scene has to be staged, and the staging is either going to support the scene or not. Learn the dynamics of supportive staging and you will be able to make any scene work.

Self-Staging

Let's deal with the myth of self-staging and get that out of the way first. Many directors feel that they are best off allowing the actors to stage themselves first and then make what little adjustments might be necessary. For the most part this does not work, and here is why. We have all been raised to do two very important things in our daily existence: seek comfort and avoid conflict. We do this every day, every moment of our lives. Wherever you are, as you are reading this, most likely you have found the most comfortable position you can achieve in relationship to others, the environment, and yourself. And, in order to make your day as stress-free as possible, you have most likely been avoiding conflict (with others, yourself, and the environment). The point is: if I permit two actors to stage themselves, within moments they will have found the most comfortable and conflict-free situation possible. They will have successfully removed most of the tension from the scene. Then they'll "act" in order to create the tension that is missing.

> *It is the director's job to get the character into trouble and the actor's job to get the character out.*

The actors, as the characters, are actually attempting to get the characters out of trouble (discomfort, tension) when they seek the comfort and balance. So, as they seek comfort, they are operating well within the parameters of the characters. But if I, as the director, do not allow them this luxury (comfort) then I will be creating tension within the scene (obstacles) against which they can push (creating conflict).

For example: The other day we were working on a scene from *The American President* in one of my directing workshops. It's the scene where the President has called Sydney into the Oval Office after she made a derogatory comment about him. The actor playing the President placed himself behind the desk and the actress playing Sydney stood behind one of the guest chairs and that's where they played the scene. But the scene lacked any dimension or tension and the actors started to act. I asked my student director if he was happy with the scene. He told me he thought they needed to create more emotional distance and the feeling that this is the *President*. He then asked the actor to be more presidential and the actress to be more ill at ease. Right away I knew that this was not going to work because he was talking to the actors (rather than the characters), and these requests would only force the actors toward result acting. The next run-through proved my suspicions. Then I asked the director, "What does the President want and what does Sydney want?" He answered: "The President would like to be free to come and go as himself and free to approach her on a personal level. And Sydney would like to be anywhere but here; she's uncomfortable and embarrassed." I then placed the President looking out the window (with his back to Sydney) and Sydney in the middle of the room away from all the furniture (giving her no support). We ran the scene again and the change was extraordinary. All the elements the director wanted were suddenly there, and they didn't need to be discussed or requested. The President was removed, powerful, isolated. Sydney felt trapped, unsupported, embarrassed. And the moment in the scene where the President attempts to make a personal connection with Sydney was all the more moving when we suggested that this be the first time he turns away from the window and faces her.

This is not staging that the actors would have come to on their own. But by placing them in positions that replicated their feelings they were able to connect with the characters in a visceral way without having to act.

The actors (left on their own) will seek comfort and balance, and the scene will lose its tension once they achieve it. The audience desires balance and closure and they will lose interest the moment they get it. It is the imbalance and tension in your staging that will help maintain the pressure and conflict in the scene.

METHODS OF STAGING

There are three key relationships in staging:
1. The characters in relationship to each other
2. The characters in relationship to the environment
3. Each character in relationship to himself

Note: Since staging is a *result* of the dynamics of the scene you need to keep in mind the objectives of the characters, the character arcs, the adjustments, and the shifts in the relationships while you are staging.

Staging In Relationship To Other Characters

Every scene is a struggle for power, control, or comfort and at any one time one character is dominant while the other(s) is subordinate. The power will shift frequently between characters which gives the scene movement and growth. You can stimulate and reflect these changing dynamics in how you stage one character in relationship to another.

Staging In Relationship To The Environment

Each character will have a different relationship to the environment. Some will be comfortable, some uncomfortable, some familiar, some strange. To determine the areas of comfort and discomfort for each character within an environment, let them walk around the set. Have them tell you where they are feeling strong, weak, secure, and vulnerable. Make note of these locations. Then ask them how they feel in relationship to each other in the set. You are beginning to form an emotional diagram that will help guide you in your choices.

Staging In Relationship To Self

This is actually body language. How the character holds herself, how she sits in the chair, walks through the room, holds the book, adjusts her clothes will tell us much about the emotional state of the character. For instance, imagine two characters in confrontation; ask one of them to do the scene looking at her feet and ask the other to hold himself tall and rigid. Then read the scene again and ask the actress to look directly into the actor's eyes and have the actor search his pockets for a lost item. You will have two very different scenes, and different relationships.

We'll look at a scene from *Forrest Gump* and explore the three levels of staging. The scene where Jenny invites Forrest into her dorm room after Forrest has protectively interrupted her back seat lovemaking. It's raining, both Jenny and Forrest are wet, and Jenny tells Forrest to "come on in . . . you're soaked." She is angry at him for the interruption, yet still protective.

```
INT. JENNY'S ROOM - NIGHT (1963)

There's a guitar in a corner. Jenny's roommate is
asleep.

                    JENNY
                [whispers]
            Give me your clothes to dry.

                    FORREST
                [embarrassed]
            What if you see something?

                    JENNY
                [smiles]
            I won't look.
```

226

She turns her back. Forrest, awkwardly, takes off
his shirt and pants.

> JENNY
> [continuing; as he undresses]
> Do you ever dream, Forrest?

And like a little boy, he shuts his eyes, as if
he's dreaming.

> FORREST
> Sometimes I can't tell what's a
> dream and what isn't.

> JENNY
> [smiles]
> No, I mean dream about who
> you're going to be.

> FORREST
> [doesn't understand]
> Going to be?
> [concerned]
> Aren't I going to be me?

> JENNY
> [reassuring him]
> You'll always be you. Just
> another kind of you.

He tries to understand. He gives her his wet
things. He sits like a little boy on her bed in
his underwear, his hands over his privates. She
puts his wet clothes on a radiator.

             JENNY (CONT'D)
          [after a beat]
      I want to be famous... I want to
      be a folk singer... like Joan Baez.

He doesn't know Joan Baez from Joan of Arc. And
there's a sadness...

             JENNY (CONT'D)
        [collegiate, overly serious]
      I want to be on an empty stage,
      with just a microphone, a
      guitar, and my voice... Where I
      can say things, reach people on a
      personal level, just one to one...

He doesn't know what she's talking about. And it's
quiet, the rain falling on the window. She comes
to stand by him. After some moments:

             JENNY
        [whispers]
      Have you ever been with a
      girl, Forrest?

He doesn't know what she means.

            FORREST
      I sit in home economics class
      with them all the time.

She looks in his sweet eyes. She looks over at
her roommate, her head turned to the wall, fast
asleep. Jenny quietly unbuttons her blouse, slip-
ping it off. She takes off her bra. He looks at

her naked body. It's like he's looking at an angel.
She takes his hands helping him to his feet.

>   JENNY
>   You can kiss me anywhere you
>   want.

He hesitates, and then touches her breasts. He
can't help himself and he shudders, ejaculating.

>   FORREST
>   [looks down, sorry]
>   I got all wet.

>   JENNY
>   [tenderly]
>   It's all right. You didn't do
>   anything wrong.

Taking his hand she lies on the bed with him. She
lays her head on his chest, closing her eyes. It's
quiet. Forrest, for a moment, painfully aware of
his inadequacies, has tears in his eyes. As they
lie in her bed, the best of friends, the rain is
running down the window.

>   END OF SCENE

We'll look at the various staging possibilities in terms of character
to character (c-c), character to environment (c-e), and character to
self (c-s).

This is Jenny's room and her invitation. So she is obviously in control.
But, who enters first? We could have Jenny enter first, move into the

room with familiarity (c-e), leaving Forrest in the doorway feeling slightly awkward (c-e). Or you could have Jenny open the door for Forrest and allow him to enter first (c-c) giving him more of a feeling of a wanted guest (c-c) and then as he moves into the room we could see Jenny for a moment watching him and then her body slumps slightly (c-s) as she takes in the situation. She could give a look to her sleeping roommate (c-c) and then pull herself together (c-s) and move confidently across the room to her closet (c-e). At this moment Forrest might be in the center of the room feeling awkward yet mesmerized by where he is (c-e). Jenny is at the closet, her back to Forrest (c-c), then she turns to him for her first line (c-c). "Give me your clothes to dry". Forrest feels suddenly observed by Jenny (c-c) and, embarrassed, he pulls his wet jacket a little tighter around himself (c-s) and says, "What if you see something?" Jenny responds, "I won't look," then turns her back to Forrest (c-c) giving Forrest a greater sense of privacy (c-e). During the next beat of the scene Forrest is undressing (c-s) and Jenny is asking him about his dreams and tells him of hers. What you chose to have Jenny doing during this sequence will greatly affect the nature of the scene. She could be taking her wet clothes off (her back still to Forrest) allowing him to observe her apparent comfort in the room (c-e) and giving him a greater sense of ease and permission in removing his clothes (c-s). Or, you could have Jenny looking at items in her closet or at her guitar (c-e). Perhaps she is merely staring out the rain-soaked window (c-e) and unconsciously playing with her hair (c-s). Jenny and Forrest are very disconnected at this point (c-c) which is intentional, not only to support the text at this moment but also to allow the characters greater distance to travel in order to achieve the intimacy they will reach at the end of the scene.

> Note: If you know where the scene is going to end (in this case intimately) then begin the scene as from that point as possible (disconnection). This will allow for greater movement (both physically and emotionally) during the scene.

After Jenny's speech about "reaching people on a personal level, just one to one" there is a moment of quiet and a major adjustment in the scene. Jenny is about to ask Forrest if he has ever been with a girl. How you stage this moment will tell us much about Jenny's attitude and intentions. She could still be looking out the window, lost in her dreams when she says it (c-e and c-s). She could turn first and see Forrest sitting there in just his underwear and then say the line (c-c). She could turn from the window, see Forrest, see her roommate (c-c), look at Forrest again, move across the room to him and speak intimately (c-e). Each one of these will create a slightly different moment.

And how is Forrest sitting on the bed? Facing Jenny? His back to Jenny? In profile? On the edge of the bed? Comfortably deep into the bed? Maybe the pillow across his lap? Each of these gives us a different picture of Forrest.

And how does Jenny approach Forrest? Aggressively? Tentatively? Cautiously? Apologetically? It's just a walk across the room but the manner of the walk will tell us much of what is going on inside Jenny. And as she shifts from openly talking about her dreams to privately offering herself to Forrest we will see character/character shifts, character/environment shifts, and character/self shifts.

Even the slightest adjustments in staging with two people sitting side by side can be significant. Jenny sits next to Forrest on the bed (c-c), Forrest shifts slightly away from her in embarrassment (c-c), he holds the pillow tighter (c-s), she glances at her roommate (c-e), she removes her blouse (c-s), he notices (c-c), and then she speaks, "You can kiss me anywhere you want." How he reaches for her, where he looks, where she looks, when he releases the pillow, when she drops her blouse — all affect our experience of the scene and the actors' experience. This is all very delicate work which requires attention to detail. The changes in Forrest's body language — from shyness, to embarrassment, to attraction, to excitement and orgasm, back to

231

embarrassment, and finally to sadness as they lie in bed together — tell the whole story.

Staging Triggers

You can trigger a response from one character by making an adjustment in another. Like the President turning away from the window, suddenly Sydney's world has changed and she will make an adjustment. She may feel less isolated but certainly more observed, on the spot. It will also cause a change in the President. He may feel more connected yet more vulnerable.

If you want to explore Jenny's vulnerability as she is telling Forrest about her dreams, find a moment when she stops talking and looks to Forrest only to see him staring at her in wonder. She will feel the exposure and will have to adjust.

If you want to show how awkward Forrest feels removing his clothes, have him do it in the middle of the room (c-e, no support); perhaps he is trying to do it with one hand while slightly covering himself with the other (c-s). Or he immediately sits on Jenny's bed (c-e), then realizes where he is and slides to the edge, or end, of the bed. Maybe he attempts to remove his clothes without rising from the bed (c-e) because he feels more protected in the sitting position (c-s). And at what point does Jenny turn and see him (c-c) and how does that affect him?

This should begin to give you an idea of how the staging is generated by the dynamics of the scene while at the same time stimulating the dynamics between the actors.

Use Of Rhythms In Staging

Each character has his own distinct rhythm. In some situations, especially comedies, these rhythms can be fairly extreme. Whether fast, slow, casual, impatient, impetuous, relaxed, or nervous, you need to find the physical behavior that will help support the individual's rhythm.

> In our husband and wife scene, you may want the husband's rhythm to be slow and solid, showing confidence and stubbornness, while the wife you may see as quick and erratic showing that she is edgy and uncertain. Sit the husband at a table, a strong table with a man's chair, so he feels as if he's on his throne. Place the wife at a counter with mismatched objects that she has to sort through. Keep her off balance. They'll feel the distance and the separation as they attempt to reach an agreement.

Consider having one character stationery while another is constantly moving. Or one could be involved in an activity while another isn't. Then when you suddenly allow one character to get pulled into the other's rhythm, there will be an enormous shift in the relationship.

Have the wife stop fiddling with the object and sit at the table with her husband. She'll feel stronger, he'll feel threatened. You may elect to keep him in this now uncomfortable position until he feels he <u>has</u> to leave.

Staging is a trial and error process. The more your experiment with it, the better you will be able to employ its benefits.

For those of you venturing into directing episodic television, soap operas, and low budget films (where there is almost no rehearsal time and a high daily page count requirement), this tool is invaluable. In fact your staging may be the only rehearsal tool you can use. You'd better be good at it!

Stage vs. Film

In a play, staging is the only tool you have for creating composition and it is through staging that you can focus the audience. Stage is like one master shot (within the proscenium arch) but the audience's focus can be pulled into two shots and even close-ups through a mixture of staging, lighting, and performance.

In film we have the luxury of multiple angles, framing, and editing. The camera gives us the power of the frame (more powerful than the proscenium) and of the two dimensional image. The director can stage the action which can then be enhanced by the framing, lens selection, camera moves, and finally editing.

The Single Shot Exercise

One of the best exercises for learning staging for the camera is to take a 3-4 minute scene and stage it so that it can be covered in one shot.

Here are the rules:
1. Camera is on a tripod - any height you want.
2. You're allowed to use only one lens size, fixed lens, no zooming.
3. You may tilt and pan.
4. The scene has to be staged so in one continuous take you get all the coverage you want.

This means all the coverage — all the singles, two shots, masters, over-the-shoulders, details, etc., at the moment you want them — in one continuous shot.

> For example: Let's say with your husband and wife scene you envision it begins with a single shot on her folding the laundry. Set up the camera so you get the single you want. But then you want a raking two shot showing the husband watching television. You can't move the camera (only tilting and panning, remember?) so you will probably have to move her so that she brings you to a two shot. Perhaps she takes a couple of steps toward the couch,

you pan with her, and now you have your two shot. But she's in the foreground and he's in the background and you had envisioned that he would dominate the scene. So you may have to have her move to the far side of the couch. Now he will dominate the scene and you have your two shot. Let's say next you wanted a single of the husband as he begins to channel surf. You could let the wife walk out of the shot leaving you with the single or you could have the husband move (to the television perhaps) to get the remote and as you pan with him you have the single you had imagined. You can pan down as he reaches for the remote and as he lifts it up to change the channel you can have restaged the wife so we see her in the background looking at the remote (because you had originally planned a cut to her reaction).

You are moving the actors in order to achieve the staging, framing, and coverage you want - moment by moment - so that you will have the entire scene contained in one shot, fully covered, fully edited.

Developing An Eye For Staging

There are many ways you can train your eye for more imaginative and creative staging.

Look At Photographs.

LIFE magazine is great. Each still photo has a story. Study the picture. Ask yourself what's going on in the picture. Why is that woman standing way in the back? Why does that young man have one foot placed solidly on the log? What does that say about him? And what about those three little girls in the foreground? Each one of them in a different pose. You can tell a lot about them just by these poses.

Watch People.

In a park, on a bus, in rooms. See how their inner dynamics are reflected in their physical behavior.

Watch Films — Without The Sound.

See if you can determine the content of the scene from the staging. Then watch the scene with sound.

Experiment With Actors.

Work with actors in workshops or classes (without the pressure of production) and experiment, experiment, experiment. The best way to learn directing is to keep directing — every chance you get. The more you experiment the more tools you will acquire.

The Deconstruction Exercise (For Staging)

- Watch a scene from a movie (on video so you can replay it).
- Watch it again but this time draw yourself a floor plan of the set as best as you can.
- Watch it again and draw on your floor plan the staging that was created for the scene — and write it in detail, every move, every nuance.
- Watch it again and ask, "What are the essential dynamics of this scene and how are they supported by the staging?"
- Watch it again and ask, "How else could I have staged this scene to further support the dynamics?"

STORYBOARDS

There is a reason why we haven't discussed storyboards until this point. Other than action or special effects sequences there is little value of storyboarding a character scene prior to exploring the physical and emotional dynamics of the scene. Once you have explored the scene, the coverage will become evident. The staging and the emotional connection between the characters will draw you into looking at the scene from very specific angles and perspectives. Let the coverage of the scene be a natural outgrowth of the actors' work as well as yours. Forcing actors to fit into a predetermined visual style, pattern, or look will only rob them of the integrity of their work.

DAY TEN (FRIDAY)

THE FINAL READING

If at all possible, end your rehearsal period with a final reading of the script. It is invaluable to have the entire cast together one more time, allowing them all to hear and experience the growth that has occurred in rehearsal.

PREPARING THE ACTORS FOR THE PRODUCTION PROCESS

Congratulate the actors on the work they have done in rehearsal. Whatever progress has been made is extremely valuable and will pay off in the production process.

Then take a few moments to focus everyone on the production process. Give them an idea how you will be working. Let them know that you might be incorporating some exercises or improvisations, and that you will be rehearsing with them while the crew is preparing the set or location. Most importantly, let them know that you are there to provide an environment within which they can do their best work.

Now you are ready for the production phase.

CHAPTER 8

PRODUCTION

As you have probably realized by this point, the first seven chapters of this book focus on the preproduction process and the last two chapters cover production and postproduction. "Preparation is everything." Once you have your script, your team, your actors, and you are all prepared to make the same movie, you have only two tasks in front of you: (1) create the material you need, and (2) assemble the material into the final film. Production and postproduction. This may sound overly simplistic but in essence it is the process. Let's look at production.

First you create an event and then you record the event.

The production process is the second telling of the story (the first telling being the creation and development of the script), and in this second telling we suddenly have living and breathing human beings in real sets and real locations, having genuine interaction with each other. Very different from words typed on a page. The story is no longer in our imagination; it is now happening right in front of us. This is the closest we will ever get to a live creation or embodiment of the story. Even then we will not experience it from beginning to end, only in pieces — scene by scene — out of order. And only a chosen few (the cast and crew) will witness this event.

It is our job, during production, to create this event (performance) and then record the event (camera and sound). It is not this event itself that we are going to show to the public (that would be theatre) but rather a record of the event, reassembled so as to create a semblance of the original event. This assemblage is the *third* and final telling of the story — the film.

239

THE NIGHTLY RECONSIDERATION PROCESS

The production process is one of constant fluctuation, reconsideration, and redesigning. As you complete one scene you find yourself reconsidering each new scene not only in relationship to the entire film, but most significantly in relationship to the scenes that have already been shot.

You will make discoveries when you shoot a scene. Maybe it didn't play exactly the way you anticipated. Maybe it worked better than you thought, taking on a different tone, or did not work as well as you thought it would.

As you sit down and contemplate the next day's work keep in mind what you have shot and how that might affect what you are about to shoot.

A hypothetical example:

Let's say that you have already shot a scene between the husband and wife where they were discussing their vacation plans and you were unable (for whatever reason) to reach the emotional depths you had thought possible and perhaps necessary. But this scene is part of your movie; you can't go back and reshoot it. Now you are looking at another scene, perhaps the one following the argument where we see the husband and wife in their car, on their vacation with the kids in the back seat. It's clear who won the argument. You are considering this new scene and how it should play in relationship to the earlier scene. In the new scene the argument continues (but now the subject matter is where they're going to stay, not whether or not to take the children — the husband wants to stay at a nice hotel, the wife wants to stop and visit relatives). Your thoughts run to, "Can I get the emotional depth in this scene? Can I reveal the pain and hurt that didn't quite happen in the first scene? And will that still track? I had originally thought of exposing the depth of the animosity, hurt, and anger in the first scene and then see it repressed in the second scene when the children are present. But now the first scene is done and I didn't get it. What happens if I go for it in front of the children? Maybe that will prove to be even more interesting. Unpredictable and interesting. Or do I want to hold back and show even more repression in front of the kids than when they were alone? Maybe this will work better."

These are serious questions that deserve consideration. Every step you take will have its effect on every future step. You are always in the gap between what has been done and what is waiting to be done, and in that gap is reconsideration and reevaluation.

Through slight adjustments in staging, objectives, intentions, or obstacles you can make significant alterations in the tone, depth, and direction of a scene. You may say to yourself (considering our hypothetical example above), "Fine, I've got four people riding in a car, how can I alter the scene through staging?" Put one of the kids between the parents in the front seat. That will change the dynamics. Put the mom in the back seat with one of the kids. Have the mom driving and the dad in the passenger seat. Each of these changes will significantly alter the dynamics of the scene. Give them all consideration. Try to imagine the change in dynamics (although it may not become totally clear to you until you have actually seen the actors in rehearsal). The more experience you acquire working with actors in the rehearsal process the more you will be able to project the actual consequences of such alterations.

DEVELOPMENT REVIEW

Review the scene again, considering the nine basic steps of development we have outlined in this book:
1. What is the story really about?
2. What is this scene about?
3. Why is this scene in the movie?
4. What must I as director achieve with this scene so that it will function properly within the movie?

5. What are the character objectives, obstacles, arcs, means, actions, activities, adjustments, windows of true nature, risks, stakes, etc?
6. How can I direct and stage the scene in order to clarify and underline the essential dynamics within the scene?
7. How can I capture (record) this scene in order to enhance the essential dynamics of the scene?
8. How do I rediscover the story that is contained within the material I have created?
9. How do I reassemble this material in order to create the most dynamic version of my story?

We are now at steps 6 and 7 and you have an opportunity at this point to adjust the dimension, perspective, and tone of your scene through your staging and the manner in which you record the scene.

STAGING

Take another look at the scene in terms of how you want to stage it and shoot it. You may have already gone through this in detail (in rehearsal, with your storyboard artist and your cinematographer), but you want to examine it again.

Staging, as we discussed in Chapter 7, is one of the most powerful directorial tools at your disposal. You can make a mediocre scene reach new heights with the proper staging. You can also rob a scene of its impact and nuance with improper staging. Good staging reflects the emotional dynamics of the scene; it grows out of the relationships and adjustments that occur within the scene. Just as our body language and physical behavior are reflections of our emotional state, staging is a metaphor for the emotional dynamics of the scene. You can enhance the dynamics of a scene by staging it in such a manner that two things will happen: (1) the audience will make certain assumptions about the relationships in the scene, <u>and</u> (2) the actors will respond emotionally in direct line with the desired emotional responses of the characters.

Once you have your staging design worked out you are ready to reconsider your coverage.

CAMERA COVERAGE

This is a key transition in the process in filmmaking (translating from live performance to recorded performance). The question is: How do you record the scene in sufficient detail so that you can recreate it in post? Can you film the work of the actors in such a manner as to enhance the dynamics of the scene? To a certain extent it is true that if the scene is well performed you can simply record and it will work. To a certain extent. But you can enhance the audience's experience and appreciation of the scene depending on how you cover it (and eventually edit it).

There are a variety of styles of coverage and cinematography starting with the extremely basic (and mostly pedantic) approach of master, two-shots, over-the-shoulders, and singles. Most scenes can be staged in such a manner that this coverage will give you sufficient material to cut your scene together. A lot of television directors and even many feature directors work this way. But the work suffers for it. The story suffers. Next time you're watching television (or film) watch the coverage. It won't take long before you find a scene that is covered in this very traditional manner. Ask yourself if this manner of coverage is adding anything to the scene or just merely recording it. A director might make the choice to shoot a scene in this manner, and it might indeed support the dynamics of the scene. Maybe the director just wants the camera to sit back and record and not bring any additional values to the scene. And that's fine <u>if that is the director's artistic choice</u>. But too often this method is used only because it is expedient and simple, not because it supports the scene.

Coverage must grow out of the dynamics of the scene (rather than something that is conceived initially with the staging then designed to support it). Look at your scene. Sense the dynamics. Watch the interrelationship between the characters. Be aware of where your eye is going, where you want to be, what you want to see. It is through your coverage (and eventually through your editing) that you will control the audience's perception of these events. Let them see it through your eyes. This is organic, subjective filmmaking. If you want the audience to just sit back and watch the scene from a distance, then put the camera there. If you want the audience to be up close and intimate, then put the camera there. If you want the audience moving within the scene, then put the camera in the scene and have it moving. Don't think of it as beautiful shots or award winning cinematography. Think of it as you telling the audience: "Look at it from here. Can you see what's happening? Now look at it from here." This is major manipulation and control — storytelling through the camera.

The Camera As A Character

I like to think of the camera as a character, and I play that character. Because in essence, the camera is showing you the scene the way I see it. I know how I want to engage with the events and emotions of the scene. Sometimes I want to keep a respectful distance, and other times I want to be right in there with the characters. I like it when I, as the camera, can move within the scene and find the details I like. Then, at other times, I feel it is important for me to react to the scene, to be literally physically moved by the characters and to respond to them.

A camera at any one time is either active or passive. An active camera moves on its own, not necessarily in response to the events or movements within the scene. A passive camera will only respond to the movement or energy within the scene. An active camera is curious, provocative — it has a point of view and an attitude. A passive camera is just that — passive, nonintrusive, respectful, cautious.

If you see the camera as being you, your character, then think about your point of view of each scene. Do you want to be actively or passively involved? And realize that your attitude will affect our experience of the scene.

There is no way anyone can tell you where the camera should be. There are a lot of people who can make a lot of good suggestions, but you are the only person who really knows where the camera must be. It is your story. It is your vision. Listen to everyone and then make your decisions based on your vision of your movie.

COMMUNICATIONS WITH THE CREATIVE TEAM

As we have stated repeatedly (and it can't be said too often), communication is the director's main (and only) tool. It is during production that your communication skills are really going to be tested. The question is: How do you keep the communication flowing while dealing with everything else and still maintain your focus on the work of the actors? Priorities and focus. What are your priorities and where do you want everyone focused? The answer is in your preparation.

At the end of a day's shooting the last thing you are going to do is make sure you are taking home everything you need for the next day's work: your notes, a copy of the scenes themselves (and the scenes preceding and following), your storyboards, and whatever other materials (e.g., research, tapes of rehearsals, technical notes) that you may have generated during preproduction.

In your preparation, focus first on the story itself and the function of these particular scenes within the story, then on your specific needs and what you have to achieve with these scenes in order to insure that they support the story. Write it down, again. I know you have already done this many times, but talk to yourself one more time — in writing — so that you are clear on your objectives, priorities, and focus. And then, write a short paragraph to each member of your creative team dealing with just these scenes. Some creative team members will not be involved in the next day's shooting (such as casting and editorial), but most will (cinematography, sound, set dressing, wardrobe, makeup, special effects, and of course the actors). Do not include writing to the actors, which we'll discuss in a moment. Write a short paragraph about what you are expecting from each team member, and where you want priorities and focus.

Here is a sample form that I have used:

Director's Notes

Production: _____ Date: _____
Day: _____ Scene and Location: _____
Actors: _____

General	
Director of Photography	
First A.D.	
Production Designer Set Dressing	
Costumes	
Sound	
Makeup and Hair	
Special Effects	
Locations	
Miscellaneous	

An example of how these notes might look:

<u>Director's Notes</u>

Production: FORREST GUMP   Date: 11-8-96
Day: 14   Scene and Location: BEDROOM - STAGE 14
Actors: FORREST, JENNY, ROOMMATE

General	This is going to be a difficult scene because of its intimacy and close quarters. I will need everyone's help in maintaining a comfortable and secure environment for the actors.
Director of Photography	As discussed, let's work with source light as much as possible. Even though this is a romantic scene I don't want to glamorize it. I want it to feel sacred and real. I don't mind shadows. I would like to feel some light (street light? moon?) coming through the window to help highlight the rain. See the storyboards for camera coverage. As discussed I will be very passive, unobtrusive, respectful. I never want to be aware of the camera either through its movement or odd angles. It should disappear so that we genuinely feel that we are in the room.
First A.D.	Since we are concentrating on just this scene today there should be a quiet and relaxed atmosphere on the set. I don't want any visitors or unnecessary personnel (even crew) hanging around.
Production Designer Set Dressing	The set looks great. I will see how much of Jenny's belongings we actually see through the camera. I do want to get a sense — all the time — that this is her room.
Costumes	We're dealing with wet clothes and partial nudity. I will do my best to work in continuity, but I do know that we will be resetting often so we will need at least two of your crew on the set all day. Also, of course, bathrobes for them after each take. Thanks.
Sound	I don't want to have to ask for volume from either of them so we need to be able to "dig" for the sound. Let me know how I or cinematographer can help you.
Makeup and Hair	Minimum make up for both. This is the two of them as raw as we may ever see them. Be aware that we have to deal with wet hair and Jenny having her lipstick just a bit smeared at the beginning. I am going to explore maybe her wiping all makeup off before she approaches Forrest at the end.
Special Effects	Rain on the windows.

On The Set

When you arrive on the set, one of the first things you want to do is have a 10- minute meeting with all the department heads. This is a brief but crucial meeting. Your objective is to bring all the department heads into focus on the day's work. Hand them copies of your notes which include storyboards, notes to creative team members, and any items that deserve special attention. Talk about the scenes you are going to shoot that day. Make them aware of the difficult shots, the importance of each scene, where they need to focus their energies. You will be saying much of what is written, allowing your notes to serve as a backup, a reminder.

Knowing that your crew is now pulling in the same direction you can focus on the actors and creating the event that is today's work. The reason we do not put the notes to the actors in writing, or share them with anyone, is that this kind of input in the wrong hands can only lead to trouble. The communication between actors and director is private and must be kept that way. The privacy honors the sensitivity of the work.

Working With The Writer And The Actors On The Set

As you move out of rehearsal and into production, your relationship with the writer and actors will shift. The closer you move to the point of actually shooting a segment of your movie, the more authoritative you must become. But this does not mean that your collaboration suffers. Not at all. If anything it actually intensifies. You, the actors, and the writer are headed toward that magical moment when all of your work reaches its full expression.

The Writer

Assuming that you have been able to establish a healthy working relationship with the writer and have maintained mutual respect, the writer can become "the listener" on the set. You will be totally involved in performance, staging, lighting, framing, camera moves, eyelines, and all those little nuances that the camera will pick up. Thus it can be helpful to have someone on the set who is merely listening to the scene and can give you feedback from a different perspective. This feedback must be given to you and *only you!* Otherwise there might be the impression of two directors!

> I was recently consulting on a feature film. I, as a director, was actually consulting with the director of the film *while he was filming*. But, as far as the rest of the cast and crew were concerned, I was a *writing consultant*. If the cast and crew had know that the director was getting advice from another director while shooting, then he would run the risk of losing the authority and respect he had already earned. You must protect your own position as director as ruthlessly as you protect anyone and anything else.

> No one, not even the writer or producer, ever talks to the actors about their performance. No matter how tempted the writer may be and no matter how in sync the two of you are, do not let the writer talk to the actors about their performance. This is not out of some director ego trip or need to control. It is for the sake of the actors. They need to hear direction from only one source and that source has to be you.

The Actors

Working with the actors on the set has become one of the big mysteries and challenges for many directors. If you are well prepared, have done your homework, and have created a foundation in the rehearsal process, the experience of working with the actors on the set can be quite simple and very stimulating.

REHEARSALS THE NIGHT BEFORE

As you complete a day's shooting remember that it only takes a few moments to sit down with the actors and review the work for the next day. This is of course assuming that you have these particular actors available to you. You want to send the actors home focused on the next day's work, not the work completed today. Sit with them for 10 or 15 minutes and read through the scenes you will be shooting the next day. Walk through the sets (if you have time and the sets are there). Remind them of the basic ingredients in the scene as discussed and discovered in the rehearsal process. Ask them if they have any questions or concerns, and then let them go. If the actors are coming to dailies with you, you may want to have this short rehearsal after dailies or at least remind them of the focus of tomorrow's work before they leave.

Spend time with members of your creative team discussing the next day's work. The nature of the work coming up will determine with whom you need to meet, but at minimum talk with your cinematographer and first A.D. Taking 10 minutes to discuss and focus on the work for the next day can save valuable time. Go over your notes. Remind them and yourself of the priorities and potential problems. I find invaluable the reviewing of rehearsal tapes, discussing the scene's dynamics, and going over storyboards and coverage.

All this work is also helping to shift your focus to the next day's work. The more you communicate with others, the more you discuss your vision, your priorities, and your concerns, the clearer you are going to be.

MEETING ACTORS ON THE SET

The actors have spent the night thinking about and working on the material for today. There may be questions, concerns, and ideas and you want to be there to address them; don't wait until you're on the set when the clock is ticking. Greet the actors. Take a few moments to share your thoughts. Keep it simple. And then let them go to wardrobe or makeup or wherever they need to be. You have connected with them and focused them in the direction of the day's work. Very important.

Also, when you first meet with the actors, take note of their energy and state of mind. Each actor will come on the set dealing with whatever has been going on in his life prior to this moment. Be aware of it. Acknowledge it if necessary, but don't ignore it.

> Note: Your energy is always infectious. If you are down and depressed and feeling negative the actors will pick up on it and it will affect them. If you are up and bubbly then they will have a tendency to become lighter as well. Your attitude is one of the greatest directorial tools you have. You can give them a sense of the energy you want in the room without even mentioning it. For example, with a comedy your mischievous, funloving, impish energy will bring the actors up. With a heavy dramatic scene, your serious contemplative tone will set the mood. Be aware of this.

Before you go on the set, talk to them about the day's work. Let them know where your focus is, what your priorities are. You may want to talk about the characters again, the objectives, the needs, or the obstacles. This is a gentle conversation (not a heady discussion) just to bring the actors from their own lives into the lives of their characters. You will be able to judge with each actor how much of this preparation process is necessary or useful. Instinct will tell you. The point is we are attending to the process and not just assuming that everyone will be focused once we hit the set.

THE REHEARSAL ON THE SET

During rehearsal on the set it is very important that <u>nothing</u> else is happening. No lighting, construction, meetings, or discussions. This is a sacred time as is the time of actual filming. It is very important that

251

you and the entire crew treat the actors' time on the set with the respect it deserves. (You have been giving other members of your creative team the time and space they need on the set.) This is not to imply that the actors are fragile or delicate or that we need to treat them with some sense of reverent awe. But rather that they, like all artists, deserve an environment in which they can do their best work. Your demand for attention and quiet during these rehearsals will show that you too respect this time, and the rest of the crew will follow suit.

You are not going for full performance in this first rehearsal. This is a gentle placing of the scene within the environment so that all department heads can see what you are doing and assess and adapt their own contributions. Check the staging, see how the actors are relating to each other and the environment. Does it have the feel that you want? Walk around the set with your cinematographer and watch the scene from the various angles you are considering for setups. Check backgrounds, foregrounds. Feel the scene.

Run the scene as many times as you need to until everyone, including the actors, feels comfortable with the staging, the lighting, and sound demands. Then release the set to the crew. Depending on the intricacy of the staging and the demands on lighting and complexity of camera moves, there may be a significant amount of time before you and the actors will be needed back on the set. This is your final preparation time. Your cinematographer, production designer, sound recorder, and the rest of your crew will be taking care of all the technical elements on the set. Your primary concern is the performers and the performance and this is time that you can use for rehearsal.

The nature of this rehearsal will depend on three factors:
    1. the amount of time you actually have,
    2. the nature of the scene, and
    3. the disposition and temperament of the actors.

Under certain conditions you'll just allow the actors some quiet time while having their makeup or costumes touched up. You may find that the activity of the set and makeup and other concerns will be distracting to your actors and you will want to spend this time with them, sheltering them from these distractions by keeping them in conversation that focuses on the dynamics of the scene. Or you may want to engage in some intense preparation with the actors just before they go back on the set. Remember: whatever the actors are involved in prior to the actual filming of the scene will affect their performance.

This does not necessarily mean that each and every actor has to remain intensely involved in the emotional dynamics of the scene in order to perform the scene. Some may have to. And others you will find need to do the absolute opposite.

Create an environment that will allow each actor to work at her best. If you are not sure what a particular actor requires (or desires) prior to shooting a scene, just ask her. She usually knows better than anyone and will tell you.

REHEARSAL EXERCISES IN PRODUCTION

There are many rehearsal exercises that can be used just prior to filming that will help refocus or trigger the actors into the scene. The use of any of these preparatory exercises will depend upon the process of the actors and the needs of the scene.

Here are a few exercises that can be very effective:

1. What Do You Want?

This exercise focuses the intensity of an actor's objective.

Stand in front of the actor and simply ask one question over and over again: "What do you want?" The actor must keep answering the question from the point of view of the character. You do not need to stop and listen. Just keep asking the question "What do you want?" The longer and more forcefully this exercise is done the more intense will be the character's objective. This exercise works best when the actor gets beyond thinking about what the character wants and just responds intuitively to the question.

2. Simultaneous Conversation

This exercise is intended to focus the two characters on their individual attitudes or points of view just prior to the scene. As opposed to "What do you want?" this exercise places the two characters in direct conflict with each other.

Each character selects (or you select for him) a specific attitude about the other character, the content of the scene, or an issue between the two characters. They speak simultaneously, attempting to convince each other of their point of view. The objective is to get the other actor/character to stop and listen. This will result in a very intense confrontation and the duration of this exercise will determine its effect.

If such a confrontation were written out, it might look something like this:

Husband	Wife
You're always doing this to me. Always. You keep putting the kids before me. You put them between you and me. I can't take it anymore. This is it. This time we're going off by ourselves and we are going to spend time together and it's going to be peaceful and quiet and we're not going to talk about the kids — not even once. We're going to eat, swim, play golf, and make love. That's it.	You resent me, don't you? You resent me because I was the one that wanted to have kids. And now you're going to hold it against me. You want to make it all my fault that we're not getting along. Well, it's not my fault and it's not the kids' fault. You have to take some of the responsibility. Look at yourself. So caught up in your work that you don't even want to spend time with your family.

3. Pep Talk (Solo)

This exercise is done by the actor alone, without you or a partner.

As we discussed earlier in this book, each character has a very clear objective for each scene. In a pep talk the actor is simply talking to himself and convincing himself that he will indeed be able to achieve his objective. It is pure mental stimulation and can be very effective. Many actors do this exercise without really realizing it. It sounds like this:

> Okay, you can do this. You can convince her. It won't be that hard. She'll understand. She has to understand. Just tell her that it's important for the marriage. The marriage. She's always saying she'll do anything for the marriage. This'll be good. It'll be great. A vacation with just the two of us. Alone, peaceful, quiet. Don't lose your courage, don't let her talk you out of it.

4. History Of Relationship (Pulling Against)

This exercise infuses the scene with an element that is part of the relationship.

There are aspects of every relationship that are either obstacles for the characters or inform the scene in some other way. For example: an argument between husband and wife which is more about their fear of losing each other than it is about whatever they're discussing. Or, same scene, the tremendous love these two have for each other is not evident but a sense of it would give the scene more depth.

Exercise: Just before performing the scene have the two actors engage in an improvisation that directly addresses their fear of losing each other (or expresses the tremendous love they share) so that when they eventually do the scene these aspects of their relationship are very present and immediate.

5. Subtext Exercise

This exercise helps focus the actors/characters on the emotional subtext of the scene in an organic way.

Ask each actor: "What would you really like to say to each other, but can't because the repercussions would be disastrous?" This is their subtext, their deepest feelings, their most honest expression. Reduce each character's subtext to a single yet profound line. Then have the actors run the scene (it could just be sitting in two chairs at the side of the set), but this time they will say their subtext line directly after each written speech. You will notice an immediate sharpening of the scene and a profound focus on intentions.

> Note: This exercise can also be used while shooting over-the-shoulders and singles. Allow the off-camera actor to say his subtext which will in turn strengthen the emotional focus of the actor on camera.

While the actors are involved in other activities (makeup, wardrobe, hair) and your D.P. is lighting the set, you can sneak in some of these rehearsals. One of my favorite places to rehearse is in the makeup room or trailer with the actors looking at each other in the mirror. This is a very direct but different relationship, and simply the act of running their lines in this configuration will keep them focused. Despite the rigors and rigidity of the production schedule, there are many opportunities to work with the actors.

Here are a few more examples:

1. Run the lines as you walk to the set. Fighting their way through various physical obstacles will add a physical tension.
2. Run a simple improvisation on the way to the set (such as recreating the moment just before the scene). This will have the same effect as the exercise above except that it will focus the

actors on yet another aspect of the scene or their relationship.

3. Devil's advocate. While waiting for the set to be ready, let the actors (as the characters) try to convince you of the importance of their individual objectives within the scene. You play devil's advocate to help sharpen and focus their points of view.

BACK ON THE SET

Run the scene once or twice just to make sure that everything is in place, that the camera moves are working, the lighting is okay, etc. (You may have already gone through this with the second team, but it's always different with the first team.) For the moment you need to refocus on to the technical aspects of the scene (camera, sound, effects), and once you are satisfied that all is working appropriately return your attention to the actors. You are now ready to shoot.

It's important at this time to remember what your task is during the filming process. This is not about achieving that one perfect performance. It is about recording a sufficient range so that you can recreate the performance in the editing room. Yes, of course you are looking to capture those extraordinary moments that will occur, but this process is more about creating and collecting a range of material for postproduction. As you record the performances keep in mind that you are limiting your choices and defining the potential range of the scene. This is when you need to think about bracketing.

CREATING CHOICES THROUGH BRACKETING

As stated earlier, the objective during the production process is the creation and collection of a sufficient range of performances and material that will give you significant and reasonable options in the postproduction process. In still photography bracketing means the adjustment of the

257

aperture a half a stop (or more) on either side of your optimum reading, permitting you to later select the most desirable exposure. We're doing the same thing here, but in this case we are adjusting the *performance* just slightly on either side of the original.

> For instance, let's say that you have a scene between a husband and wife and it's an argument. The husband is trying to convince the wife that they should spend their vacation alone while she's trying to convince him that they should take the children. In the performance the husband is exhibiting a lot of passion, resentment, and anger. As you're watching it you may be wondering if it's a bit too much. Too much anger, too harsh? Or should he let himself go a little more and really expose the depths of his feelings? These are valid questions to be asking at this time and quite honestly you probably won't have the answers. The answers will come in postproduction when you finally have the scene all cut together and you have the opportunity to view it in the context of the entire film. Right now you are just witnessing this one scene, and it is extremely difficult to imagine how it is going to play in context.

Bracket the performances ever so slightly. Once you feel you have recorded a suitable performance go for another take, but this time request that the actor(s) make slight adjustments on one side or the other. You can even say, "I need some options in editing" so that the performer(s) will understand what you are doing. When you have recorded a performance that is, let's say, a bit calmer and more restrained, go for one that is a bit looser. How many of each of these performances you wish to print is totally up to you (and your budget) but going into the editing process knowing that you have a range of performances is going to give you more control over your final product.

TECHNIQUES TO TRIGGER PERFORMANCE

Depending on the techniques you have employed in rehearsal, the background you have developed for the character, and the personal exploration you have done with each actor, there are several techniques that you can use to trigger a performance while in the filming process.

We have mentioned the use of the subtext exercise above as one method. Some others are:

> 1. Refocusing or sharpening the character's objective. A simple shift or adjustment in a character's objective can appreciably alter the behavior of that character.

Let's look at our hypothetical scene again as an example. The husband and wife are arguing about whether or not to take the children on their vacation. You're watching the scene and you want to turn up the burners under the wife's performance a bit. You could go to her and say, "I need a little more intensity from you," and you might get what you want. But there is a chance that you won't get what you want because you are talking to the actor and not the character (as we have discussed), and the actor has to translate that direction into something organic. You're talking in results and you need to be speaking of objectives and behavior. You could say, "You are tired of his arguments, try to end the scene on each of your lines." Now the character has a new objective (added to the original objective of convincing the husband that they should take the children), and suddenly the scene will take on a new energy. The actor playing the husband doesn't even need to know about the new objective. He'll feel it and respond to it organically.

> 2. Changing or adjusting an obstacle. Obstacles are very powerful directorial tools, and a simple addition or adjustment of an obstacle will immediately alter a performance.

We're in the same scene with the same problem. You just need a little more fire from the wife, and you would like to achieve it by an obstacle adjustment. Let's say the scene has been playing in the living room, the husband has been sitting on the couch, tired after a long day at the office, and the wife has been moving around the room. There's no time for restaging. Give the husband an independent activity that will impede the wife's progress. Let him read the newspaper during the scene. Let him go through the day's mail during the scene. Anything you give him to do that draws his attention away from her will create a new obstacle. You could even have this new activity start at a certain point within the scene, thereby forcing her to make an adjustment.

3. Making an adjustment in the means.

Another approach is to suggest to the actress that she try to achieve her objective by a different means. Where she may have been playing it with a sense of logic and tolerance, you could suggest that she try being more forceful and demanding. This is not suggesting a different result but rather a different character approach.

4. Adjusting the other actor's attitude (on camera and off).

Similar to giving the husband an independent activity as we suggested above, making an adjustment in his attitude will naturally cause a shift in the wife's behavior. If, for instance, he were to suddenly treat the whole discussion as if it were a bit ridiculous and childish, this dismissive attitude could very well raise her ire to the point desired.

> Note: This trigger is very useful when you are late in the process of shooting the scene. You're doing the wife's close-up and perhaps she is getting tired and losing her drive. Making a major adjustment in the husband's attitude or behavior when he is off camera (so there's no matching problem) can quickly trigger new energy in the wife's performance.

5. Regenerating the personal trigger. This is the trickiest, most delicate and potentially most powerful trigger. This technique is totally reliant upon the personal investigation done with the actor during the rehearsal process.

Let's assume that we have done such an investigation with the actress and we discovered that she is single but she has an issue with her boyfriend that is similar to the one being explored here. She has a cat that she adores and her boyfriend does not like her cat to the point of insisting that she keep the cat in another room when he is visiting her. During our personal exploration we have discovered that this is indeed a powerful and potentially destructive element in their relationship. In the rehearsal process we have explored this issue in improvisations so that it is indeed an operative force between the two actors.

It's guaranteed that the performance is going to change if you go to the actress just before the next take and tell her privately, "He's telling you that you have to choose, it's either him or the cat, you can't have it both ways. If you want him, you have to give up the cat. Choose now!"

Another way to stimulate the same personal trigger is to have the actor playing the husband throw in the cat's name during the scene. This works especially well when one actor is off camera and you don't need to worry about matching. As a matter of fact, if the husband is off camera he can substitute the cat's name every time he mentions the children. He can even say, "It's the cat or me."

Keep in mind that this trigger will only work if you have developed this improvisational and personal relationship between the actors during the rehearsal process. You cannot suddenly introduce this process while shooting the scene.

Using Music To Set Rhythm And Tone

If you have established the use of music in your rehearsal process as a means to setting tone, rhythm, and mood, then it is an easy transition to bring it into the production process. Music is one the of the most powerful and subtle emotional stimulators. Playing the theme from *Rocky* or *Superman* just before or as you are shooting an action sequence will certainly get everyone pumped up. Playing a "love theme" just before shooting a very intimate and delicate scene will not only bring the actors into the mood of the scene, but also everyone on the set, the camera operator, the boom man, even the electrician who is stuck up in the rafters. Music communicates quickly, efficiently, and appropriately to the entire set. If you establish the routine (you don't have to do this for <u>every</u> scene) of playing a piece of music before you begin filming a scene, you will eliminate a lot of shouting for "quiet." The music is the same signal given in a very different manner.

Dealing With Problems On The Set

You are going to run into unexpected circumstances when filming. The problems could be staging, time, wardrobe, weather, props, actors, performances, or script. There is only one way to deal with any of these: go back to the source and remind yourself what you must get from this scene in order to make your movie work. If the problems you are facing seem insurmountable, design another way to achieve what you need. If you are convinced that it is impossible to obtain what you want in the face of these problems, then you'll have to shoot something else and come back to this later. If you are very clear about your priorities and you are able to set clear boundaries and guidelines for the needs of the scene and your story, then in the face of any and all problems you will be able to make a clear decision.

If it is an actor, performance, or script problem you are facing, you need to follow the same process. Assess whether or not you are going to be able to achieve what you need from the scene even if you can't solve the problem. If you can't achieve it, then don't shoot the scene. If you can, then go ahead and shoot. If it is artistic differences between you and the actors (and perhaps the writer), then it is unfortunate that these didn't get resolved in the rehearsal process. If you are facing them now and they are thwarting your progress, then stop and deal with them. Go back to the point of agreement. Take 10 or 15 minutes. Resolve the problem. Come to some sort of agreement that you can live with and then shoot the scene. Carrying unresolved differences in production will only cause a general erosion of trust and collaboration. Remember, inclusion, not exclusion.

REWRITES

There will always be rewrites on the set. Many production managers and producers get upset with last minute script changes, but it is a necessary part of the process. Your focus needs to be on the scene and whether or not a rewrite will genuinely improve the scene and/or solve a problem you are facing. Remember, the priority is not the written word (as many writers unfortunately believe) but rather the intention and function of the scene. In many cases it does not matter exactly what words come out of the character's mouth if the intention and function of the scene are being suitably served.

Conversely, a quick rewrite of the scene may indeed satisfy the needs of the actor and perhaps even the writer, but it could at the same time thwart the intention and function of the scene. It is your job to keep an eye on all of this.

IMPROVISING THE SCENE ON CAMERA

This exercise, as we discussed earlier, is frequently used in the rehearsal process to help the actors reconnect with the core issues in a scene.

Ask the actors to improvise the scene, put the scene in their own words, and not rely on the written text. They must, in their own words, hit all the key moments and story points in the scene (see Chapter 7).

This exercise brings a freshness to the interchange that may not have been there before. You can use this same approach in production. Have the actors improvise the scene on the set with the same staging and same story points. It will regain its freshness.

But there is also the option of *filming* the improvised version of the scene. You are now moving into a delicate area and there are many concerns, the most important being: Is this actually a better rendition of the scene or does it just seem that way because it is suddenly new and fresh? Will this rewriting of the scene have a ripple effect on any other scene? And what about your writer? If your relationship with the writer is healthy and collaborative, there should be no problem with this approach. If the writer is able to put ego aside, she will be able to see the value of this approach and give you an honest, objective assessment.

I have a tendency to use this approach in a lot of my work. (Coincidentally, I am currently working on a project where the entire script is improvised.) Since I am always looking for that electric moment between actors, I am willing to push beyond the actual words of the script in order to find it. But I am aware I have to keep the essence of the script in mind, the obligations of this scene, the objectives of the characters, and their obstacles. I have to be the guardian of the script as I allow the actors to veer away from the written word. Often I am not allowing them to improvise the entire scene, perhaps only moments where I am seeking that spontaneity and rawness that is sometimes hard to get. Even though I am a great believer that a good director (with good actors) can make a scene work <u>without</u> having to rewrite or improvise the dialogue, I am also aware of the deeper levels and sense of reality you can reach when the actual creation of dialogue is put in the hands of the characters (and with good actors it <u>will</u> be the characters who are writing the scene, not the actors).

If this is an approach you want to take, begin in the rehearsal process. Unless you have had extensive experience working with actors and know your actors well, I do not advise introducing this approach on the set. If it is introduced in the rehearsal process your actors will become acclimated to it and begin to find their own voice and expression. It will deepen their awareness of their characters and you may reach a refinement of the script in rehearsal which will achieve your objectives.

There are a few directors (e.g., Robert Altman, Mike Leigh) who work extensively with improvisation. Look at their work and you will see that they have attained a different level of behavior, attitude, and relationship between the characters. There is a vitality there that most often does not exist in tightly scripted performances. Be aware of your preferences, of what you as a director wish to attain.

FINDING AND SHOOTING THE DETAILS

As you are watching your scene play out, let your eye wander. Look for details that are helping to inform the scene but that the camera may not be getting. Is your actress toying with an object that is expressive of her frustration? Is the way your actor is working his way though the papers on the table indicative of his desire to be elsewhere? Is the slow gliding of the fish in the tank an interesting contrast to the human tension in the room? Is the stillness and reliability of the clock on the mantel an ironic counterpoint to the scene? Within any scene there are many details that our eye will pick up and incorporate as we watch it on the set but which may get lost in the actual filming process. Look for these details and capture them. Whether you allow them to become the foreground of your shot (such as shooting across the papers to the husband) or to become inserts (a shot of the papers from

265

the husband's point of view) is up to you. The point is: don't leave the scene without shooting some of these. They can be done relatively quickly (especially if you are not seeing the actors speak in the shot), and they can literally save you in the editing process, not only in terms of cutaways but also by giving us a richer appreciation of the scene.

DAILIES

The viewing of dailies by the actors is also a volatile subject. I made the mistake in my first feature of not allowing the actors to see the dailies. Most didn't ask or show much interest, but some did. And I felt it was my right (which it is) and obligation (which it is not) to keep this part of the process private. I think I believed that if the actors saw their work it would affect their future work in the film. I had heard horror stories about actors being so upset with how they look and perform on camera that it took days for them to recover. But I now genuinely believe that these are isolated cases and it is just best to deal with them when they come up.

As we have said many times, this is a collaborative process and for me not to allow the actors to witness the results of this collaboration was wrong. It was actually a form of exclusion.

> I learned my lesson when I asked Bill Pullman to look at one of the scenes we had cut together. His response was so strong and appreciative and his awareness of where I was going with the movie in terms of style and rhythm greatly enhanced his work from then on. I only wish that I had taken these steps earlier. We live and learn.

If an actor has an adverse reaction to seeing dailies, then you might suggest that he stay away. It is of no value to an actor to see his work if the subsequent work is going to suffer because of it. Some actors will tell you that they prefer not to, others will show a strong desire to see specific scenes, and some may be ambivalent.

During the viewing of dailies it is important that you set the tone in the room. Let everyone know that the purpose is simply to view the dailies. This is not a time for critique or selecting favorite performances (especially with the actors in the room). Just sit back and review the day's work.

The questions are: Have you shot (and printed) a sufficient range of performance for the scene? Have you covered it sufficiently? Have you recorded enough detail? Can you see any reason why you would have to return to this scene? If you are satisfied that you have sufficient material, then let the scene go. Instruct your editor to look at the scene in the same manner (most will do this automatically) and let her know that you can discuss preferred performances and takes at another time.

Let the material wash over you. Enjoy the performances. Let yourself be an audience and allow yourself the luxury of responding genuinely to the material.

COMMUNICATION

Communication is the key.
It is the key to creating and maintaining a collaborative attitude in your entire crew.
It is the key that sustains the trust and the security that is so necessary for honest performances.

It works two ways:
> From you to the actors, your team members, and the members of the crew. Their response to you through their work which becomes the material for your film.

Once you have created and gathered all the material you feel you need in order to assemble your movie, then you are ready for postproduction.

Chapter 9

Postproduction

The production process is a grind. It is excruciating and exhilarating all at the same time. You're up against schedules, budgets, attitudes, and opinions with not enough time and not enough money. And once it is over you enter a process that couldn't be more opposite. The postproduction process is lonely, quiet, and exceedingly slow.

This is a time when you can easily lose your way or your vision. The production process has most likely tapped all your energy, and now you have to be careful that you don't let up. You need to renew yourself because <u>now</u> you are finally going to make your movie. Everything you have done up to now has only been to prepare yourself for this final phase of the process. This is where the movie is really made.

This is the <u>third</u> and final telling of the story.

Editing As A Rehearsal Process

We have spoken of this earlier but it bears repeating: The editing process in film is like the rehearsal process in theatre. During the editing process you are making your final selections in terms of performance, rhythm, pacing, continuity, and structure. As you enter this process you really have no idea what selections you are going to make. Start with an open mind. Don't begin editing with a firm conviction that you know exactly the choices you are going to make, but rather with the notion that you are going to discover the story that is lurking somewhere within the material you have created in production.

REVIEWING DAILIES WITH YOUR EDITOR

During production you have been spending time reviewing the dailies with your editor. During this process there are specific steps you need to be taking:

1. Remind each other what the scene is all about.
2. Talk about how the scene supports the story.
3. Point out preferred takes or moments, and the reasons why.
4. Let the editor do his work.

GET AWAY

The first step of postproduction is quite simple: Get away from the film! You have spent the past several months (and maybe even years) working diligently on the script, casting, preproduction, and production and now you need to get away, to regain your objectivity. Take two, three, four weeks, and do something else. Take a vacation. Read a lot of books. Sit by the seaside. Climb a mountain. Do anything except think about your movie (lots of luck!). You will be the best director you can be in postproduction if you can approach the process with a clear, fresh, and rested mind.

FIND THE STORY

Before you commence this third "telling" of the story go back to the initial stage of your process. Remember when you first starting working on the script? You read the script several times and allowed it to just wash over you. The "script wash" we called it. And during this "wash" you allowed the script to affect you so that you might discover its essence. You tried to make no judgments as you allowed the script to impact you. Well, you are going to follow a similar process in postproduction, but now you are faced with the fact that you have limited possibilities. You need to *discover the story that is within your material*. You may think you know what the story is, but I guarantee that you will be surprised. Your postproduction process will be the most successful if you allow yourself to *find the story* rather than try to force your material into the story you *think* you have.

> Anecdote: At the first preview of my film *Going Under*, I was deeply disappointed that the audience was all preteens rather than the adults that the film was made for. After the screening the response was predictably discouraging. I was in the lobby with one of the top executives from Warner Bros. (who had never read the script or seen the film prior to this moment) and I told him that I knew the film would play well for the adult audience we had scheduled in two days' time. He looked at me and said, "No, this is the audience that this film was intended for and we will make it work for *this audience*." I didn't know it then, but that was the beginning of the end of my movie. After my director's cut, the producers and the studio attempted to create a totally different movie. It didn't work. It wasn't in the material. The storyline, behavior, and attitudes that entertained an adult audience were totally unsuitable for preteens.

THE EDITOR'S CUT

While you have been on your vacation, your editor has been assembling a rough edit of the entire movie.

It is very important that you allow the editor the time and space to make her own cut of the film. This is not just a courtesy, it is an important step in your collaborative process. Just as you have allowed all other members of your creative team to give their input (in response to your vision) it is important that you allow the editor to show you how she sees the movie you have shot.

It is going to be a shock when you first see this cut. It will not seem like your movie at all. The rhythms will be off, the pace will be off. The scenes will not contain many of the dynamics you saw on the set. The editing may seem rough and jarring. So, you say, why go through all this if this is going to be the result? Because this result is only *your* reaction to the editor's cut. You are merely responding to someone else's assemblage of your movie. And even though you may have all the experiences I mentioned above, it does *not* mean that any or all of them are accurate. Before you panic look at the film again. Listen to the film. Understand where these choices are coming from. The editor's job (in this first cut) is to deliver a version of the film that is as true as possible to the original script and to the footage you delivered. The editor has yet to respond to the more profound story that is lurking beneath the material.

Before you jump to conclusions, watch the film a few times. Ask your editor about the choices made in rhythms, pacing, and performances. You are not questioning these choices but merely beginning to understand how the editor is responding to your material

> Note: This is similar to a writer hearing actors read their material for the first time. Often horrifying. But once the writer understands the reasons for the actors' choices in performance, he learns something new about the script.

Like the writer, (as we discussed in Chapter 3), may not know what he has written, you may not know the movie you have made.

Take the time to listen to the editor. Some of the choices may be of great value to you, and some may not. But before your dismiss or accept, listen to them all.

> For example: let's say that you are looking at a particular scene and it is playing much more seriously than you had intended. The editor has found all the intense moments and serious reactions

and has constructed a scene that is a bit too somber for your taste. This can easily happen. Before you jump back into recutting the scene to meet your vision, discover why the editor had this response to the material. Maybe there is an undercurrent in the scene that is giving it a more somber tone. It may be a more interesting way for the scene to play. Or not. That will of course depend upon the entire fabric of your movie.

It now begins to become quite clear why it is so important that you deliver a variety of material from the production process. The greater the variety (within reason), the more latitude you have as you begin to make the discoveries and choices that will determine the final telling of your story.

THE DIRECTOR'S CUT

According to the Directors Guild of America (DGA) Creative Rights you have 10 weeks within which to deliver your director's cut. The DGA fought hard for this number of weeks (and they are barely enough) because editing is a discovery process that demands and deserves time. Think of it like the writing process. No matter how clear you may be about a script you want to write, it takes time to find the best way to express the story that is in your head. And even though the editing process is quite simple technically (cutting pieces of film and taping them together, or now with computerized editing it seems even simpler), the process is quite complex artistically. It is a process of discovery more than assembly. This is what many studio and production executives don't seem to comprehend. It takes being with a film for weeks upon end, watching footage, looking at scenes, reviewing dailies over and over again, before you can even begin to "feel" the movie that is lurking within the material. It is a trial and error process.

The DGA (and I realize that many of you may not be members of the Guild but it is important that you realize what the Guild has accomplished in the name of <u>all</u> directors) also stipulates that you are permitted to complete your cut of the film without the interference of producers, writers, studio executives and others. This is to be your version of the movie, exactly the way you want it. No one is allowed to interfere or to be assembling another version of the film somewhere else.

With this in mind it becomes apparent how important it is for you to create and maintain a clear and clean way of working. Once your cut is done and previewed, all these other parties are going to make their opinions known and felt. There's nothing quite like a nervous producer or backer who feels strongly that a different version of the film will be more successful to put your teeth on edge.

ESTABLISHING YOUR PROCESS

You've probably been left alone for the most part during preproduction and production. For good reason: No one else knows how to make the film. Now, in the final stages of postproduction everyone will become an expert on how the film should be completed. You realize, of course, that these were the very same people who were clueless when it came to story structure, character relationships, casting, cinematography, performances, lighting, and locations. But now with the footage at their disposal they are suddenly filmmakers.

As you begin working toward your director's cut establish a working process that will give you the maximum security, clarity, and ability to consider all possibilities before you make your final decisions.

As you view the editor's cut don't get caught up either in scenes that don't work at all or in scenes that work magnificently. Start with the overall film. Ask yourself: "Is this the story I want to be telling?" If you can look at the film and feel confident in the overall story, then you can begin looking at its strengths and weaknesses.

Be aware of when you are drawn into the story and when you slide out of it. This is your internal barometer. If you find that you are concentrating on performance, the editing or production design, or that beautiful camera move you fought so hard for, then you are <u>not</u> involved in the movie. But when you find yourself concerned with the characters, their objectives, and their struggles, then you <u>are</u> involved in the movie. When you pull out again and become aware of the film itself and its mechanics, make a note, the film isn't working. This is where you need to do your work.

Look at the weak scenes and ask yourself:
1. What is the function of this scene within the overall story?
2. What do I need to accomplish with this scene in order to insure that it supports the story?

Review all the footage you had printed for this scene. Look at the performances (and hopefully you have a range to consider) and reacquaint yourself with the material you have on hand. Then, in response to the two questions, begin to reshape your scene.

As you recut the scene you may begin to get the feeling that certain moments or beats are not necessary. Maybe a point is made once too often. Maybe an actor's performance is adding another dimension making a certain line redundant. Maybe a certain thought or idea or statement is thwarting the flow of the scene, or is stated better in another scene. In other words, you will be discovering, as you rework the scene, the urge to rewrite the scene, make cuts in dialogue, move speeches. This is a good sign. Remember, this is the third telling of the story and doesn't have to replicate either of the first two. You are now in the process of discovering the story within the material.

You may even have the feeling that a certain scene isn't necessary, or is in the wrong place. For the moment leave it in, where it is. You want to give each scene its best shot before you decide to move or extricate it.

Go through this process with each of your weak scenes, reassemble the movie, and look at it again. This time you may notice something odd. The scenes that you thought were strong are suddenly not so strong. This occurs all the time. It is a natural part of the editing process. Nothing has happened with those scenes except that the surrounding scenes have improved. They seem weaker only by comparison.

Go through the process again, find the weak spots, reexamine them, and rework them. You may find that one or two scenes, or perhaps an entire sequence, are thwarting the progress of the movie. Consider whether or not they belong in the movie, or belong where they are in the movie. You are at the stage where you may need to make bold moves to make your film work the way you want it to. You are finding the story within the material and are sensing the best way to tell that story. Be bold. Remember, you can always put it back the way it was. Nothing will have changed.

Listen to your editor. Just when you may be thinking that you have to reshoot something or lose an important moment, your editor may come up with an imaginative way of solving the problem with the footage you have. (Read *When The Shooting Stops* by Ralph Rosenblum and Robert Karen for a fascinating look inside the world of editing. It's amazing what a good editor can do.) It's your job to maintain the vision of the movie and the editor's job to express that vision through her craft.

MOLDING THE ACTORS' PERFORMANCES IN POSTPRODUCTION

An actor's final performance is made in postproduction; there is no question about that. This is why actors are often disappointed or shocked when they see a film in which they have performed. There is no way that the final edited performance is going to meet all their expectations.

Look at it from an actor's point of view, from the actor's experience. The actors have just spent a certain number of weeks (or even months) delivering a performance with many variations and nuances that have helped define the complexities of the character and the character's experience. And they have personally experienced every moment of this character. That is what is living inside them. That is the emotional memory they carry with them as they sit down to watch a screening of the film. There is no way that it can all be there on the screen. This is why film is a director's medium. You have final say, final selection, over the performance of the actor. On stage, the actors are in control of their performance. (In theatre the actor is actually functioning as the editor as he performs.) Film is frustrating for many actors, and this is one of the primary reasons why some actors are attempting to wield more control not only in script and director selection, but even venturing into directing and producing themselves.

As you watch your film keep your eye on the characters and the character arcs. Ask yourself "what would happen if..." What would happen if you lightened a certain actor's performance in one scene, or allowed it to be more intense? What would happen if the conflict between the two characters became apparent a scene or two later? You have a good idea of the range of performances available, so you know in your mind the latitude you have. It is in these small (and sometimes not so small) adjustments to performance that you can refine, tighten, and hone the dramatic telling of your story.

As we discussed earlier, there is good reason for the editing and postproduction process to be as long as it is (often longer than preproduction and production combined). This process takes time because as you make slight adjustments in one performance you will feel the story shift. Then you may desire to make adjustments in another character's performance and that will cause another shift. Hopefully all of these shifts will bring you closer to your vision of the film, but the trick, and mystery, in editing is that you won't know until you try it. Trying to imagine how an adjustment to a performance in one scene will affect that scene and consequently affect the entire movie is very difficult, and remains highly speculative. Seeing the change, feeling the repercussions — that's where you find the answers. You may try several good ideas and find that they don't work, that there's no improvement in the dramatic flow of your story. And then you may try one more idea that perhaps seemed like a long shot, a slightly outrageous choice, and you find that the effect is significant. You never know until you hear it and see it, and this takes time. Allow yourself the time.

KEEPING THE AUDIENCE DISSATISFIED

As we discussed earlier, the audience is always seeking closure. They want the hero or heroine to achieve their objectives. They want the two lovers to get together. They want the good guys to beat the bad guys. And as soon as they (the audience) get what they want, they want to go home — the movie is over. So it is incumbent upon us, as storytellers, to keep the audience dissatisfied. We intentionally do not let scenes reach total balance or resolution, and we certainly do not let our protagonists and antagonists achieve their overall objectives before the end of the scene (or the end of the movie).

As you are watching your movie, be aware of your feelings and your desires for resolution. There is power in the inconclusive scene, the unanswered questions, the little beats or moments that can signal that all is not as well as might be assumed.

> For example: Imagine our husband and wife arguing about their vacation plans and at the end of the scene the husband agrees to take the children. Then we cut to the wife and see a very satisfied look on her face. That's one ending. But let's imagine that the final cut is to the wife and she has a hurt look on her face. Now, what's that all about? Didn't she get what she wanted? Does this mean that she wanted the husband to fight harder for what <u>he</u>

wanted? A very different scene. But you may be asking, "What if I didn't shoot that moment, the hurt look?" If you didn't shoot a variety of endings, look through your dailies. I would find it hard to believe that in all the footage you shot in that entire scene there was not one moment of the wife with a hurt look. That's where you find it. (And these are the moments that truly, and understandably, throw the actors when they see the film!)

Now you have altered the ending of a crucial scene and presented some questions. Why did she have this response? How is this going to affect future scenes?

Let's look at the scene in the car and suppose that within that scene there is a moment when the wife has a few sharp words with the children. They are acting out and getting rambunctious and suddenly the wife snaps at them. Now this moment is going to play very differently depending on the ending you have in the previous scene. If you leave the argument scene with the wife's satisfied look, then this moment with the children will just look like she's upset with them. But if you leave the earlier scene with the wife's hurt look, then this snapping at the kids could be seen as an expression of her disappointment that her husband gave in. But you won't know until you play the two scenes together with the different endings. (Oh, the joys of digital editing where you can quickly make two versions of a scene, without cutting film, and show them both in one screening!) And as you look at the two versions of this sequence, consider whether you want to alter the confrontation with the kids in any way. What happens if you heighten it, if you soften it? Each alteration will affect the development of the wife's character and the nature of her arc and her relationship with her husband and with her children. And consequently all of this will affect the nature of your story.

This is a simple but clear example of the significance of exploring the range of possibilities for every moment within each scene and the resulting ripple effect. We talked in Chapter 3 ("Working with Writers") about the ripple effect when the writer makes a small change in the script, whether it's in a character or an event or a piece of behavior. The same effect is in operation here. That one moment when we see the wife's disappointment in her husband's acquiescence to her strong request will most likely affect every scene (having to do with this family) that follows.

Don't feel obligated to maintain perfect clarity. Allow yourself the luxury of the unknown and perhaps indecipherable. The audience, always thrilled by the unexpected, loves a good puzzle and thrives on the unanswered and the beguiling.

ADR As An Area For Performance Adjustment

ADR (Automated Dialogue Replacement), or "looping" as it is commonly known, has become a standard practice in all filmmaking. There is always the sound problem (airplanes flying over, noisy sets, overlapping, camera noise, insufficient volume) that will necessitate bringing the actors back to replace their lines with clean recordings. Without getting into the mechanics of this process, we need to consider this phase of postproduction in terms of our ability to refine the telling of our story.

You will open up a large can of worms if you begin to consider looping every scene just in order to alter performance. Besides the expense it is indicative that you have an even bigger problem. It has been done though. There are instances where entire performances (*Knife in the Water, Greystoke: The Legend of Tarzan*) have been replaced by another actor. This is not what we are discussing here. If you feel convinced that a slight alteration in performance in particular scenes or moments will significantly strengthen your movie, then you have the option of bringing the actors in for that purpose.

It is one thing to bring actors in to replace dialogue because the original tracks are unusable; it's another thing to alter performance. Prepare the actors. Bring them into your process. Let them know how the movie is coming together. Tell them of the strengths and again express your enthusiasm. Let them know of the scene or scenes you are considering for performance alteration, and why. You may even want to show them the latest cut of the film so that they can see exactly what you are talking about. The bottom line is to make them part of the process, and allow them to collaborate. There is even the possibility that they might come up with different solutions to the same problem. Remember, they are still working from within their characters and they will view the film from a slightly different perspective. They may see a way to rerecord those problematic scenes in a manner that you had not considered while maintaining a consistency of character.

When rerecording in ADR you are suddenly back in production. You are creating and gathering material. Go for a range of performances. Bracket, especially with the dialogue that must be replaced because of faulty sound recording. Don't limit yourself.

NARRATION AND VOICEOVER

Narration has been around since sound was added to film. Sometimes it works very well, sometimes it sort of works, and sometimes it is a dismal failure. Depending on how it is used, it is no different than any other storytelling tool. Read *Forrest Gump*, Academy Award winner of Best Picture and Best Screenplay (adapted from other material) in 1994, and you will see that there is an extensive use of narration and voice-over. It works. It was well designed.

But now we are in postproduction and we are bringing up the issue of voice-over and narration. If it has been a part of your original script then the extended use of this technique could fit nicely into the fabric of your film. If you have not employed voice-over and narration in

281

your film so far, then the addition of this technique could be disruptive. But if your film is in trouble and there are some holes that just can't seem to be filled by any other process, you still have the option of pulling it all together with narration. This means that you will be creating a whole new thread in the fabric of your story. Don't make the mistake of just adding narration here and there in order to clarify. Look at the whole film. You are, in effect, considering a rewrite so you need to look at the entire script. Who should your narrator be? And at what age (i.e., is she narrating from the time of the story or from a more objective point of view after the story is over)? When would be the best point in the film to establish the narrator? At the very beginning? After a specific scene? Remember, you are creating a whole new character — the character of the narrator — which is not the same character as the one in the film. The character in the film is operating in relationship to the other characters in the film; the narrator is telling a story to the audience. Consider the objectives, obstacles, and general arc of this new character. What is the narrator's point of view on the story, and how does this point of view affect our understanding of the very same character who is in the film? In other words, if the wife was narrating our hypothetical film, how does her point of view as narrator affect her character as we see her on the screen? And how often do we need to hear from the narrator? Is it only in relation to certain events in the film? Does the narrator reach closure at the end of the film? A lot to consider.

There is another important consideration. How does the narrator's input affect the rest of the film, the characters, and the individual scenes? Will you have to change any of the other material in the film because you now have a narrator who is altering the audience's experience of the story?

If you don't consider all of these points, you run the risk of the narration seeming to be exactly what you initially considered — a device to cover up problems in the script. Narration done properly can be that one element that pulls your story together.

POSTPRODUCTION SOUND

There are three categories of sound in postproduction: dialogue (production and ADR), sound effects, and music (original score and prerecorded). And each has its own team of editors.

THE SOUND EFFECTS TEAM

You are now at the point of locking your picture for your director's cut so that other members of your postproduction creative team can do their work. All the time you have been working on this cut, your sound effects team (and your music editors which we will get to in a moment) have been viewing the various stages of the film and have been gathering their material. During this time you have been communicating your thoughts on the nature and type of sounds you want, scene by scene. Let's look at one of our hypothetical scenes and consider the range of sounds that could be part of that scene.

> The husband and wife have an argument. Let's say that it takes place in the living room of their home about 3 p.m., before the kids have come home. What are the possible sounds you could add to this scene? It's a tense scene because of the argument, although at the end of the scene there is a resolution, of sorts. Let's say that there is little within the environment that suggests specific sounds. No evidence of a stereo playing or television on. No source sound. But what else could there be? Is there a clock in the room? Yes, an old pendulum clock on the mantel. The ticking of the pendulum clock could certainly add tension to the scene. How about that aquarium in the corner that you did a very clever shot through? How about an occasional burst of air bubbles as air is forced into the water? Could there be sounds from outside the house? Cars passing by? Sirens? Children playing joyfully (in contrast to the way they are being considered in the scene)?

283

Now these are all realistic sounds. Sounds we can identify with the environment. But then there are the nonrealistic sounds, or sounds that are seemingly inappropriately placed.

> There is a wonderful scene in Peter Weir's *Dead Poet's Society* that takes place in the living room of the home of one of the boys, Neil. There are three characters in the room — Neil, his mother, and his father. They are discussing Neil's future. The father had insisted that Neil abandon his ridiculous dreams of being an actor. Neil defied him and the father has just witnessed Neil's performance in a school production of *Midsummer Night's Dream*. The father presents an ultimatum. He is taking Neil out of this private school (and away from the teacher, played by Robin Williams, who had nurtured Neil's creative soul) and placing him in a military school. Neil is devastated. The mother is silent. And what is the sound we hear under the scene? Wind. The wind across a plain. Empty lonesome wind. There is no wind in the room. It's seemingly a totally inappropriate sound for the scene we are watching, but emotionally it is totally accurate, expressing the emptiness, the vacuum felt by Neil. Peter Weir, the director, knew exactly what he was doing. *Dead Poet's Society* is a fascinating study in the use of "inappropriate" sound. Rent the movie, listen to the sound. The rush and call of birds in flight segueing into the chattering and stampeding of students down a schoolroom staircase is brilliant.

So, imagine for a moment what other sounds you could employ in our husband-wife argument scene. Wind would be interesting, wouldn't it? It would, like in *Dead Poet's Society*, underscore the emptiness. But what if you wanted to make a different statement, emphasize a different aspect of the scene, such as the mounting tension that you feel is about to snap? The clock could help you do that. Maybe the clock's rhythmic ticking changes during the scene and increases in tempo, or slows down. What would that do? Or the ticking becomes harsher, or softer. And maybe at the point when the husband agrees to take the children, the ticking stops. What does that mean? What would that do to your audience? Suddenly there's silence. No ticking, no cars, no children playing. The sudden absence of sound can be just as powerful as the sudden addition of a sound. There are endless choices and possibilities.

MUSIC

Due to the manner in which films are made, the actual score of the film is usually not even roughed out until the picture is locked in its final version. This makes score consideration and the collaboration with your composer a very difficult process. Many times directors don't actually hear the score for their film until the moment of recording with a full orchestra. This is why the creation of a "temp" track on your director's cut becomes important in many ways.

We will talk more about the final score and working with the composer when we lock the picture.

THE TEMP TRACK

As you are assembling your director's cut, your music editors (with the advice of your composer) will be creating a temporary sound track using existing music. Once again, as with your consideration of your sound track, you have an opportunity to color your work with the addition of this new element. Because this initial music track will be composed of existing (prerecorded) music you have at your fingertips an extraordinary range of material from which to choose.

In your consideration of an editor, we talked about the editor's appreciation and use of music while editing. An editor who has a good sense of music and the power of music in filmmaking will begin to place music under certain scenes as she is working. I have found it very difficult to *imagine* how a certain scene is going to work with music under it, and I am constantly amazed at the powerful effect of underscoring and background music.

> In Linda Seger's *From Script to Screen* she reveals how Peter Weir selects a piece of music for each scene. The music gives him a rhythm and pace. He'll play the music during rehearsal, while the crew is lighting and even up until the moment of shooting. He says that the music is crucial to the rhythm and tone of the scene, that it will influence the actors' performances and reaction time. John Seales (Peter Weir's cinematographer for *Dead Poet's Society*) says that the music helps him determine the speed of the camera moves, or how fast to pan or tilt or track. And this may even be the exact piece of music that will underscore the final version of the scene.

In my last film *Going Under*, I had the composer, David Michael Frank, create themes for each of the characters prior to production and I played these themes for the actors so that they would have an idea of the musical moods that would be supporting them. It made a big difference. My editor for the same film, Paul Seydor, had a tremendous knowledge and appreciation of music. He was constantly experimenting with various musical themes and ideas. I was amazed at what he would come up with, what would work and what wouldn't. It was a great learning experience for me.

I think that there is an imbalance between how much we rely on music to create and support the ultimate tone and rhythm and mood of our movies and how little we use music during the preproduction and production phases. It is an element that is too often left to the last moment (sometimes composers aren't even hired until the film is nearing completion), and too often there is an undue reliance on the music to "save" the film. I don't know how many times I've heard during the final stages of postproduction, "the music will make this scene work." It may be true, but if so, why wasn't this crucial element of music taken into consideration earlier in the process?

As you are creating your director's cut and your temp track, you will be laying in music you have been considering since the script breakdown and rehearsal processes as well as pieces that have been suggested by your editors and composer. You are now getting a first look (listen?) at the blending of these sound elements with your picture. Remember, this is trial and error. One of the best ways of testing a piece of music for your film is to simply play it in the editing room while you are running the scene on the moviola or Kem (or whatever editing system you have chosen). You don't need to transfer every piece of music you are considering. You'll know if it's right as soon as you hear it with your picture.

THE FIRST MIX

As you go into your first sound mix (mixing the three sound elements into one sound track), you are going to get the first taste of your completed movie. Even though it is still your first cut and you're dealing with a temp track, this is close to what your film is going to look and sound like. Quite a thrilling moment. And now you also realize how important each element is to the making of your movie.

PREVIEWS

Once again we have a topic about which there is a wide range of opinions from directors, producers, studio executives and others. Many directors resent the whole preview process because they see it as a means used by producers and studios of unfairly assessing audience response to the film (thereby not trusting the sensibilities and tastes of the very people who made the film) and consequently catering to the lowest common denominator. Question: if a preview audience (through their written questionnaires) show that they don't like a certain character or certain scene, is this good or bad? If a majority of the audience feels that a certain moment was too violent, or too explicit, is that good or bad? If the audience for the most part was displeased with the way the movie ended, is that good or bad? In other words it is the *filmmaker's* assessment of the *audience's* assessment that is the critical evaluation. You see, we are right in the middle of that discussion we had chapters ago, the audience's desire for balance and closure and for a satisfying ending. We all saw that it was our job as storytellers to "frustrate" the audience, to not give them what they want, and that was one of our most powerful tools as storytellers. So, when we show our film to a preview audience, we have to be very clear with ourselves what response we are looking for. What negative responses will we find totally acceptable and what positive responses will we find disturbing? Is the response of laughter good or bad? It all depends on the scene and the nature of the relationship we are trying to maintain with the audience.

There are many directors who value the preview process because they see it as a means of genuinely testing their film in front of the public. They want to see it in a roomful of eager listeners and they want to hear the reactions to specific moments. They feel strongly that they can use these responses to effectively fine-tune the final cut of the film.

Then there are those directors who feel strongly that they must complete their films as they see them (perhaps showing them to a select group of friends and colleagues) and not allow themselves to be swayed by the responses and apparent needs of the audience.

This is obviously an individual choice. Many artists work in almost total isolation and don't reveal their work until they are satisfied. Others are constantly testing the waters of audience reaction and adjusting their work accordingly. I warn only of the extremes. Those filmmakers who work in total isolation are in my opinion cutting themselves off from the potentially healthy and constructive feedback from the very audience they wish to reach. And those filmmakers who excessively present the material to anyone who will watch run the danger of hearing so many opinions that they will eventually lose sight of their own vision.

I have found the reading of screenplays for a select audience of professionals stimulating and enlightening. I have found inviting one or two friends into the rehearsal process constructive and informative. And I have found the screening of various cuts of my film for trusted directors, editors, writers, and actors a very appropriate counterbalance to the isolation of postproduction. In the preview process, I have found that the feedback from a caring and concerned audience can be enormously helpful.

Now, I say "caring and concerned" target audience. "Target" means selecting a preview audience that reflects the demographics of the general populace that you intend to reach. My last film, as I mentioned, was a disaster in previews for an audience of preteens, but played very well for the young adults for whom it was intended. No one film is going to please everyone, and if it attempts to, then it will fail.

The creation of a caring and concerned audience depends on the manner in which they are invited and how the film is presented. If the audience is told, "Free movie, bring your friends," then you will get one attitude. But if the audience is told, "We're previewing a new movie and the filmmakers would like your response and feedback," then you will get another kind of attitude. Prepare the audience for the screening. When we go to the movies we usually have some idea of the movie we are about to see either from word of mouth, advertising and promotion, or articles and reviews. Even the presence of a star or a line on the one-sheet will give us an idea. In previews the audience only knows that it's going to see a new movie. Taking a couple of minutes to prepare the audience for your movie will set them in the proper frame of mind. Just saying "this is a comedy, a very different kind of comedy" will mean one thing, while saying "this is a serious film and we know it may not be for everyone but we think it is very special" will set the audience in a different mood. Don't just assume that the audience will come in, get their popcorn, sit down, and be ready to see *your* movie. Prepare them.

And be prepared yourself. Perhaps the most difficult part of the preview process is allowing yourself to be a member of the audience. Don't judge the audience. Don't judge the film. Be a member of the audience and enjoy the experience.

You're right. We're back at that point again — the script wash. Once again it is time to allow the film to just wash over you. Let it affect you. Don't judge it and don't get overly focused on the audience. An amazing thing happens the first time you sit in an audience and watch your film — you suddenly see a whole new movie. There will be parts that suddenly work that didn't seem to work before, and other parts that don't. You'll see it differently, you'll hear it differently, and only because you are now a part of a community, the audience, and you are seeing it through their eyes. It is a wonderful and mystical phenomenon.

THE FINAL CUT

You are now approaching one of the most nerve-racking moments in filmmaking — locking the picture. There comes that moment when you have to say, "That's it. That's the movie. Lock it." This is the beginning of a series of final decisions, choices, and selections. The picture is locked and you are approaching the creation of the final sound tracks, the composition of the final score, and eventually the final mix. In the back of your mind will be questions: "Would it work better if I shortened that moment?"; "Should we take one more pass at that action sequence?"; "What if we spent more time on the opening?" Those questions will always be there and as Martha Graham said there is always that "divine dissatisfaction." That artistic restlessness is part of your creative soul and will not allow you to see any work as complete. It is important that you understand this as you begin the sequence of slowly letting go of the movie.

SPOTTING THE PICTURE

This is a process quite simply of "spotting" those points in the picture where you and the composer will be placing the music. You have been using a temp track up until this point so many of these points are going to be obvious to both of you, but make sure that you are not limiting yourself. Reconsider every moment and what you expect the music to accomplish. In many ways this is the beginning of the creative process between you and the composer. Up until now you have been talking about music, maybe heard some samples of what might play under a scene or character, and you have had your discussions about the temp track. Now you are truly venturing into the world of the original music track for your film. A new element and another opportunity to fine-tune your story.

Be specific as you describe the effect you expect the music to have. Discuss why you want music at certain points and not at others. Review the temp track and how it worked (or didn't work) for you. Keep in mind: the essence of each scene and how that scene needs to support the overall story; the character arcs and how music might enlighten or clarify aspects of a character; the mood and attention of the audience and how music might keep them dissatisfied or promise that resolve that they so desire. Talk about mood, tensions, suspense, romance, humor, pathos, and whatever you want to support (or counterpoint) with the music. Be specific and the composer will respond with music.

THE SCORING SESSION

The first time you hear the musical score may be at the scoring session. If so, this is unfortunate. With synthesizer's and samplers it is so easy for a composer to give you a clear idea of the score he is composing long before you hit the scoring stage. Insist on hearing the score, even on just a piano, before you hit the stage. Due to economics

291

and budgeting (by the time some films hit the scoring stage they have often run out of money) many producers will give you very little time to actually play with the score. Get all that you can. Remember, the score is one-sixth of your movie. One-half of your movie is visual and one-half is sound. Sound is composed of three parts: dialogue, effects, and music. One-sixth of your movie! It deserves as much attention as any other of the key elements.

As you listen to the score don't be too analytical. Allow it to wash over you. Let it take its effect on you. Like any new element it will sound strange at first, but give it a chance. And remember, just like with performances and ADR you are suddenly back in production again. If you think a certain piece of music is too harsh, ask your composer if there is a way to soften it, to record it in two or three versions. Sometimes softening the percussion or emphasizing the strings will make all the difference in the world. You don't have to have extensive musical knowledge in order to communicate with your composer. If you feel the music is inappropriate you should be able to explain that in dramatic terms — not musical terms. If it feels intrusive, say so. If it feels too timid, say so. Be aware of your emotional reaction to the music and that will guide you.

THE FINAL MIX

As you go into the final mix you are going to have three distinct areas of sound to consider: dialogue, effects, and music. Up until this point you have been considering each one individually. The dialogue tracks were selected from production and ADR sources. Many of the effects tracks may be the ones you used for your temp mix and there will most likely be new material. And you will have the music tracks as we discussed above.

Depending on your dialogue, sound, and music editors, these elements may be assembled on as many as 20, 30, 40 or more separate tracks. What this means is, as you go into the mix you still have control over many separate elements. Depending on the capability of your mixing stage, your music track could come in still on 24 separate channels (allowing you and the composer to actually do your final music mix at this point). So, even though your picture is locked, your sound is far from locked and you are once again in a position to make significant choices about and contributions to your movie.

There is no way I can impress upon you how important this moment is, and how frustrating it is when producers schedule too little time for this process. You are now approaching the final edit for one-half your movie, the sound, and unlike the picture edit, this edit is done on the fly. It is the best way. You are going to have at least three mixers working (dialogue, effects, and music) and each of them is going to have several tracks at their fingertips. It is an exciting, exhilarating, and often frustrating process.

ACHIEVING THE MIX YOU WANT

There is no way anyone can tell you what you want or what the best mix is. It is totally subjective. Even though you are going to be in a room full of mixers, editors, producers, your composer, and other collaborators (who of course will all be giving you advice), you are very much alone in this process and it is imperative that you maintain your individual focus. Once again, and for the very last time, you need to go back to your source — the script, the story. Focus on the story you want to tell. Focus on your vision, your overall objective. You're taking the audience on a journey. Keep the journey in mind.

As you listen to each reel:

> Step one: Listen to the whole reel, all the way through. Let the mixers do the best they can with what they have. You just listen and take notes. After the first ten minutes of your movie (and hopefully you are doing the mix in order), ask yourself where you want the audience to be at this point. What have you achieved so

293

far in your story and how can the mixing of the sound elements help you support that? What is the emotional journey that you want? Remember that effects and music are able to affect the audience on an emotional level more effectively than picture and dialogue. You are the emotional barometer. It is your reaction that is being used to make these final selections.

Step two: Talk to the mixers, talk to the whole room. There are many people working simultaneously (not just the mixers but everyone in the room) and they all need to be focused on a singular objective. Each is handling a different element and needs to know how you see (hear) that element contributing to the final mix, the final effect. You want to make sure that the mixers and editors are all working together in an ensemble effort. You are the conductor of this symphony.

Step three: Let them take another pass at the reel. You just watch and listen. Don't interrupt. Take notes. You may find that you are spending a long time on the first reel but that's okay because you are pulling together a team — the team that is going to finish your film. The time you spend now will pay off handsomely in the reels to come.

Work from the general to the specific. Talk about the whole movie and then talk about this specific reel. Then after a couple of passes work your way down to specific scenes and specific moments. Listen to your mixers, your editors, and to everyone in the room. Then make your decisions on your own.

As you finish two reels play them together. Make sure that you are building the momentum you desire. No one wants to go back and remix a reel that has been "locked," but if it's necessary, then it's necessary. Take your time. These are major decisions you are making and every decision will affect the eventual experience of your audience.

Once you have locked all the reels it's time for another screening. You may elect to have your trusted colleagues present (maybe some of those who were present at some of your previews), or you may wish to do this alone. That's up to you. Let the film wash over you and screen it more than once if you need to. Be aware of your reactions. Be honest with yourself. You may elect to have another preview at this point. Again, that is up to you (although producers or studios may insist). Take your time. Don't rush. This is where mistakes can be made because of exhaustion, impatience, and approaching release dates. You are as alone at this moment as you were when you began this project, when it was just you and the script. Now it is just you and the movie. When you say "it's not done yet" then it's not done yet. And when you say "that's it," then it's done.

LETTING GO

The hardest moment of making a movie is the moment you stop making the movie.

Even though your movie has a few more stages to go through before being released to the public (cutting negative, color timing, addition of titles), you are basically done and you are facing the moment of letting go. A tough moment, a very tough moment! You have been singularly focused on the telling of one story for months or maybe even years and suddenly it's over. The story is told. It is in its final form. All that is left now is the richest part of the experience — joining the audience as they listen to your story. Enjoy it. Relish it. You have certainly earned it.

And now some closing thoughts . . .

MARTHA GRAHAM TO AGNES DEMILLE

"There is a vitality, a life force, an energy, a quickening that is transcended through you into action , and because there is only one of you in all of time, this expression is unique. And if you block it, it will never exist through any other medium and be lost. The world will not have it. It is not your business to determine how good it is nor how valuable, nor how it compares with other expressions. It is your business to keep it yours clearly and directly, to keep the channel open. You have to keep open and aware directly to the urges that motivate you . . . no artist is pleased . . . there is only a queer divine dissatisfaction, a blessed unrest that keeps us marching and makes us more alive than others."

Martha Graham

NELSON MANDELA

"Our deepest fear is not that we are inadequate.
Our deepest fear is that we are powerful beyond measure.
It is our light, not our darkness, that most frightens us.
We ask ourselves, 'Who am I to be brilliant, gorgeous, talented and fabulous?'
Actually, who are you not to be?
You are a child of God. Your playing small doesn't serve the world.
There's nothing enlightened about shrinking so that other people won't feel insecure around you.
We were born to manifest the glory of God that is within us.
It's not just in some of us; it's in everyone.
And as we let our own light shine, we unconsciously give other people permission to do the same.
As we are liberated from our own fear, our presence automatically liberates others."

1994 Inaugural Speech
Nelson Mandela

AND FINALLY...REMEMBER THE BUMBLEBEE

In my office, in my home, and even in my car . . . there are bumblebees. Not living, flying, pollinating bumblebees, but stuffed, carved, painted, glass, plastic, wooden (and even a gorgeous kite) bumblebees. I collect bumblebees and of course many people ask "why the bumblebees?"

Here's why. According to the laws of aerodynamics the bumblebee can't fly. Its wings are too small and its body is too big. There is no way this little insect can fly, but (and this is the key) *the bumblebee doesn't know this*. All the bumblebee knows is that he has to fly, and so he does.

The next time you hear "it can't be done," "that's not the way it's done," "it has to be done this way," "that will never work," "we've always done it this way and that's how it works," or "you can't do that, it's impossible" — just remember the bumblebee. And if you feel you have to fly — then just fly.

See you at the movies.

CHAPTER 10

RECONSIDERATIONS AND RECAPITULATIONS

IT'S JUST STORYTELLING

We are storytellers first and foremost — filmmakers second. We have chosen to tell our stories through the medium of film. We have chosen to tell our stories in one of the most complicated, complex, confusing, expensive, and convoluted ways possible. This process of storytelling is so fraught with traps and black holes that master writer and director James L. Brooks was once quoted as saying, "My job as a film director is to make sure that a really bad movie isn't made." And this is from the man who brought us *Terms Of Endearment*, *Broadcast News*, and *As Good As It Gets*.

A majority of the films attempted are never finished. A majority of the films that are finished are not released. A majority of the films that are released go straight to video. A majority of the films that are released in theatres aren't worth watching. "Make sure a really bad movie isn't made." Not an inappropriate motto. And yet, we keep choosing to tell our stories in this form fraught with minefields while the vultures of bankruptcy hover overhead. We need to ask ourselves: Why? What is it about this form of expression that is so enticing, so seductive, that we keep plunging ourselves into the arms of this mother who could just as easily smother as soothe?

When I began teaching directing over fifteen years ago, I was arrogant enough to think that I could actually impart some useful knowledge to my students. And I was clever enough to convince heads of major schools that I was their man. It wasn't long before I realized that I was scrambling through each class, merely inches in front of the students' questions that were pursuing me like bloodhounds. I would struggle to concoct an answer that would seem reasonable and carry a certain amount of "authority" and "experience," while barely keeping my nose above the water line. After years of this dance (with bullets skimming past my ever-hopping feet), I started to understand that I was not the teacher. I was the student. I was the student looking for the answers in the best way I knew how. I like the high-wire act. I feel most alive when attempting to maintain balance when there's no net. After fifteen years of teaching I haven't found the answer to "Why film?" Fifteen years ago the question didn't even occur to me. And that was the problem. How can you answer some of the most essential questions regarding your chosen form of expression if you don't even know what the questions are?

All I know is that I believe that if I keep telling stories, whether it be through film, theatre, oral storytelling, short story, or novel, I might eventually begin to understand what it is that I am trying to say. And if I can have even that little moment of clarity before I say "The End," then I will have at least soothed myself.

DIRECTORS DON'T MAKE MOVIES

What a radical thought! As much as I take great pride in the films and the television shows that I have made, I have slowly come to one sobering realization. I don't make movies (or films, whichever you prefer)! I don't. Think of it this way. I read a script that I feel would make a great film and I convince myself that I am the director to bring this story to the screen. Then what do I do? First I form a personal relationship with the story and determine my vision. Then I work with the writer and pull together my creative team. Now I have a cinematographer, production designer, casting director, editor, composer, etc. I tell them my vision and they start their work. Then I get the actors, I inspire them (hopefully), and they create these remarkable characters. We go into production. The actors act. The cinematographer films them on the sets designed and built by the design team. The costumes are great, the lighting is great, the performances are great, and we finish shooting. Then in postproduction the editor and his team cut the film to fulfill my vision and the sound editors build the sound tracks, the composer writes and records the music, and then we're in the final mix. And soon it's all done. And when it's being projected up there on the screen I say, "I did that!" But, in reality, I did none of it. I didn't write it, design it, perform the roles, light the sets, build or design the sets, cut the film, write the music — none of it. Still, I get to say it's my film. And if I want, I can have the credit that says "A film by Mark Travis."

But what did I really do? I did one main thing: I became inspired by the story. And I was inspired enough to want to enter into this massive collaboration trusting that I could gather around me artists of sufficient talent to bring my vision to the screen. And I trusted. I trusted these other artists. I was willing to collaborate. I was willing to be challenged. I was willing to let them do the hard work. And, most importantly, I was willing to trust my own instincts and intuitions. But, did I make that film? No, not really. I inspired the film to be made. I think it was producer Lynda Obst (I may be wrong about this) who said, "Films are not made, they're forced into existence." I've always loved that quote. And it's true. Films are forced into existence. And the primary fuel that drives the process is the passion and the vision of the director. With our passion, films get made.

ONLY THE CHARACTERS CAN TELL THE STORY

Here's a simple concept that took me years to understand and appreciate. Little of the art or the artifice of narrative filmmaking can tell your story. You cannot tell the narrative story through cinematography. You cannot tell the story through production design, costume, make-up, or special effects. You cannot tell the story through editing, sound effects, or music. All of these elements are a part of the filmmaking system, but they are merely the support system. They are there to support, enhance, and clarify the telling of the story. But they would be useless without the primary element of narrative storytelling: the characters. It is through the characters that the viewing audience gets drawn into the story and is able to take the ride.

We are merely human beings trying to survive on this Earth, and storytelling is an essential tool that allows us to share the experiences of other human beings. It has been this way long before stories were written down, before there was writing, even before there was language. Our stories establish and maintain our connections with the rest of humanity. So when we go to a movie, we don't go to "see a movie." We go to immerse ourselves in the personal journeys of other individuals. We go to experience a movie.

Once you understand that it is through the characters and their behavior, choices, desires, dreams, successes, and failures that you connect with the audience, you are now on the path to the essence of storytelling. And once you see the rest of the filmmaking process as being a support and delivery system for your story, you might be able to avoid the traps and the pitfalls that consume so many directors. And once you realize that the most essential tool you must develop as a film director is the ability to work with script and actors, you are well on your way to becoming an effective storyteller.

But, unlike other forms of storytelling, filmmaking is uniquely complex and fraught with danger.

THE JIGSAW PUZZLE MODEL

Imagine this. I'm your good friend and I come to you one day with a great idea. I tell you, "I'm going to make a 40-piece jigsaw puzzle of a George Washington portrait and sell it." You probably react with something like, "Okay. Not a bad idea." But then I tell you how I am going to make this jigsaw puzzle.

First I show you a picture of George Washington. And I say, "This is what it's going to look like when I'm all done." You say, "Fine."

Then I tell you how I plan to make this jigsaw puzzle. I say, "First I'm going to cut out pieces of cardboard that will look like this, and then I'm going to

paint each one individually, one at a time. And then I'll cut out another piece and paint it, and then another and another and another until I have forty pieces. Now I have forty puzzle pieces and they've all been individually painted.

"Now I'm going to fit them all together and hope that they look like the George Washington portrait!" And at this point, you, as my good friend, would probably say, "Good luck!"

I'm still very proud of this idea because I believe that I have come up with a unique way to create a work of art. But now you tell me how truly insane I am and that this is the most ridiculous way to create anything. Then, of course, because you are still my good friend, you present me with a simpler and more realistic approach: "Why don't you just take the print of the painting, mount it on cardboard, and then cut it up into forty pieces? Then you'll have your jigsaw puzzle. All the pieces will fit together and you will be guaranteed that the final product, once assembled, will resemble the George Washington portrait." And, because I feel I am still your good friend, I am not offended by this idea but truly see the wisdom of it. "Great! What a great idea. I don't know why I didn't think of that earlier!"

Well, of course, that's the way jigsaw puzzles are made. It's obvious. But, the first approach I suggested, my "insane" approach as you called it — *that's the way films are made!*

That is the challenge. That is the reality.

Let's say we have a 120-page script (two hours) and we have a 40-day shooting schedule. This means that on the average we will be shooting about three pages a day. Let's also say that we are working a typical 12-hour day. And our typical 3-page scene will have standard cover-age, which may average twelve setups per scene. Now, this means in our 12-hour day we'll be spending less than an hour in each setup. So, at any particular time during our average production day, we will be concentrated on a single setup which is one of twelve setups, which will eventually be re-constructed to create this 3-minute scene, which will then eventually be joined by the other thirty-nine 3-minute pieces, which will then become our movie. What a ridiculous way to create anything! And it becomes even more ridiculous when you realize that the first time you will get to see all the work assembled into some kind of cohesive whole won't be until you are in postproduction. And, by that time, it's too late and too expensive to go back and re-shoot.

So, what do we do? We must have a plan. We must have an approach to this process that can insure, as best as possible, that once our jigsaw puzzle goes back together it will look like the picture we have in our imagination.

And this is where we come back to the Nine Basic Steps (see Chapter Seven) and realize how totally essential they are. We realize that the only way to insure that our puzzle will look like the picture in our head is to have a very clear vision of each individual piece and how it will fit into and support and enhance the rest of the picture. But now I want you to look at the Nine Steps in a whole new light. These

Nine Steps are slightly different than those in Chapter Seven. These steps have the same intention from a different perspective.

THE NINE STEPS REVISITED:

1. What is the story really about? What does it mean to me? What does the whole picture look like? What are its rhythms and its tones? What are its impact, intention, and purpose? What do you want it to say? What do you want it to imply, provoke, question, or stimulate?
2. Why do I want (need) to tell this story? What within you insists that you make the telling of this story a part of your life experience? What part of you is stimulated or provoked by the themes and the questions and the world of this story?
3. What is my (the storyteller's) journey through this scene, this story? Every time you read this story you are taken on an emotional journey. You need to look at this journey. You need to recognize it and accept it. You need to embrace it, as this is the first indication of the potential audience journey.
4. What do I want the audience's emotional journey to be as they experience this story? Now you must begin to imagine the audience's experience — not only for the entire story, but also for each scene (scene by scene) and for each moment (moment by moment). And here's a tougher question: What do you want your audience thinking about, talking about, and feeling as they leave the theatre?
5. What is this scene (piece of the puzzle) really about, for me? Each scene is a story in itself and a part of a larger story. What is really happening in each scene (beneath the content, the lines) for you? What issues, questions, concerns, or aspects of the human condition are addressed in each scene?

6. What is my emotional journey through this scene?

> The answer to this question is your guide to insuring that the pieces of the puzzle fit together. Experiencing a story is an emotional journey. Each scene is part of that journey. How does each scene contribute to your emotional journey of the story?

7. How can I structure this scene (event) so that it generates the effect that I desire?

> Now we're into the mechanics of directing. How can you direct the actors (see Chapter Seven) in such a way as to stimulate the characters to engage in the events of the scene in such a way as to trigger the emotional response in the audience that you require? Now you are at the core of directing. It is these colors and this shape that will ensure that this piece of the puzzle fits and enhances.

8. How can I structure and deliver the entire story so that it generates the effect that I desire?

> Now we're putting the puzzle back together and, unlike the picture puzzle, the story will be delivered one piece at a time. And the choices of sequence and structure will affect the audience experience.

9. Through which medium do I wish to tell this story? (Film, theatre, oral, etc.)

> The puzzle is put together. The story is complete. Now you have the choice of delivery systems. Where do you want to hang this picture? Through which medium do you think the story will be best received?

Clarity of vision. Clarity of intention. Clarity of story. Clarity of purpose. Once you are clear on the story you want to tell, the reason you want to tell it, how you want to tell it, and how each element completes the puzzle... then it will all fit together beautifully.

Now all you have to do is be willing to take charge, take control, and lead.

THE ALPHA HORSE

There is an extraordinary dynamic that occurs in the filmmaking process. It occurs mostly in production (at least that's where it can be felt the most) but it is also operative in preparation, preproduction, and postproduction. It's what I call the "Alpha Horse Syndrome." You have to think of the collection of artists and technicians working on the film like a herd of horses.

First, a few simple facts about horses: The horse is an animal of prey. It is not a predator. Horses spend most of their time concerned about whether or not another animal is going to come up behind them and eat them. They are always on guard. Also, horses, by nature, are herding animals. They stay in herds for protection. And they have a system. They select one horse to be their leader. They have a very complex communications system (which we do not need to go into here) by which they actually say, "Are you going to be the leader?" And one horse says, "Yes, I'm the leader," then the other horses respond, "Good, then we'll follow you." And follow they do. Within a short period of time a herd of horses will have found its leader and they will begin moving as a unit. The lead horse is called the Alpha Horse.

The director of a film *must* be the Alpha Horse. He (or she) must be willing and able to lead. The director must be willing to lead even if he doesn't know exactly where he is going. The director must always assure the rest of the cast and the crew (the rest of the herd) that he has everything under control and that they will indeed arrive at their destination safely and intact.

Horses know of the necessity of having an Alpha Horse. And if the selected Alpha Horse fails or falters or is injured, another horse will become the Alpha Horse within moments.

If the director of a film fails or falters or is indecisive, another member of the crew (or cast) will by instinct assume the role of Alpha. If you are directing a film and one of your actors seems to be taking over the reins and undermining your efforts, don't blame the actor. That actor is only responding, by instinct, to her need to have a strong leader. Blame yourself. If you show the confidence, vision, and clear determination to bring this film to completion, that actor will remain a loyal follower. But if you show that you are uncertain, unwilling to take control, unwilling to protect your vision, or unable to create a safe environment for your actors, you have demonstrated that you are not capable of being the Alpha.

I was consulting on an independent film last year. When I arrived on the set one day and asked the director how it was going, she said, "My cinematographer is taking over." When I asked her why, she said: "He thinks he knows how to make this film better than I do." I told her she was wrong. I told her that most likely her DP had lost confidence in her and that he felt that the whole system was in danger of falling apart.

A few moments later I was talking with the cinematographer. When I asked him how it was going he said, "I think it'll be okay. (The director) just needs time to clarify her thoughts. She's struggling right now. She needs more time to prepare, so meanwhile I'm just keeping everything moving." This was a first-time director and a veteran cinematographer. He knew exactly what he was doing and he knew exactly what she needed. She just needed someone else to be the Alpha for a while until she was ready to resume the role. After about a two-minute conversation between the three of us, everything was smoothed out and the production continued without a hitch, the director firmly in the role of the Alpha. It's interesting that no one else on the crew knew what was happening. There was never a lack of an Alpha and the herd kept moving in the intended direction.

My friend, Mark Rydell, has a great story about the first day of production for *On Golden Pond*. It's important to know that the cast of
Jane Fonda (who purchased the property for her father), Henry
Fonda, and Katherine Hepburn had been set before a director was
attached. Many directors were considered but Jane Fonda was
recommending Mark. Katherine Hepburn certainly knew of Mark
but had never worked with him. So she arranged screenings of all of
his films, which she watched. And then she met with him. And after
a long discussion about the film and her role, she gave her approval.
Now, you have to ask yourself, "Who, at this moment, is the Alpha?"

Come the first day of production. The first scene they are going to
shoot is the first scene in the movie, Hepburn and Fonda's arrival at
the cottage. It's a simple moment, Katherine Hepburn and Henry
Fonda driving up the road. The camera crew is ready. The car is
ready. Henry Fonda is ready. Katherine Hepburn is still in her trailer.
The word comes to Mark through the First AD, "Miss Hepburn
doesn't want to wear her wardrobe." Mark Rydell, being the meticulous
director that he is, had spent weeks with the costume designer selecting
just the perfect wardrobe for Miss Hepburn and Mr. Fonda, as well as
for the rest of the cast. Henry Fonda and Katherine Hepburn play
two New Englanders who feel most comfortable in practical clothing.
Think L.L. Bean. Accordingly, Mark had not only been very specific
about each item of wardrobe, he also had Miss Hepburn and Mr.
Fonda (as well as the rest of the cast) approve all of his selections. And
now, at the commencement of principal photography, Katherine
Hepburn had suddenly changed her mind.

Mark marched directly to her trailer. And there she was, dressed as
only Katherine Hepburn could dress — in a fashionable outfit with
scarves, a high collar that was her trademark, elegant boots, and
matching jewelry. "I think this is what I should wear in the opening
scene," she announced to Mark. Now there was no question that what
she was wearing was totally wrong for the character and totally wrong
for the film. But, to Mark, it was also very clear that this was a test.

He looked her directly in the eye and said, "Do you know why I love directing so much?" "No," she said, "I don't." "I love directing because I get to make all the final decisions. When you're in the outfit we agreed upon for this scene I'll meet you on the set." And with that he turned and left the trailer. Mark told me that as he walked back to the set he was thinking that one of two things was going to happen. He would get a phone call from the studio telling him that he had been fired. Or she would show up in the appropriate outfit. Minutes went by like hours as he, and the rest of the crew, waited. Finally, Miss Hepburn came around the corner, dressed in the appropriate outfit. Mark said nothing. Then Katherine Hepburn walked up to Henry Fonda and handed him a rumpled old hat. "This was Spencer's hat," she said. "He would have wanted you to wear it." Henry put the hat on. Katherine turned to Mark Rydell and said, "Mr. Director, what do you think? Does this meet with your approval." "Absolutely." "Fine, I'm ready whenever you are." And from that moment on, there was never a problem. There was never a question as to who was the Alpha.

This was a test. The real question Katherine Hepburn was asking Mark Rydell was, "Are you going to be strong enough to lead all of us through this production? Are you going to be the Alpha Horse?" If Mark Rydell had acquiesced to Katherine Hepburn concerning the wardrobe, he would have lost. She didn't want a director who would buckle. She wanted a director who was confident enough and strong enough to lead. And that's what she got.

THE 90% RULE

As I teach or consult with other film directors around the world there are certain questions that continually pop up and reveal what little practical information is available concerning the economics and practicalities of filmmaking. Here are some of these revealing questions:

1. What's a setup? (This question tells me we're in for a very long consultation. See Chapter Eight.)
2. If I only need a few lines in this setup, why would I shoot the whole scene from this angle? (This time, a shorter consultation.)
3. What is a shooting ratio? (Now we're into math, ratios, and equations.)
4. I'm going to be okay with a shooting ratio of 10:1, aren't I? That means I'm going to be shooting ten times more film than I need. That's a lot! (And now we start entering the 90% Rule.)
5. Why do major filmmakers only shoot 3-4 minutes of their story in a day? Why does it take so long?
6. Why can't I shoot 10–20 minutes of my film in a day? I'm shooting all day and it's only 10–20 minutes.

You get the idea. We are now in the area of logistics, economics, scheduling, and division of time and labor. It's not a terribly creative area. If anything, to many artists, it is a frustrating and annoying area. But it is necessary to understand the basic concepts so that you don't get caught in assumptions.

We'll look at a film model.

The Premise:
- We are shooting a 100-page script. A 100-minute film.
- We plan a 20-day shooting schedule.
- We will average five pages per day.
- We plan to shot 35mm film at a 12:1 ratio.

Note: A 20-day shooting schedule means this is a relatively low-budget film on a tight schedule. There is going to be very little room for error, experimentation, or exploration. And a 12:1 ratio is very tight, as you will see.

311

The Footage:
- It takes 900 feet of 35mm film for every ten minutes of running time.
- The final product (100 minutes) will be 9,000 feet of film.
- We want to shoot at a 12:1 ratio.
- Therefore we will expose 108,000 feet of film.
- On an average we will expose 5,400 feet of film per day.

Note: Exposing 108,000 feet of film for a final product of 9,000 feet means that 99,000 feet of exposed film will be thrown away. *92%* of the film you exposed will be discarded. And this is not taking into account pre-runs (before the slate), over runs (after the scene is over before the director calls 'cut'), and short ends (when there is too little film left in the camera for the next take and you load a fresh roll).

The Shooting Schedule:
- We will average five pages per day. (five minutes of material)
- We will average four setups per scene. (a very low coverage rate)
- We will average three takes per setup. (each take running the length of the scene).
- 5 minutes X 4 setups = 20 minutes of film.
- 20 minutes X 3 takes = 60 minutes of film. A 12:1 ratio.
- 60 minutes of film = 5,400 feet.

Note: If you are allowed (on an average) only four setups per scene and only three takes per setup, this means that your visual palette is very limited and that with only a 3-take allotment there is little room for error or experimentation. There is definitely not enough room for extensive bracketing.

In the average day of shooting 5-minutes worth of material, we will expose 5,400 feet of film for a final product that will use only 450 feet of film. (*92%* of the footage will be discarded.)

The Daily Schedule:

- The average shooting day is twelve hours. Subtract one hour for lunch and that leaves us with eleven hours of actual production time.
- In the average 11-hour shooting day we will shoot 5-minutes worth of material.
- We will average four setups per scene and three takes per scene.
- As stated above, we will end up with sixty minutes of exposed film by the end of the day.
- We exposed sixty minutes of film in an 11-hour day. That means that ten hours of that day were spent not filming, but actually in preparation for filming (lighting, rehearsing, prepping, etc.)
- Only sixty minutes of the 12-hour day were actually spent filming.

Note: There are ten hours of preparation time in a 12-hour day to produce one hour of material for a 5-minute scene. (*91%* of the production day was spent in the preparation for filming.)

So, now you can see it: **The 90% Rule**. 91% of the average day is spent **not** filming. 92% of the day's film that is shot (during that one filming hour) will be discarded. 92% of the total footage that will be exposed for the entire film will be discarded. (And if you want to get into how much of your budget is spent on items that have absolutely nothing to do with your film or getting your film made — have a good time. Personally, I don't want to go there right now. It's much too depressing.)

What's a comfortable shooting ratio? I like a minimum of 20:1. My last film, a half-hour short called *The Baritones*, came in at a 22:1 ratio. This means I shot eleven hours of film.

There is one scene in *The Baritones* where I wanted to have the actor improvise. It is a moment when the lead character is driving alone, talking to himself. I knew it would be only about forty seconds on the screen. I had five different setups (the editorial plan was for jump cutting) and shot nearly a half-hour of material for those forty seconds. The ratio: 45:1. It is one of the best scenes in the film thanks to Gene Butler's performance and the brilliant editing skills of Suzanne Spangler. There are other scenes in the same film that were shot in one setup and in only two or three takes.

I prefer to shoot on digital tape. It seems that we are always working on very tight budgets and time schedules. It's hard enough to have "too little money" and "too little time" to shoot your film. But when you add "too little film" to the mix, it becomes unbearable. Fight against the 90% Rule. Work with your cinematographer to shorten the lighting and the prep time on the set. Give yourself more time for shooting. Increase your coverage (within reason) and allow yourself multiple takes so that you have sufficient material from which to choose in postproduction.

The more you are aware of the realities and the practicalities that limit or confine the filmmaking process, the more you will be able to work reasonably within them.

CHAPTER 11

NO MORE ACTING, NO MORE DIRECTING

RESULT DIRECTING

This is probably one of the most discussed and least understood aspects of directing. Just say "result directing" to an actor and you can feel the hair rising on the back of her neck. Mention it to many acting teachers and you'll hear the snort of disdain. But mention it to most directors (and I mean "most") and they won't really know what you're talking about. They'll have heard about it, but can't imagine what the problem is. It seems simple to them. "Results? That's what my job is, getting results. What's the problem?" And they are right. Their job is getting results.

First, a brief definition of result directing: The director knows precisely the emotion, the attitude, and the behavior that the character should express during a scene, and his method of directing is to simply tell the actor what he wants and then expect the actor to deliver the requested results. That's result directing — going for the result.

Here's the problem: Result directing works perfectly when you are collaborating with any member of your creative team *except the actors*. You can tell designers, cinematographers, editors, and composers what you want and they can give it to you. This is a major part of the directorial process as we have discussed earlier. But, when you tell an actor the result you want (i.e., the specific performance or emotion or behavior) then there is a problem. Entire books have been written on this subject. So I've decided to join the fray and add my own perspective to the discussion: *Result Directing — Good or Bad?*

You're in rehearsal. You're about to talk with the actor and again you have a very clear idea of what you want. You see it as no different than talking with the designer, cinematographer, editor, or any other member of your creative team. You tell the actor exactly what you see his character going through — physically, emotionally, and spiritually. You tell him when the character is feeling good, when he is feeling bad, when his confidence is high and when it is low. You tell him where you see the character moving, standing, sitting, walking, and turning. You give him such a graphic depiction of the whole scene that anyone can see it. It's clear. It's precise. It's moving. It's electric. But inside the actor is a voice that says, "I can't do that." And you ask yourself, "What's the problem? I was clear, precise. He agreed it sounded great. Why won't he do it?"

Here's the answer. He's a talented actor and of course he can do it. He can do it precisely the way you designed it. He can do it better than you could ever imagine. But he won't. He won't because delivering the result is antithetical to his process. His process, quite simply, is to create a character that is a living, breathing, feeling human being. Part of the actor's job is to allow the actor to disappear into the character. And once he has disappeared into the character he will allow the character to function *as the character*. The character doesn't want to be told where to move, sit, and stand. The character doesn't want to be told how he is feeling and what he is thinking — no more than you do. As a matter of fact, the character doesn't know that he's in a film. He has no awareness that his life is being recorded. The character's focus is totally different than the actor's. For the actor to try to force the character to act and behave in a pre-described fashion will actually cause resistance within the character. And the actor knows that, he can feel it. The actor knows that if he goes into the scene with "results" in his head, he will not be able to disappear into the character. It will become an actor-driven scene rather than a character-driven scene. And I can tell you right now you don't want that.

So what do you tell the actor? How do you talk to the actor if you can't talk in results? It's very simple, really.

First, talk to the actor *about* the character. The character is created in the collaboration between the script, you, and the actor. When you are designing and discovering the character — you are talking to the actor. When you are discussing the scene, its function in the story and how you imagine it working — you are talking to the actor.

Then, when you start directing the scene, you must stop talking to the actor and start talking to the character. That's right. Talk to the character. Talk to the person who has no idea that he's in a movie. Talk to the person who is actually in the scene, not the person who has lost himself into the character. You don't want to see the actor in the scene. You don't want to see him, hear him, or feel him. You want to lose all awareness of him. You want to see the character. If you direct the actor, that's who you'll get — the actor, acting. If you direct the character, then it is the character that will be there. It will be the character, not acting but simply behaving. Guaranteed.

As we discussed in The Rehearsal Process, emotions arise out of circumstance. Emotions are generated within a character due to her history, her objective, her obstacles, and her expectations. We don't ever create emotions. We try to create circumstances wherein we may experience a desired emotion, but we do not, and cannot, create emotions. So asking an actor to create an emotion is asking him to do something that is not only unfamiliar, but also impossible. Talk to the character about how he might achieve his objective, thereby creating a situation that may elicit the emotional response you want.

The key is: How do you talk to the character? You know you can't talk to the character in acting-result terms because the character is not thinking about acting or performance. The character is only thinking about the needs, desires, fears, and concerns of the character. He is not thinking about staging, lighting, moves, emotions, lines, cues, or any of the actor's considerations. He is only thinking about what he hopes to achieve in the next moment of his life (the upcoming scene). Basically, you need to abandon "directing" in its most dogmatic form. You need to stop directing and start coaching.

Coaching is talking to the character about his objectives, expectations, needs, and desires — about his fears and concerns. Coaching is modifying the behavior of the character just as you would with a child. Coaching is urging the character to seek a different result. "You can do better than that. You know you want to convince him to hire you. But he's winning. He's a bigger obstacle than you thought. What are you going to do? I'll give you another chance. Don't disappoint me." That's coaching. There is no discussion of the results of the behavior. There can't be. The character has no control over the results. There is only the encouragement and the permission to try again. There is the encouragement to seek a better result, not a specific result. Every character wants to fulfill his objective. Every character in every scene will come up short (see Mind the Gap) or overshoot the objective. Or the character may arrive at the objective only to find that is it not what he expected. Either way, there is disappointment or surprise or confusion.

In life we rarely get a second chance. In the world of acting there are many second chances. The question is not "How am I going to play it this time?" The appropriate question is "What can I do differently this time in order to come closer to my objective?" The first question is the actor speaking. The second question is the character speaking. The character, seeking a different result, will have to modify his behavior. This modification is encouraged and coached by the director. And here's the downside with this style of directing: You never know what the character is going to do, partially because the character doesn't know either. And the upside: Whatever the character does will be genuine, it will be real, and it won't be acting.

Result Directing In The Casting Process

As we discussed in Chapter Six, the casting process is significantly different from the rehearsal or the performance process. In the casting process, result directing is not only permitted, but welcomed and advisable. The casting process is a test, an audition, a job interview. The prospective employee (actor) just wants to know what you want. And you, the potential employer, just want to know if the actor can deliver the goods. Because result directing is acceptable in the casting process, many directors feel that they can continue that approach into rehearsals and performance. And then they wonder why the best performance they got was in the audition! Well, that great performance that they got in the audition was under the stress of the test. The pressures were enormous: too little preparation, too little time, not sure exactly what the director is looking for, not sure I can deliver this character, maybe even not sure I want to do this character. Then there are other pressures that the actor can be dealing with that are more personal: family, finance, scheduling, health, etc. We never know all that is going on at the time, but whatever is going on is affecting the audition.

Now the actor has been cast. The pressures are still there but most likely they have changed in complexion and definition. The major change is two-fold: The actor has the part (the test is over) and his focus now is on creating the truth of the character (a new pressure), which means that much of the actor's personal pressures may not apply anymore. It's a decidedly different process. The actor has discarded the performance that he did in the audition because it is no longer applicable. It was false. It was created out of instinct, intuition, imagination, and drawing on the reality of the actor in the moment. It was a sketch. It was simply a brush stroke implying what the fully rendered painting might look like. It was not a performance. It was a result.

WHEN RESULT DIRECTING DOES WORK IN PRODUCTION

Okay, I'll admit it: There are times when we need to use result directing in production. It's usually when we are under pressure that we must resort to the "by any means necessary" approach. You're in rehearsal. You've spent hours exploring all the nuances and the various approaches to the scene and the characters and the relationships. But there is still this version of the scene that is just floating in your head. It seems perfect, or at least acceptable. But the actors aren't getting there and for some reason you don't seem to be able to communicate it to them. You're frustrated. They're frustrated. You're considering a career change and very likely the actors would encourage you to do just that. It's time for result directing. It's time to bring out the big guns. But the problem with big guns is that they can often blow a hole right through the middle of that thing called "truth." You know it. You can feel it. Here's how it can work, without damage.

Let's imagine that you have a scene between a brother and a sister. It's the brother's performance that feels inadequate. Simply approach the actor playing the brother and say, "I hear the scene in my head. I want to let you hear what I hear and then I want us to figure out how we might get there." Then give him the result. Give him a line reading if necessary. Let him listen to you. Let him observe and absorb the performance that you imagine. Then the next question is, "How can we get there?" Two things are important about this question. First, the question puts you back into the realm of the character. Result directing is talking directly to the actor ("Do this!"), process directing is talking directly to the character ("How do we get there?"). Second, the question is, "How do we get there?" It's collaboration. You're suggesting that the two of you work it out and find the means for the character to get there. You both have the goal (result) in your heads and the only question is justifying such behavior or attitude for the character. Under what circumstances would this character behave that way? Can we create those circumstances and is it reasonable for the story we are trying to tell?

Yes, there are a lot of questions. But that's the process of rehearsal: questions, exploration, and discovery. Rehearsal is not "just do it this way." Naturally, there are a lot of questions. But these questions will eventually lead to behavioral solutions that will become the result you so desire.

Remember, results are just that — results. They are the end product of the blend of objectives, intentions, obstacles, adjustments, and expectations, just like the chemical reaction that is the result of the mixture of certain chemicals under certain conditions. When we're dealing with human behavior we have to remember that the result we so desire or imagine can only be obtained honestly when the chemical mixture of objective, intentions, obstacles, and attitude is specifically appropriate to create that result. We cannot *create* results (that's called "acting"). We cannot *create* emotions (that's called "indicating"). We can create desire, need, objectives, and even obstacles, which will stimulate certain emotions, which cause certain attitude and behavior (i.e., results). It is crucial that you understand and honor this sequence.

Imagine that you are in the middle of production. The cameras are ready to roll but the actor isn't going anywhere. His performance is as flat as a page from your script. The clock is ticking. The producer is pacing and the sun is setting. What do you do? It's result-directing time! This is one of those moments when you simply walk up to the actor and say, "Here's what I need. We only have a few minutes to get it and I need it. Sadly we don't have the time for rehearsal or exploration and barely enough time for justification. So, we're going straight for the result … and here it is." And this is where you tell the actor exactly what his character's objective is, what he wants, what he fears, what the stakes are, how high the risk is, what the obstacles are, how formidable they are, and why all of this creates the exact result that you want. Any actor who is worth anything will listen to that and say, "I've got it. Let's do it." But you can see in this example that we have taken the time to justify the behavior. We never stop with the result itself — because then the performance will be behavior on command.

And you've seen this kind of acting. You've seen if from some of the most talented actors and directors we have. No artist intentionally gives a mediocre performance, so the only rational reason for a less than stellar performance is a weak script coupled with unclear, inorganic direction that finally leads to the condition of "I'll just do the best I can."

In conclusion, "results" simply means that you know what you want. You have an idea of how the performance can manifest itself. But what you need to know beyond that (or need to discover during the rehearsal process) is what attitude, behavior, situation, obstacles, or means will get the character there. You need to create a situation within which the "results" you imagine are genuine emotional responses to real conditions. In other words, you want your "results" to actually *be* results — the resulting actions, attitudes, behaviors, and emotions that are stimulated by characters in relationships.

DIRECTING THROUGH QUESTIONS RATHER THAN STATEMENTS

Here's another way of approaching the same issue. The question is: "How do I stimulate or inspire the actors to do what I have in my mind?" Or, "How can I get the actors to discover within themselves those emotional truths that are applicable to this character in this situation, and then bring those truths to the surface and eventually (hopefully) deliver the performance that I have in my head?" One very powerful approach is to not only stop telling actors what you want, but to also stop telling them anything. When the blind seem to be leading the blind, eventually someone has to acquire vision.

I have mentioned many times over the past ten years of teaching that my goal is to bring the actors to a point where they will no longer be acting — where they no longer will be expected to act or need to act. I want to eliminate acting. Acting, by definition, is pretending. It's make-believe. I have no interest in watching people pretend. I have no interest in observing the extraordinary talents of an actor as she creates a dazzling display of physical and emotional tics. This holds little interest for me. It's just technique. It is a calculated and studied process that will deliver specific results. It is so far removed from genuine human behavior and emotional truth that we have to call it "acting." In my films I want no more acting. And the way I am going to be able to achieve this is two-fold: I will no longer ask the actors to act, and, within the best of my abilities, I will stop directing. If I'm not directing and the actors are not acting, there is room for only one thing to happen: genuine human behavior. And that's what I want to capture on film. My goal as a filmmaker is very simple: When the camera is rolling I want to capture magic. And the magic I want to capture is genuine human behavior. When the camera is rolling I want to be in a position where I am not totally sure what is going to happen and neither are the actors. All we know is that something genuine is going to emerge in front of the cameras and I will have it on film. Now I understand that this is very risky. And I understand that for many directors this is frightening because it means a loss of total control. For those directors who insist on total control, don't try this. You won't like it. For those who are willing to take the risk that you might not get what you imagine and very possibly you will get something radically different — and quite possibly stimulating and intriguing — then keep reading.

Stop directing. Stop telling the actors what you want or even what you envision. Start asking questions. Be naïve. Be innocent. Be willing to be surprised and challenged. Be open to the human experience. Ask questions to which you do not have the answers. Let the answers guide you. Let the truth of the actor guide you. Be willing to let yourself be led down a path where neither you nor the actors have any idea of the final destination.

Here's an example of how this can happen. Let's take a scene from *American Beauty* by Alan Ball. It's the final scene in the garage where the Colonel comes to confront Lester. Here's the scene in its entirety from the shooting script:

EXT. BURNHAM HOUSE - GARAGE - CONTINUOUS

We're MOVING SLOWLY toward the Burnham's GARAGE DOOR WINDOW through the RAIN. Through the window, we see Lester, wearing only his sweatpants, per- forming bench presses.

INT. BURNHAM HOUSE - GARAGE - CONTINUOUS

Through the window, we see the COLONEL, standing outside IN the pouring rain, watching. We ZOOM slowly in on him as he watches, transfixed.

EXT. BURNHAM HOUSE - GARAGE - CONTINUOUS

His POV: LESTER finishes his last rep, straining, then racks the weights and sits up, sweaty and out of breath. He lights a half finished JOINT and inhales deeply, running his free hand over his chest... and then he glances at us, suddenly aware he's being watched.

INT. BURNHAM HOUSE - GARAGE - CONTINUOUS

LESTER and the COLONEL stare at each other through the window.

INT. BURNHAM HOUSE - GARAGE - MOMENTS LATER

The rain is coming down IN sheets now, and there is a sharp CLAP of THUNDER. We're directly out- side the GARAGE DOOR as it slowly lifts to reveal Lester smiling at us.

                    LESTER
        Jesus, man. You're soaked.

INT. BURNHAM HOUSE - GARAGE - CONTINUOUS

LESTER pulls the COLONEL inside. The COLONEL
moves stiffly and seems preoccupied, slightly
disoriented.

                    LESTER
        You want me to get Ricky? He's up
        in Jane's room.

The COLONEL just stands there, looking at Lester.

                    LESTER (cont'd)
        You okay?

                    COLONEL
            (his voice thick)
        Where's your wife?

                    LESTER
        Uh... Probably off fucking that
        dorky prince of real estate
        asshole. And you know what?
            (laughs)
        I don't care.

                    COLONEL
        Your wife is with another man and
        you don't care.

                    LESTER
        Nope. Our marriage is just for
        show. It's a commercial, proving

                    325

how normal we are, when we are
anything but.

He grins... and so does the Colonel. LESTER
realizes the Colonel is shivering.

> LESTER (cont'd)
> Dude. You're shaking.

He places his hand on the Colonel's shoulder. The
Colonel closes his eyes.

> LESTER (cont'd)
We really should get you out of these clothes.

> COLONEL
> (a whisper)
> Yes...

He opens his eyes and looks at LESTER, his face
suddenly filled with an anguished vulnerability
we wouldn't have thought possible from him. His
eyes are brimming with tears. Lester leans in,
concerned.

> LESTER
> It's okay.

> COLONEL
> (hoarse)
> I...

> LESTER
> (softly)
> Just tell me what you need.

```
The Colonel reaches up and places his hand on
Lester's cheek... and then kisses him. Lester is
momentarily stunned, and then he pushes the
Colonel away. The Colonel's face crumples in
shame.

                    LESTER (cont'd)
          Whoa.  You got the wrong idea,
          pal.  I do not go there.

The COLONEL stares at the floor, blinking, and
then he turns and runs out the open garage door
into the rainy night.
```

I'm sure all you very talented directors out there have already conceived of how you would like the scene played. And, unfortunately, there are many of you who can't get the scene in the film out of your head and see beyond those two fine performances. (In this scene, Chris Cooper gives one of the most startling performances that you will ever see.) But the question is, how did the director, Sam Mendes, get this performance? I don't know. I wasn't there. But since Mendes comes from the theatre, I am going to assume that the process — simple to conceive but difficult to achieve — might have been something like what follows.

You lead the actor to discovery through questions, not statements. You don't try to control the scene; you let the characters take control. Let's say you're talking to the two actors playing these parts. The question and answer process might go something like this:

You: Lester, what's going on in this scene?

Lester: Let's see. I'm working out, feeling good. I see the Colonel outside in the rain. I know something's going on, but

327

I don't know what. I open the door for him. He comes out of the rain. I can see that something is wrong and I think it's the rain and the cold. I want to help him. I do help him. He's shaking and I think it's from the rain. And then, before I know it, I'm holding him and suddenly he kisses me. I'm shocked. I'm upset. (pause) I don't know. I thought I knew but I don't know what's going on in this scene.

You: Colonel, what do you think is going on in this scene?

Colonel: I have no idea. I have no idea because I'm not sure what I'm doing. Not as me the actor but as me the character. I have no idea why I'm here or what I want. I just know that I need to be here and I need to talk to him.

You: There's no plan?

Colonel: No. No plan. I know I'm in trouble. I know I can't stop myself. I just know I need to be here with him, close to him. I know somehow he has the answers.

You: The answers to what?

Colonel: The questions.

(silence)

You: What are the questions?

Colonel: (pause) I don't know. I mean I do know (as the actor) but I don't know (as the character). I just know that there are a lot of questions. Old questions. Heavy questions. And I think he has the answers.

You: Lester, do you have the answers?

Lester: I don't even know what the questions are.

You: Neither do I.

(silence)

You: Lester, do you know what he wants to ask you when he's standing there in front of you?

Lester: I think I do, for a moment. I feel a cry for help, I think... a reaching out. I think I can answer that. But I really don't know what he wants.

You: So, what are you going to do?

Lester: I don't know. At first it seems simple. Reach out. Be there for him. First thing I say is "Do you want Ricky? He's in Jane's room." That seems simple and direct and clear. But after that it all starts to slip away.

You: What starts to slip away?

Lester: My sense of knowing... my sense of knowing what's going on. It feels like I get further and further away from it as the scene goes on.

You: And how does that feel?

Lester: Like shit.

You: Colonel, how do you feel at the opening of the scene, before he opens the door for you?

Colonel: Not good. Lost. Not good.

You: And how do you feel at the end of the scene as you are leaving?

Colonel: Like shit. I feel awful.

You: Worse than the opening?

Colonel: Yeah. Much worse.

Be aware of what has happened in this conversation. You have asked a lot of questions. You have supplied no answers at all. All the answers have come from the characters (actors). You are simply asking them to look deeper into their understanding and their experience of the scene. You are forcing them to discover the truth of the scene, not create a truth. A question at this time might be "What if what they discover is not what I want in the scene?" This is a good question and a legitimate fear. There are two aspects of this process that you must understand. Number one: Whatever the actors/characters discover during this question and answer period will be the truth; it will be honest. Number two: Any actor, at any time, is always doing the best he/she can *with the information they have*. So if you are not satisfied or pleased with what has been discovered, change the information, alter the circumstances, alter the input, change the questions. Here's an example.

Let's assume that you don't like the response that the Colonel gave:

You: There's no plan?

Colonel: No. No plan.

Let's assume you believe the scene would work better if the Colonel did have a plan, if he did have an idea of what he wanted. Of course you could just tell the actor to make the change. But this won't be as effective as leading the actor/character to the discovery of what you want.

You: There's no plan?

Colonel: No. No plan. I know I'm in trouble. I know I can't stop myself. I just know I need to be here with him, close to him. I know somehow he has the answers.

You: You need to be here with him?

Colonel: Yeah.

You: Close to him?

Colonel: Yeah.

You: And how do you imagine that will feel?

Colonel: Better.

You: Safer?

Colonel: Yeah, much safer.

You: So, if that feels safer, then what feels dangerous now?

Colonel: Dangerous?

You: Yeah. Dangerous. Unsafe. What feels unsafe?

Colonel: Everything!

You: Everything feels unsafe? But to be close to Lester would feel safer? More secure.

Colonel: Right.

You: Like in Viet Nam. You feel safer in a fox hole than you do out in the open.

Colonel: Yeah. Right.

You: So, that's the plan?

Colonel: Ahh. Yeah. Safety. Find safety. Get out of the dangerous area. Something like that.

You: Sounds like a plan.

Again, mostly questions. Leading questions to be sure. And there are some statements that help solidify a discovery or an idea. But for the most part it was just questions. You were successful in shifting the development of the character in terms of this specific moment and doing it in such a way that the discovery came totally from within the character. What's interesting about this process is that the actors know exactly what you're doing. They know that you are leading them to the discoveries that you want them to make. And they are all right with that. And, most importantly, they know that you are willing to allow them to make the discoveries on their own. And that builds confidence and trust.

This is a process that is difficult to develop. It has taken me many years of directing, studying, therapy, and trial and error to be able to build the confidence that I now have. It won't take you nearly so long if you are simply willing to take the plunge and try it. Be smart; try it outside the risk zone. Don't try it for the first time on your next production. Try it now. Invite some actor friends for a rehearsal. Tell them that you want to experiment with some different rehearsal techniques. I can guarantee you: Any actor worth anything will jump at the chance to explore new ways of rehearsing. We are all so keenly aware that it is in the rehearsal process (second only to the casting process) where the project either comes together or falls apart. We've all had too many of the latter experiences and too few of the former. To discover new and better ways to rehearse is an actor's (and a director's) dream.

THE LINK BETWEEN OBSTACLES AND STAGING

One of the greatest joys in teaching, consulting, and lecturing is those magical moments of discovery. You know me — I love the high-wire act. I love launching myself into a relationship (either as director, consultant, or teacher) not knowing exactly what is going to happen or if I am going to be able to handle all the challenges, questions, and problems that may arise. I do have the confidence, though, that whatever happens I will be able to survive. I may fall off the wire but the sudden contact with the hard ground won't kill me, it won't even injure me. In fact, it will make me more knowledgeable or more aware. Ironically, it won't make me more cautious.

Years ago when I first began lecturing about the phenomenon of Obstacles, I felt I knew what I was talking about (see Chapters Two and Four). And in each subsequent lecture it all became a little clearer to me. First of all, there are always Obstacles. Secondly, there are three categories: Other Characters, the Environment, and the Self. Then, it became clear that the Environmental Obstacles had two categories: the Physical Environment and the Social Environment. Later, just as I was suggesting that most characters did have Internal Obstacles (within the Self), I realized that they *all* had Internal Obstacles. Finally I audaciously stated to a very large class in Munich, "Every single person in this room struggles with Internal Obstacles every moment in his/her life. Even at this very moment." And as I made this statement (a totally new one for me), I realized that I was absolutely right. And the more I could see the profound parallels between what I understood about dramatic material and what I saw and felt in my daily life, the more I realized that I was just viewing the tip of an extraordinary iceberg.

And then I was talking about Staging (see Chapters Seven and Eight) and I was mentioning the three relationships in staging: Staging in terms of other Characters, Staging in relationship to the Environment, and Staging in relationship to the Self. I think it took me longer than it should have to recognize that the three areas of Obstacles were the same as the three areas of Staging. My first reaction (when I did see it) was that it was just coincidence. My second reaction was that it was totally meaningless since I had come up with these three areas to begin with. It just showed my limited imagination or insight — I would be lucky if no one else noticed. But then, after more months of teaching and lecturing went by, the connection started to plague me.

In yet another reckless moment, in front of 50-60 students some-where in the world, I launched into the explanation of this revelation — having no idea where I was going. The high-wire act. There was definitely no net this time. Hitting the ground could be very painful. But I kept going.

"There is a link between Obstacles and Staging. They share the same areas of relationship."

That was pretty obvious but the connection between Obstacles and Staging was totally eluding me. Then clarifying words just came out of my mouth.

"Staging is working with Obstacles and we reveal our reaction to Obstacles through our Staging."

Boy, that sounded good, but I had no idea what I had said. This was one of those moments when you look out at the students and all you see is a room full of stunned faces. They're not too sure what you said either but they have a feeling it was profound. In other words, no one in the room has a clue as to what is going on. But I'm the instructor. I have to keep going.

"There is an inextricable link between Staging and Obstacles."

At times like this it is always a good idea to throw in a big word, even if you don't know what it means. It's a verbal smoke screen. It caus-es confusion and disorientation and buys you time to dance out of the woods.

"Whenever you move actors in relationship to each other, the environment, or themselves, you are playing with the position and the power of obstacles."

Alliteration is also good. It's not quite the smoke screen of a big word like "inextricable" but it has a cool numbing effect. "Playing with the position and the power" is good alliteration. I'm halfway out of the woods.

"We move in our everyday life avoiding obstacles. We seek areas of comfort. We yearn for the comfortable proximity with other individuals. And everyday our body language is revealing the true internal conflicts, the internal obstacles."

Now this was sounding better, more confident at least. Even though I was clueless as to where this was going, I had a feeling I was now dancing near the edge of the forest.

"Objectives and achievements don't reflect who we are. They are only what we wish to do and what we have done. Obstacles and how we deal with our obstacles, that's what really defines us. We are not what we achieve. We are what we overcome."

Boy, this was sounding good. At this point I was only hoping that I could keep it up and land somewhere in the neighborhood of confidence.

"And like I have said many times, 'The dialogue in a scene is not the scene, only a result of the scene.' And even the behavior in the scene is not the scene. But in the staging, in the very graphic and subtle battle with one's obstacles, we reveal the core of the scene. Even in the most benign scene there is a war raging under the surface. Through staging we define and exacerbate this war and we reveal it in all of its complexities and incongruities."

Now I was certainly on a roll. Three big words (okay, they're big for me, maybe not for you) and a near miss at alliteration. I am definitely out of the woods.

"The two most powerful directing tools you have are Obstacles and Staging. And now we can see that they are intricately entwined. I have often said, 'A director's job is to get the character into trouble and it is the actor's job to get the character out of trouble.'"

Who knows how often I've said that? But I do know that if you precede any statement with "I have often said," suddenly you give it history, dignity, and credibility. And God knows I needed a little credibility at this point. I'm still on the wire and there could be a

335

false step at any moment. And of course, having made a bold and seemingly disconnected statement like that, I had to somehow loop back to the original premise — otherwise all dignity and credibility go in the crapper.

"The best way to get a character into trouble is through the manipulation of the character's obstacles. Intensify them, change them, or add new ones. And the cleanest and most efficient way to manipulate the obstacles is through the staging."

I think I just avoided the crapper. This is actually starting to make sense.

All teachers have one thing in common, the sheer joy of the "Aha Moment." That's when we see the looks of confusion or deep concentration (why do they have to look the same?) on the faces of our students suddenly change into that wide-eyed look of comprehension (usually accompanied with a sudden inhale or exhale). That's the Aha Moment. Something got through. Something registered.

Well, in this particular moment, those "aha" looks were saying that *someone* understood what I was saying (even if it wasn't me). When I'm on the high wire, I live for these moments. If one person in the room understands what I'm saying, then there's a good chance it'll become clear to me before I stop talking. And then all will be well with the world.

With a belief that there was a light at the end of this tunnel, I plunged forward.

"The world is a minefield of obstacles. Some will annoy you, some will trip you up, others will stop you, and a few will even destroy you. It is our intention to navigate this minefield as smoothly and comfortably as possible. This is what we do everyday in life. Each of you is doing it at this very moment. Every character in every story is navigating his/her own personal minefield

at every moment. It will be the character's instinct to avoid the obstacles and stay out of danger. It is your job as the director to create a journey for that character that is full of genuine obstacles and reasonable danger, thereby thrusting the character (who is driven by the actor) into a survival mode which will result in the expression of organic behavior... the magic."

This is what happens when I once again survive my own personal minefield. I just confidently plunge into graphic descriptions, metaphors, and parallel human experiences with such confidence that I am sure no one (except myself) will question the initial premise. It's a final gutsy maneuver that usually works. But I have to go for the gold now, the final connection, the ultimate Aha.

"Staging is undeniable and specific. It is not intellectual, spiritual, or emotional. It is purely physical. It is physical movement that triggers emotions. The emotions can be questioned and analyzed, justified, or denied. Physical motion cannot be challenged, questioned, or analyzed. It simple exists. The reason for the motion can be questioned but not the motion itself. And the results of the motion are undeniable. Motion generates emotion. And visa versa. Move a character and the character responds emotionally as he/she feels the shifting in the obstacles of other characters, the environment, and within him/herself."

And that's where I end up. For now. For today.

My Process

I decided to take you through my discovery process rather than just give you the conclusions, the results, the wrap-up. Because it's not about the conclusions. It is not about the final discoveries and the statements of fact. It is about the process. Directing is less about knowing something and more about taking yourself through a process that leads to a discovery of a truth, your truth.

I am very aware as I write this new material (and as I hear from the thousands that have read my book) that so many directors are looking for the answers. There are too many of you out there that want a formula. You want tools that you can pull out at specific times that will give you guaranteed results. It doesn't work that way. We aren't carpenters reaching for a hammer to drive in a nail. We're interpreters of the human condition who reach inside ourselves to understand the human experience. We are a process. We are not a product. We are all about process and we create through process and that process always includes self-discovery, self-doubt, self-questioning, self-assurance, and self-revelation.

I take great pride when I bring a concept (such as the Link between Obstacles and Staging) to students and other film directors and I see them grasp the idea with relish and joy and a sense of empowerment. But I take greater joy when I am in the presence of a student or a director who is working through a problem, digging within herself to find the connection, the reasoning, or the key that will bring her a moment of true discovery. And when she gets there — it's her discovery! She owns it.

THE ACTOR'S GREATEST OBSTACLE

Let's go into the process again. This time it will be shorter. That's the wonderful thing about this process. You really have no idea how long it will take or where it will lead you. It's like life.

We've already discussed that we all have obstacles that we deal with every day. It's not just characters in our stories who are trying to overcome seemingly insurmountable mountains of resistance. You and I do this daily. You, as a director, have incredible obstacles to overcome in the making of a film, whether it's a 5-minute short or a 2-hour feature. There are so many walls for you to hit and holes for you to fall into that we consider it a minor miracle that the movie gets done at all.

For the moment I want you to consider the actor's obstacles. Remember, this is for the actor, not the character. The actor's objective is fairly simple: He wants to embody the character as deeply and as fully as possible, thereby allowing himself to behave, think, and react like the character.

What are some of the obstacles in that process? I'll state them from the actor's point of view:

- I'm nothing like this character. I'm nowhere as intelligent and don't have his life experience.

- My priorities and my political leanings are totally opposed to this character.

- My character is married with two children. I am single with no children.

- My character has a passion for golf and scotch. I don't particularly like golf and I don't drink.

- My character is a brilliant writer. I only wish I were.

- My character is an adoring husband. I'm having doubts about my relationship with my girlfriend.

All of the above obstacles have to do with the differences between the actor and the character; indeed, these are significant obstacles to overcome. There are other obstacles that have to do with the filmmaking process:

- We have to shoot this film out of sequence. It will be hard to get a sense of the arc of the character.

- We're shooting in Montreal and pretending that it is New York. I was born and raised in New York!

- The actress playing my wife is involved in another project and won't have time to rehearse at all. I may have to rehearse with another actress.

- The actor playing my son is only 10 years old and has to spend a certain number of hours each day in school with a tutor. When I do my scenes with him, for my coverage and close-ups, he won't be there. I'll be performing to another actor.

- The director likes to do short takes in the coverage, sometimes just one line, so I don't get to feel the flow of the scene.

That's enough. You get the idea. So the question now is "What is the actor's greatest obstacle?" Yes, this is a test. You can skim forward quickly and find the answer or you can look over the two lists above and make up your own mind. And maybe it's not even in those lists.

The greatest obstacle an individual can face is anything that can totally derail her from the pursuit of her objective. The actor's objective is to embody the character physically, spiritually, and emotionally. Yes, any one of the above obstacles will impede that process, but none really has the potential of derailing the character from her intended goal. None — except the *script itself*.

That's right, the script! The script is the greatest obstacle to the actor's process. Simply knowing how the story turns out is an obstacle. Knowing whether or not her character is successful or fails. Knowing how each scene ends. Knowing what scenes exist and which don't. Knowing exactly what she says and does in every scene. And even what the other characters do and say. All of this information is totally antithetical to the process of creating a credible character because it is antithetical to life. An actor is trying to create a sense of reality and what is thrust right in front of her is pure fantasy. It's more than fantasy; it's an accurate prediction of the future. Now as much as we would like to have a prediction of the future, can you imagine how miserable our lives would be if we knew exactly what was going to happen? Knowing the future removes any need to challenge, excel, struggle, persuade, charm, or seduce. The essence of life is gone.

Now you're asking, "So I know this, now what do I do about it?" Good question. Remember, your job is to get the character into trouble and it's the actor's job to get the character out of trouble. Play with the obstacles. Play with the objectives. I remember reading an interview several years ago with Jason Robards. He was performing *The Iceman Cometh* here in Los Angeles. He had been performing the play for months on the road and on Broadway prior to that. And the interviewer asked him, "How can you go out on that stage night after night in this very taxing play and keep it all fresh for yourself?" His response (paraphrased from recollection): "You see, my objective in this play is to convince these men to stop living in their fantasies and dreams and to get up and take action. I don't succeed. But every night I go out there and I know that I will succeed. I believe that tonight the play is going to end differently than it ever has before, because tonight I will convince them. If I knew and believed that I was going to fail I could never do the play."

What you need to instill in the actors and their characters is the belief that they can make the scene turn out differently than it is written. The actors need to push against the obstacle of the inevitability of the outcome. Try it. It's amazing how an actor's performance will change when she shifts from concentrating on her lines and staging to concentrating on forcing the scene to go in her direction. There's no need to change the lines. As a matter of fact, the lines will come out with a new intensity and a new meaning. And no one will be more surprised than the actors themselves. This is the magic you want to capture. Challenge your actors to be daring. Challenge them to break the rules. Challenge them to push against the script and its demanding structure just as we in life must push against the events that try to derail us from our intentions.

Understanding our obstacles makes us wiser. Challenging our obstacles makes us more courageous. Overcoming our obstacles makes us stronger. And just as the actors have the challenge of dealing with their knowledge of the script and its outcome, directors have their own unique challenge: the audience. The audience is the great unknown in the theatrical equation. The audience is unpredictable, indefinable, and often unreachable. Without the audience, there is no event. Without the audience, our storytelling has no purpose.

THE THEATRICAL CONTRACT

It's 1966 and I'm an undergraduate student at Antioch College in Yellow Springs, Ohio. I have finally connected to my passion: theatre. And I know what I want to do in theatre: direct. I am putting all of my energy into a major production (my first effort to direct a full-length play) of *A Streetcar Named Desire*. I am pushing against all odds and obstacles. Student directors aren't allowed to direct full-length plays. There isn't enough money. (So I raise the money.) We don't have an appropriate actor for Stanley. (So I adjust the rest of the casting to accommodate the best actor I do have.) There is only one available weekend to mount the show on the Main Stage. (So I agree to a one weekend run. The weekend happens to be my birthday. An omen I am sure.) We have to rehearse around other Main Stage productions. (We rehearse in the middle of the night.)

And now we are coming close to Opening Night. My nerves are on edge. I'm exhausted but exhilarated. The head of the drama department, a lovable curmudgeon named Paul Treichler, calls me into his office for a final review.

I'm nervous. I know how tough this guy can be. I know he's worked with some of the finest actors and directors in regional theatre. I know he's watched some of my rehearsals, checked out the set (I had to get his approval on it, which I did), and even sat in on the tech rehearsals.

Paul: How's it going, Mark?

Mark: Fine.

Paul: You're happy with the performances?

Mark: For the most part. There's still some work to do but I have the time.

Paul: Good. The set looks good.

Mark: Thanks.

Paul: I saw some of the lighting during your tech rehearsal. Looks very nice.

Mark: Thank you.

I'm wondering where this is going. If he's so happy with everything then why is he taking up my time when he knows, at least he should know (he's directed hundreds of plays), that I need every moment I've got to do the final touches on this production. Time is running out. I mean I'm very happy that he seems pleased, but I've got work to do.

Paul: So the play is pretty much ready? Performances, costumes, make-up, set, lighting. What else is there to do?

Mark: Uh, that's about it. The music. The music I've got is great. You'll see.

Paul: Good. So everybody's ready. What about the audience?

Mark: The audience? Well, we're almost sold out for the whole weekend. We've all been working very hard ...

Paul: Are they ready?

Mark: Ready?

Paul: Yes, is the audience ready for what they are going to see?

I have no idea what he is talking about. The audience? Are they ready? I guess so; they know where they are supposed to be and at what time. What else can I do? Feed them?

Paul: Mark, the performances of *Streetcar* that will occur on the Main Stage this weekend are only half of the event. Only half. The other half is the audience. Without them the show is superfluous. It's a blind date and you are the matchmaker. There are expectations and trepidations on both sides. It's your job to take care of both sides so that the date might possibly turn into a romance.

I was stunned. I felt like I had been hit by a sledgehammer. Something deep in my gut told me that I had failed, that I had overlooked an essential part of what I was trying to create. My stomach was in a knot because I knew that I had no idea what to do.

Mark: What do I do?

Paul: Imagine the event from the audience's side. Mark, when we direct we project ourselves into each character and to the best of our ability we imagine and feel what it would be like to be them. You have to do the same with the audience. Imagine what it will be like to be them. As they read your ads, what are they thinking? As they arrive at the theatre, what are they seeing and hearing? As they enter the theatre, what are the impressions they are getting? Ask yourself, what do you want them thinking, knowing, feeling, wondering, and imagining before the play begins. You need to prepare them for the date.

There are key moments in every artist's life that help define the artist and the art. This was one of mine. Mr. Treichler (who sadly passed away many years ago) probably would not have remembered this conversation. But it was a moment that suddenly clarified for me what indeed it was that I was doing. I wasn't just trying to direct a play that hopefully a lot of people would like. I was trying to create an event that could possibly have an effect on both participants: the performer and the audience member. And I had an obligation to both parties.

But how do I "rehearse" an audience? How do I prepare them for the event? I don't even know who they are! And then I realized that I do know who they are. They are the people who want to see my show. They are the people who are interested in the material, the writer, the actors, etc. They have a desire to be there. Otherwise they wouldn't be coming. And they have expectations and trepidations, just like Paul Treichler said. But how do I prepare them for this event? I don't have any time with them! Then, remembering what Paul said, I understood that the "rehearsal time" with the audience had already begun. Some had read our ads. Some had invested in the production (and wanted to see what their investment had produced). Some had been contacted by cast or crew members. Regardless, they all had started to form some expectations. And the rest of the "rehearsal period" with the audience would consist mostly of the time between arrivals at the theatre until the beginning of the production itself. This was precious time. And I realized that I had to make the most of it.

I got into my car and drove off campus, turned around, and started to head towards the theatre. The moment I saw the theatre itself (an old converted warehouse), I was suddenly aware of how depressing it was. I asked myself if this was good for my rehearsal or not. Deciding that it was not, I made a note to place colorful lighting outside the theatre to create the feeling that something special was going to happen inside.

Then I drove up to the entrance. Again — depressing. Just a big factory door leading into a dark building. Decision: more lights and a single sign, *Streetcar*. I walked inside the lobby of the theatre.

Concrete slab floor, concrete block walls, a box office at one end, very high industrial ceilings. Cold, impersonal, not inviting. Decision: Find as many posters from earlier shows as possible for the walls, and find elements (drapes, props, furniture, and costume pieces) from those shows. Let the audience feel that they are walking into a sacred area. The artifacts are reminders of past "dates," past "romances." Music: Find music that welcomes and embraces and comforts. The theatre is a cathedral, a place of honor for all involved. The audience needs to feel privileged and honored to be there.

The box office. Typical box office. Decision: Change the lighting inside. Make it warmer, more inviting. The program (at this point it was finished except for the cover). Decision: Eliminate tickets; the program *is* the ticket. The program is your dance card. Tickets are too impersonal and (in this situation) not necessary. Another decision: an insert in the program welcoming each attendant to the theatre and to the production. Make the entire event as personal as possible.

Walking into the Main Stage space. What music is playing? (I never like silence in a theatre before a production.) Is it the same music as the lobby or different? How do I want the set lit? How do I want the audience area lit? By whom and how are the audience going to be greeted as they enter the theatre space?

By this point in my "projection" into the experience of an audience member, I realized that I had almost another entire production on my hands. And it was exciting because I knew it was manageable. I knew that I would be able to create an entire environmental experience that would genuinely prepare each and every audience member for the production he or she was about to see.

I sat in the audience staring at the stage. I'm looking at the stage where in a few days my production of *Streetcar* will unfold. And as I'm sitting there calmly, quietly, and peacefully, I am suddenly struck by a realization. I realize what this audience rehearsal has done to me. It has totally put me into the mindset of the audience member. And now I am sitting there in the audience and I realize that my mind is slowly going quiet. I am relaxed. I am at ease. I am excited, anticipatory, and maybe a little nervous. But I am willing. I am willing to give over two hours of my time to whatever this event is going to be. I am not only willing, I am eager to give over this time. And then this thought runs through my mind: "I am here for you. I am here to experience you. I am ready for you to take me on a glorious ride. And you can do whatever you like to me. You can make me laugh, make me cry, scare me, thrill me, tickle me, challenge me. All I ask is please don't bore me." And in that moment I realize that the audience and I have a contract, an agreement. They give their time, they release themselves totally to the experience. And I do my best to entertain, challenge, and provoke. This is an awesome responsibility. There is so much trust inherent in this agreement. How often do we enter a situation and say to the other party, "Do whatever you want to me, just don't bore me"?

In the world of cinema, little attention is paid to this phenomenon. We spend millions of dollars creating two hours of entertainment and we seem to have no concern for the state of mind of the audience prior to the film itself. We assault an audience with fifteen minutes of previews and advertising (none of which they asked for) before the beginning of the featured film. I know, it's a business and this is a perfect opportunity to promote all the other films that are playing or coming soon. Fine. Show our ugly side up front! Why not? I'm not opposed to previews. Not at all. But what would it take to spend the 3-5 minutes prior to the showing of the featured film bringing the audience into that world and that sensibility?

I am very fortunate because as a member of the Directors Guild I get to spend most of my film-viewing time in their glorious theatre. Not only does it have a great screen, great projectors, and a magnificent sound system, but also — three minutes before the film is to start —

its lights are lowered to half. Music begins to play. Usually it is music from another film (not the one we're about to see). Always it is music that is reminiscent of a genre, style, tone, and a world that is appropriate for the upcoming film. Sometimes it is right on the nose. Sometimes (and I love these moments) it is ironic, tongue-in-cheek. Sometimes it simply sets a tone, an atmosphere. You can feel the audience in those three minutes settling in. With the lights dimming we know the event is about to begin. The music is wrapping around us and within a short time 300-500 people are entering a common world. Then, as the music draws to an end, the lights dim to black and the curtain opens (very important and unfortunately a discarded item in most new theatres) and the screen is revealed. We are in the world of magic and make-believe. And we, the audience, are ready. Three minutes of time, a little music, a little lighting control, the glorious opening of the curtains, and suddenly your film has the introduction it well deserves. I'm thinking of adding three minutes of music at the beginning of my next film. Just music, no picture. It will be music that will bring the audience into the world of the film. And the lights will go down. And the curtain will open. And...

MIND THE GAP

Several years ago I stumbled upon this unique aspect of story structure. For years I had been conducting a writing workshop for the development of autobiographical material (appropriately called The Solo Workshop). I have always found this material to be the most intriguing, far surpassing most fiction that I read. Week after week I would hear true stories crafted by some of the best writers in Los Angeles. And then something began to emerge for me. I began to sense a common pattern within all the stories. Every story that I was hearing — no matter how profound, humorous, mundane, or magical — seemed to share a similar quality. But I couldn't figure out what it was. It was there. But it was not clear. And then one day I heard myself saying to one client, "You need to recognize that in every story,

in every event, there is a common element: Expectation vs. Reality."
At first I wasn't sure what I had said. (I often discover things this way.
I say it in a class or workshop and then have to spend the next few days
or weeks figuring out what I meant.)

Expectation vs. Reality. It sounded great and the more I looked at it
the more I realized it was absolutely true. In every situation (in life
and in story) each character not only has an objective, but also an
expectation. The objective and the expectation may be the same or
slightly different. Regardless, there is an expectation. And then there
is the reality, the result. And in every case there is a difference, a Gap,
between the expectation and the result. Have you ever entered a situation with specific expectations and had those expectations perfectly
met? The answer is probably "No." Most likely you fell short of the
expectation, overshot the expectation, or, if you hit it right on, then
there was something else in this accomplishment that didn't measure
up to what you anticipated. There is always a Gap.

The energy of life exists in that Gap. We live in a world full of Gaps.
And as we observe characters trying to narrow or close those Gaps, we
understand. We understand the effort, the desire, the frustration, and
even the sense of accomplishment as a Gap is narrowed.

Then one day I was sitting in a Robert McKee screenwriting seminar
(a brilliant man — with a stunning mind — giving an inspiring lecture) and suddenly he was talking about "the gap." My heart rose and
sank at the same time. What if I'm wrong? What if I'm way off and
this is just some kind of uneducated conceit that I'm having? What if
there really is another gap, a better gap, or a more important gap?
What have I missed? And then he meticulously took us into the
analysis of character and scene and exposed the Gap. "Expectation
versus result" he said. And suddenly I felt okay. I felt validated. And
to be validated by a man as gifted as Robert McKee is quite an honor.
I was on the same path. I was in the same environment. I was seeing
it from the perspective of autobiographical stories. He was seeing it

in the world of fiction. And we were seeing the same thing. It's a fact of life. It is not something that has been constructed or conceived for dramatic purposes, but rather a reflection of the human experience.

Here's how it looks graphically:

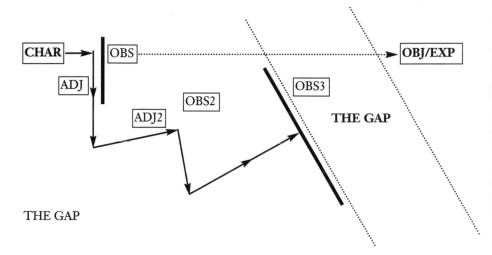

1. **CHAR** is the Character heading directly toward **OBJ/EXP** the desired Objective and anticipated Expectation.
2. ┄┄┄┄┄➤ is the intended line of travel for the Character — straight to the Objective.
3. **OBS** is the first set of Obstacles the Character encounters, Obstacles of character, environment, and self.
4. **ADJ** is the first adjustment the Character makes in order to over-come, undermine, or totally avoid the Obstacles.
5. **OBS2** is the second set of Obstacles (which may only be the first Obstacles redefined).
6. **ADJ2** is the second Adjustment that the Character makes.
7. **OBS3** is the third (and in this case, final) set of Obstacles the Character encounters, leaving the Character short of the intended Objective. The difference between OBS3 and OBJ/EXP is the Gap.

The Character's Response To The Gap

We live with the experience of the Gap in our everyday life and it is how we respond or adjust to the reality of the Gap that determines the nature of our character. When you experience the Gap there can be many different reactions. You may be motivated or re-invigorated. ("This is great. Now I know how close I got and I am convinced that I can make it.") You may be defeated. ("Forget it. I'll never make it.") You may be resolved that there is no way to close the Gap. ("It was impossible to begin with.") You may embrace the Gap as an unexpected but welcomed discovery. ("Really? That's what I have to deal with now? Wow!") The Gap may cause a loss of self-esteem. ("It's my fault. Others could have made it.") It may cause a rise in self-esteem. ("You know, it's amazing how close I came. Never imagined that I was that good.") It may cause you to go into denial. ("What gap? I don't see any gap!")

Remember:
1. There is always a Gap between Expectation and Result.

2. The energy of your story exists within the Gap and is intensified and clarified with the creation of each new Gap.

3. The true nature of your characters is revealed in their reactions and adjustments to each Gap.

And as you track your characters through your story you will see how each Gap and response defines a unique emotional journey.

The Emotional Graph

A couple of years ago I was in Cologne teaching The Director's Journey (a three-day directing seminar) and we were discussing the emotional journey of Conrad, the son of Beth and Calvin in Alvin Sargent's

351

Ordinary People. (Yes, Robert Redford directed the film, Alvin Sargent wrote the script, and Judith Guest wrote the novel. You decide whose film it is.) As we were examining young Conrad's emotional journey through a sequence of scenes, we began to see how delicate and complex this journey was — even in just two or three scenes. When we looked deeper into just one scene we began to see the extraordinary emotional twists and turns that might be occurring moment to moment. And then I found myself drawing this on the board:

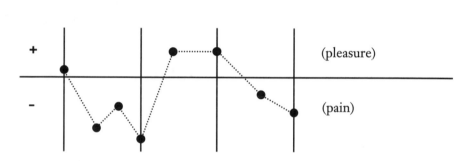

Conrad's Emotional Graph

... and saying this:

"We all move through our lives negotiating between two basic emotional states: pleasure (the + in the graph) and pain (the − in the graph). As we find ourselves facing different obstacles or reacting to new events in our lives, we experience emotional shifts (as depicted in the dotted line in the graph).

"It's important to remember that we do not create our emotions (see Chapter Seven, The Rehearsal Process). We have experiences. And in response to these experiences we have emotional reactions. We try to control these reactions as we attempt to move closer to (or deeper into) the pleasure zone. We may or may not be successful in this attempt (remember the Gap); regardless, there is usually another emotional reaction."

And as I drew this graph I began to realize that what I had was a visual picture of the Emotional Journey of a character. I was intrigued. The students in the class were intrigued. And the actors in the class were especially intrigued. Admittedly, this graph was my projection of Conrad's journey. Another person might see it differently. That's fine. This was not about a definitive depiction of a character's emotional state, but rather my finding another way to visualize what I believed was going on inside a character — making the invisible visible. I was discovering another way to communicate something that is almost indefinable and I was very excited.

I asked each of the students to make their own graphs for these scenes. And I reminded them that there was no right or wrong way to see this emotional journey, only their own honest projections. And with slight variations everyone projected a similar journey.

Then we stated talking about Beth (Conrad's mother), who was also in two of these scenes. I asked the students to imagine Beth's journey during Scenes 1, 2, and 3. I added my version of Beth's journey over Conrad's. It looked something like this:

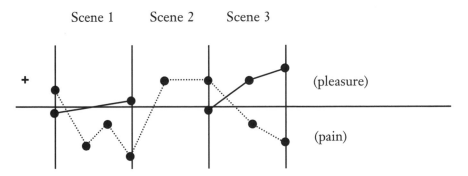

Beth and Conrad's Emotional Graph

As we all looked at our charts we began to notice two very profound patterns. Number one: As Beth moved out of the pain zone and into the pleasure zone, Conrad moved in the opposite direction. Number two: When Beth was not present in a scene (Scene 2), Conrad would move quickly and more easily into the pleasure zone. Suddenly we were seeing a very important pattern in this relationship. It was at this point that I began to realize the usefulness of this technique.

Since that time I have explored and experimented with this approach to character and relationship analysis and I continue to find it challenging and revealing. It's challenging in that I am forced to look more deeply and specifically into the emotional state of each character at each specific moment in the story. I am keenly aware that I am revealing my own personal projections. Often I learn that — prior to creating this graph — I had no idea what I was imagining the character's emotional state or journey to be. It's like looking under the hood of your car and seeing how each part of the engine functions, how well or how poorly, and how each part affects the other.

Then I took it one step further and graphed an entire screenplay, *American Beauty*, from page 1 to page 117. I averaged about one scene per graph page (sometimes several scenes on one page; some very complex scenes took two or more pages). I mounted all these graph pages end to end along my studio wall creating one long graph. The whole movie was then sitting in front of me with each character's emotional journey (in a different color) displayed very specifically. What this revealed to me was shattering. As I looked at this graph (nearly 100 feet long!) I could feel and see the delicate inner workings of this incredible script. I brought actors in to see the chart — actors who could play these specific roles. I was honestly worried what they might think of this very graphic and specific charting of the emotions of an entire cast of characters. But every actor was intrigued. Some of them spent hours tracking the characters, reading the scenes again and then checking the graph. I could feel that it was actually pulling them into the story in a whole new way. Perhaps the most revealing moments were when an actor would ask me to explain how I viewed a certain moment on the graph, how I had come to these particular projections or decisions. And what this question opened up was the beginning of an insightful and healthy discussion, which ended with the actor putting his version of the character's journey on the graph.

In a moment we'll look at a selection from that graph: the scene where Jane first meets Ricky. She has seen him earlier when he was filming her from the front of his house. Now she and Angela are in the schoolyard. The importance of this scene is the shifting Jane/Angela relationship, the beginning of the Ricky/Jane relationship, and the initiation of an internal struggle within Jane.

To get the most out of this process, I suggest that you read the scene first and make your own graph. When you read the scene, notice that it is constructed in four parts: the four-character scene with Jane, Angela, and the two Girls; the two-character scene with just Jane and Angela when they notice Ricky's arrival; the three-character scene with Ricky, Jane, and Angela; and finally the two-character scene with Jane and Angela after Ricky leaves.

EXT. HIGH SCHOOL CAMPUS - A FEW MINUTES LATER

JANE and ANGELA are seated with two other TEENAGE GIRLS. They're all smoking.

> ANGELA
> I'm serious, he just yanked it out
> and showed it to me. You know, like
> the President did to that woman.

> TEENAGE GIRL #1
> Gross.

                    ANGELA
          It wasn't gross. It was kind of
          cool.

                    TEENAGE GIRL #1
          So did you do it with him?

                    ANGELA
          Of course I did. He is a really
          well-known photographer? He shoots
          for Elle on like, a regular basis?
          It would have been so majorly
          stupid of me to turn him down.

                    TEENAGE GIRL #2
          You are a total prostitute.

                    ANGELA
          Hey. That's how things really
          are. You just don't know, because
          you're this pampered little
          suburban chick.

                    TEENAGE GIRL #2
          So are you. You've only been in
          Seventeen once, and you looked fat,
          so stop acting like you're goddamn
          Christy Turlington.

The two TEENAGE girls move away from JANE and
Angela.

ANGELA
    (calling off)
Cunt!
    (then)
I am so sick of people taking
their insecurities out on me.

The Colonel's Ford Explorer pulls up, and Ricky gets out. The creases on his trousers are sharp enough to cut glass.

JANE
Oh my God. That's the pervert who
filmed me last night.

ANGELA
Him? No way. Jane, he is a total
lunatic.

JANE
You know him?

ANGELA
He was in my earth science class
in eighth grade, and he always said
the creepiest things, and then one
day, he was just, like, gone. And
then Connie Cardullo told me his
parents had to put him in a mental
institution.

JANE
Why? What did he do?

>   ANGELA
> What do you mean?

>   JANE
> Well, they can't put you away just
> for saying creepy things.

ANGELA stares at JANE, then her mouth widens into a smile.

>   ANGELA
> You total slut. You've got a
> crush on him.

>   JANE
> What? Please.

>   ANGELA
> You were defending him! You love
> him. You want to have, like, ten
> thousand of his babies.

>   JANE
> Shut up.

JANE suddenly finds RICKY standing IN FRONT OF her, looking at her intensely.

>   RICKY
> Hi. My name's Ricky. I just moved
> next door to you.

>   JANE
> Uh, yeah. I know. I kinda remember
> this really creepy incident when
> you were filming me last night?

>   RICKY
>   I didn't mean to scare you. I just
>   think you're interesting.

ANGELA shoots a wide-eyed look at JANE, who
ignores it.

>   JANE
>   Thanks, but I really don't need to
>   have some psycho obsessing about me
>   right now.

>   RICKY
>   I'm not obsessing. I'm just
>   curious.

He looks at her intently, his eyes searching hers.
JANE is unnerved and has to look away. Ricky
smiles and walks off.

>   ANGELA
>   What a freak. And why does he
>   dress like a Bible salesman?

>   JANE
>   He's like, so confident. That
>   can't be real.

>   ANGELA
>   I don't believe him. He didn't
>   even like, look at me once.

Before you look at my graph, plot your own Emotional Graph for the
five characters. It's best to take one character at a time. Start with the
two Girls, then add Angela and Jane for the first part of the scene.
Then move on to the second part, etc. Good luck. Enjoy it.

Here is my Emotional Graph for all five characters in the scene:

Emotional Graph For Scene From *American Beauty*
(Girl 1, Girl 2, Angela, Jane, Ricky)

G1 ●·········● G2 ●—·—·● Angela ●————● Jane ●————● Ricky ●————●

Part One — The Two Girls with Angela and Jane
Notice the effect these two girls have on each other. I see the first Girl as totally admiring in the beginning and in awe of Angela (who is, of course, lapping up all this adoration). But the second Girl is skeptical, critical. And when she starts to speak I feel that the first Girl loses her confidence and switches her allegiance during the final moment and allies herself with the second Girl. (In a nutshell, this is what this scene is about: the switching of allegiance.) The two Girls leave. They are allied with each other, not with Angela.

Part Two — Jane and Angela
These individual journeys and their relationship to each other are crucially important in this scene, as they are through the entire story. In fact, what we have in this scene is a microcosm of the entire Jane/Angela relationship. At first they are both in the positive zone. Angela is feeling good about the attention she is getting and Jane is feeling good just being in the glow of Angela. Even the insults and the insinuations from the second Girl don't seem to threaten the Angela/Jane bond. But once they both see Ricky the shift starts to

happen. Angela feels more empowered because she can discredit someone who is incomprehensible and unavailable. But Jane is pulled in the opposite direction for the very same reasons: Ricky is incomprehensible and aloof. As much as Ricky annoys Jane, he also fascinates her. And here begins one of the more fascinating and complex aspects of the Emotional Graph — when a character is experiencing conflicting feelings. This is the internal struggle that brings a richness and a complexity to any character. (It is actually occurring within every character in this scene to some extent, but most profoundly with Jane.)

Part Three — Ricky joins Angela and Jane
As Ricky approaches, Angela is ready for the kill. Jane is uncertain and conflicted. Ricky is calm and confident. During this part of the scene, as Ricky introduces himself to Jane and explains his interest in her, his journey remains relatively even. But Jane's journey experiences a deeper split — her feeling of interest soars while her fear pulls her in the other direction. Most interesting, perhaps, is Angela, who plummets from an enormous high to the deepest low in this section. And she is silent; she only observes the exchange between Ricky and Jane.

Part Four — Jane and Angela after Ricky leaves
Angela tries to pull herself up, only to experience her own split, her own lack of confidence. Jane feels her level of interest increasing while her fear is diminishing, leaving her with a mostly positive feeling.

Now look over the graph at the journey of Jane in relationship to Angela. That's where the core of the scene is pulsing. The effect of these two encounters (with the two Girls and then with Ricky) on the Jane/Angela relationship is profound. Jane needs Angela as much as Angela needs Jane. In the world of young women they are bonded and firmly connected. When an interesting young man enters the relationship we see how fragile this bond really is. We see a threatened Angela and an uncertain and conflicted Jane.

Remember that these are all projections. The scene, as written, is nothing more than words on a page. My analysis of this scene is only my projection. Yours may be quite different. That's fine. Again, there is no right or wrong. We're dealing with human emotions and almost any projection is possible.

An important aspect of this process is self-discovery. You will discover what *you* believe and what *you* feel. If you are willing to let yourself go and experience the scene, you will discover as much about yourself as you do about the characters. The more we understand ourselves (as directors) and the more willing we are to expose ourselves emotionally, the more effective and honest our work will be.

Ironically, the more we experience and explore the process of creating credible moments of human behavior and interaction, the more we realize that the greatest obstacles to these truths are most likely ourselves, the actors, and the process itself.

A FRESH LOOK AT THE REHEARSAL PROCESS

No More Acting

The more I work with actors and the more I explore the unique challenge of creating believable characters, the more I discover how incredibly difficult this task really is. As you have (hopefully) learned from early chapters in this book, I have a rather unorthodox approach to working with actors. It is not unorthodox for the world of theatre but it definitely is for the world of film. As much as I love to work with actors and as much as I relish the rehearsal process, I realize that I often love the process as much as the final product. I love the exploration, experimentation, improvisation, risk-taking, and tightrope walking of the rehearsal process that will often result in an extraordinarily magical performance. I love controlling the exploration process and giving up some of the control of the performance. It's in my nature, I guess. In seminars, workshops, and consultations, I find myself making statements that I believe to be true, or at least true for me:

> "My goal as a director is to bring actors to the point where there is no longer a need for acting."

> "Acting is pretending. Acting is planned behavior and emotion. I have no interest in behavior or emotion that is planned or created. It is false and will always be seen as false."

> "The ultimate goal of the actors is to *stop acting* in order to immerse themselves totally into the world of the characters."

> "My goal as a film director in the production phase is rather simple. When the cameras are rolling I want to capture magic. I want to capture real behavior and real emotions that are happening for the first time. That is the magic."

> "The ultimate goal of the director is to *stop directing*. By this I mean we need to stop trying to make things happen the way we want them to happen. Stop telling your actors what you want them to do. Stop trying to control the behavior and the emotions of your characters. Let go. Create an environment within which the characters will become so involved in their individual objectives that real emotions and behavior will be the only result."

As I listen to myself I sometimes wonder where I am going. I wonder if I am just saying things to sound profound or revolutionary, or if I really believe my statements and can back them up. Now, years into the process, I know that they are true and that I can back them up. I also know that this is the only way I want to work. My creative life has always been a high-wire act, and as I get more settled into my own personal forms of self-expression I understand how important this high-wire act really is.

Be Willing To Risk

It's all about risk. And risk means giving up control. What are you willing to risk? How much are you willing to let go and trust? The first nine chapters of this book (written over five years ago) described and defined an approach to filmmaking that combined collaboration and compassion with control and dominance. I haven't abandoned that ideal at all. In some areas I have embraced it more passionately; in others I have reconsidered the priorities. I am fully aware that my career as a director, writer, and teacher is as much a journey of self-discovery as it is a form of self-expression. Day by day I discover what I really think and feel about this process of filmmaking and this phenomenon of artistic self-expression. Because, after all the smoke clears, that's all it is. Every film I make, every class I teach, every script I write, is really about my trying to say something to the world. That's why I chose this profession. That's why any of us choose it (or any other profession that allows an artist to be heard). We have something to say. I'm spending most of my time trying to figure out what it is I want to say, how I might say it, if I have said it — and then, if I've said enough. Or do I have to say it again? I'm stuck in this hamster wheel of constant explosion of ideas followed by self-doubt. The "divine dissatisfaction, a blessed unrest," as Martha Graham so brilliantly defined it.

In this curious art form called filmmaking we have elected to collaborate with many other artists in the attempt to express ourselves. It would have been easier to write a book or to paint a painting. Ask yourself: If you really want to express yourself, why did you pick filmmaking? Why not pick something over which you have more control, where the final product is purely you? You can create a piece of sculpture out of stone, or write a short story, or paint a watercolor, or photograph a landscape. That final product will be purely from you.

When the first edition of this book, *The Director's Journey*, came out five years ago, many people asked me, "Is this really the way you direct a film?" And I had to honestly respond, "No. My book describes the director I aspire to be." And that's true. As I was writing the book I became aware that occasionally I was describing procedures and attitudes that I had difficulty maintaining. But I could clearly see the power and the possibilities of this approach and I wanted to convey that. Since that time I have come closer to embracing that directorial image, and in some ways now I am moving beyond it, or past it, or under it. I am aware, even writing now, that I am not totally embracing these aspects of directing as I describe them. But I do want to. And someday I will.

No More Directing

I mentioned somewhere in the original nine chapters that I felt the term "director" was a misnomer. I still feel that way. Probably always will. But what's a better name? I'm not sure. The term "director" seems to elicit images of someone pointing in a certain direction. Have you noticed that most photos of film directors directing have them next to a camera and they are pointing? We never see whom or what they are pointing at. But there they are: pointing, directing, in control. And of course they are next to the camera. Most directors should be kept far away from cameras. Most of us have no idea what to do with them artistically or mechanically and we shouldn't be allowed anywhere near them. But that's not the point. You want a photo that says "film director"; well, here it is. Now, my preference would be a picture of the director talking to an actor or a writer — people in communication. To be fair, we do see these pictures, but it's usually with an actor who is so recognizable and so powerful that the director is willing to give up the image of the camera for the image of an actor. And of course, in this picture, the actor with the big name is listening intently to the director of the smaller name. It's not the other way around. We must project the image of "directing," which is the person who knows, who has the answers, who demands the respect of everyone else. Because, after all, that is "directing."

Here are the images we don't want:
- The director listening intently to a writer or a designer who has a good idea.
- The director struggling with the personal and the emotional strain of self-expression.
- The director being entertained by the insight and the daring of an actor.
- The director sitting alone at the computer or the sketchpad.
- The director arguing passionately with the producer or the studio executive.
- The director receiving the consolation and the encouragement from a friend.

We don't want to see these images because they're not glamorous or sexy. They undermine the image, the perception, and the dream. These images are too real, too honest. Directors are not supposed to struggle or argue. We are not supposed to be so dependent upon the skills and the insights of others. We are not supposed to be alone or lonely. And we certainly don't need support and encouragement like other artists do. We're directors. We're in charge. We're in control. We are what everyone else in this business desires to be. We are at the peak of our process on the top of our game... and all is well.

Maybe if we get rid of this name "director" we'll be one step closer to what this job really is. But, for the life of me, there's not another label that seems to work.

- Facilitator (boring),
- Guide (sounds like a Boy Scout leader),
- Visionary (too much ego attached to that word),
- Coach (sounds like a sporting event),
- Leader (back to that Boy Scout guy).

You see, the actor's job is to act; the director's job is to direct. But I want to get away from all that. I want to move beyond the obvious and the mundane. I want the actor to merely (and I don't mean to make this sound easy) immerse himself into the character and allow real behavior to emerge. And I want the director to merely (again not easy) allow himself to be inspired, intrigued, and passionately driven by an idea, and then focus primarily on the creation of an environment within which the inhabitants will create events of genuine behavior.

I believe that we all can learn to stop directing (in the old-fashioned way) if we will allow ourselves to create an environment (physical, social, mental, and spiritual) that will by its nature give the actors the permission and the courage to stop acting.

It's a huge risk. But we are not going to grow in this art form if we continue to play it safe.

THE COURAGE TO BREAK THE RULES

Here I am, I've written all these pages (not to mention the years of directing, writing, teaching, and discovery) giving you specific advice and tools and steps in film directing and now I am suggesting that you break the rules. That's right. Break them. But know them first. Use them first. Prove them valuable first. Master them first. And then break them. As much as I am fascinated by the structure in filmmaking, I am constantly thrilled when I see someone break the rules, push the form, challenge the expected, and arrive in a new place.

It took me a long time to realize that my edict for working with actors — "Give them strong boundaries and then give them total freedom" — was something that I needed to apply to myself as a writer and a director. But what are the boundaries for a director? The boundaries are understanding and mastering storytelling through the medium of film. Just like a jazz musician needs to master the scales, classical music, pop music, and rhythm and blues — before he can really relish the ultimate personal expression of jazz. As filmmakers we need to master the act of telling a simple story, simply. Knowing how it works, why it works, and making it work is the first step. Demanding of yourself that you master the form is a boundary. Insisting that you always stay within that form is an unnecessary restriction. One of the most difficult tasks we have in life is giving ourselves permission to be totally free while maintaining strict boundaries and discipline. The child in us just wants to play. The adult sees the edge of the cliff.

Let your mind go free. Remember the bumblebee.

CHAPTER TWELVE

THE ULTIMATE COLLABORATION: DIRECTORS WITH DIRECTORS

THE ROLE OF THE DIRECTING CONSULTANT

For the past six years (especially since *The Director's Journey* was published), I have had the privilege of being hired to consult on a variety of films — from small independent projects to major studio features. The type of consulting that my partner, Frederick Johntz, and I have been doing is rather unique. We are both directors and writers. We both have a strong background in theatre so our main strengths are story, script, and working with actors. When producers or directors call us, it is usually because they feel the director needs additional support with the script or working with the actors. At first I thought this was sad and baffling. Sad because I could see that these directors had the best of intentions and great visions but had little knowledge about the actor-director relationship. And baffling because often I would wonder why these directors were even hired if they were so lacking in what I considered the primary skill necessary to tell a cinematic story. The answers to that question were as varied as the skills of the directors themselves.

And then I started to realize that what I was doing was just a further extension of the collaboration that I had been so passionately championing — a collaboration that no one seemed to want to talk about. Several times either Fred or I have been asked not to disclose our relationship with a director. Understanding the necessity of the director to maintain the position of authority, we readily agreed. But as the years went by and our consulting became more in demand, I began to wonder about the perception of the director who is not expected to need or seek help, advice, and support. As a director, you are discouraged from announcing that you have actually engaged another director in your pursuit to create the best film possible. How sad. Other artists seek advice and support as they pursue their crafts. Why not the director?

I have often said "the best film school is the one you create yourself." You are forever a student and I highly encourage you to make assisting and supporting another director an essential part of your curriculum.

In the final phases of developing your directing skills, reach out to those who share your passion, your skills, and your insights — and collaborate. Let them support you, and you offer to support them. But before you start, there are a few questions that you need to answer.

How can one director support the other?
This is the first hurdle. Two directors — two egos. Two directors — two visions. One of the most difficult, yet fulfilling tasks that you will ever have is to allow the authority and the vision of another director to become the ultimate guide. At first you will want to assert yourself and impose your vision on the other director. But what kind of collaboration is that? Then you will want to suppress your own instincts, but will quickly see that you are of no service if your views are kept under wrap. Now you are about to enter a difficult part of the collaboration. Your job, if you are willing to accept it, is to first identify the vision of the main director. Then question that vision. Your objective is not to destabilize the director's vision but rather to strengthen it in both your mind and the mind of the director. This is a very delicate process for both of you. Remember, any director who is willing to be challenged by another is to be admired. Your questioning must have the intention of reaching deeper clarity. You are now working with a director much like you would with an actor. You are going beyond the initial ideas and searching for the sub-textual impulses that drive us all. Like many writers, many directors have

passionate ideas about what they want to say through their films, but again, like many writers, they have difficulty articulating these ideas. It is your job to help your director identify her deeper passions and then put them into words, images, and clear concepts.

Here's an example of a recent conversation I had with a first-time director:

Me: What is this story all about? For you?

Director: Reconciliation. For me it's all about the reconciliation between the father and the son.

Me: But the father doesn't want this reconciliation.

Director: No, he doesn't.

Me: And the son, who I have to assume is the protagonist ...

Director: Yes, he is.

Me: The son seems to have almost no overall objective in this story. He's almost a leaf in the wind.

Director: Well, he wants his father to notice him.

Me: Does he? What does he do to try to get his father's attention?

Director: He asks him to come watch him play baseball.

Me: That's it?

Director: Yeah, that's about it.

Me: So, what does the father want?

Director: He wants to be left alone. He wants to disconnect from everyone. Until he discovers that he is dying.

Me: And then what does he want?

Director: Then he feels he needs a connection.

Me: After he's disconnected from everyone.

Director: That's right.

Me: And when the son discovers that his father has been hiding his illness … ?

Director: He tries to destroy himself.

Me: Why? To really destroy himself or to get attention?

Director: To get attention. He's angry.

Me: At his father.

Director: Yes.

Me: For abandoning him.

Director: Right.

Me: And what about the older brother?

Director: Well, he's just a loose cannon. He seems bent on creating as much chaos as possible.

Me: Why?

Director: I think he wants to be like his father.

Me: Really? His father is a drunk and a failure.

Director: No, he wants to be like his father when his father was younger and a Marine.

Me: How do we know that?

Director: Well, there's that one scene where he tries to sign up with the Marines.

Me: One scene.

Director: Not enough?

Me: Not enough. Don't you think the older brother is acting out just to get the attention of his father who is trying to disconnect from him?

Director: That could be.

Me: And the younger brother is playing baseball and doing well in school just to get the attention of his father who is trying to disconnect from him?

Director: Yeah. Could be.

Me: And when both sons learn of their father's terminal illness, which he has kept a secret, their fear of abandonment and anger turns them against each other and they almost destroy each other.

Director: This is a better script than I thought. It's almost classical.

Me: The triangle of the father and the two sons is very powerful. The two sons vying for their father's attention is classic. The father's fear of intimacy because of his own low self-esteem is universal. And the sons' fear of abandonment and placing the blame on themselves or each other will hit a chord with everyone.

Director: It's just not about reconciliation, is it?

Me: Doesn't seem to be. Seems to be much deeper than that. It's about a struggle between a father and his two sons. It deals with the powerful fears of intimacy, failure, abandonment, and jealousy. It's a classic family struggle.

It was clear to me from the outset that the director was connecting to something deeper within the script, a script that he had written. It was my job to help him find this connection by allowing him to discover what it was — much like we work with actors in the process of developing characters.

My job, as a consultant, is to help the director get his vision on the screen. This is where one ego, one point of view, has to give way to another. As a collaborating director, your job is not to make the best movie you can from the script, your job is to help the main director make the best movie *he* can make from the script. You are now a member of his creative team. And he is the Alpha Horse.

What about the autonomy of the director?
The director's autonomy must always be protected. Even though there are many cases in which there have been two directors on a film, there can only be one Alpha Horse as far as the cast and the crew are concerned. (Some directing teams actually divide their tasks; one works with the actors while the other works with the camera and the crew.) When you are consulting with another director your main objective is to help her get the movie she sees in her head up on the screen. As much as this might feel contrary to the role of a director (your supporting another director), it really isn't. Your job, when you are directing, is to support and to guide all the other artists in the creation of a film along the lines of your vision. When you are supporting another director it is the same thing. The only difference is that the vision comes from another. Your task is still to support that artist in her work. In all the years (over thirty) that I have been directing, I have found the activity of consulting, advising, and collaborating with other directors to be most educational and humbling. It is invaluable.

The director's ego is a fragile vessel. It can be easily threatened, cracked, or even shattered. It needs strong internal glue to hold together the veneer of glass while maintaining the appearance of steel. The glue is humility. The willingness to abdicate the throne but still support the agenda of the king will reinforce that fragile vessel. We all need thick skins in this business. You can acquire that armor by developing calluses, but you run the risk of becoming isolated, unapproachable, and unavailable. Or you can reinforce your armor by stepping back and allowing the priorities and the principals of another to become your first priority. Your inner awareness, consciousness, flexibility, and adaptability will give you the strength you need.

What actually happens in the director-to-director consultation? First, you have to be clear about what must *not* happen. The consulting director must not ever attempt to tell the director how to make her movie. That is forbidden, as forbidden as result directing with the actors. The first task of the consulting director is to determine why the director wants to make this movie and what she imagines the effect will be on the audience. Once you have these expectations clearly established (and this can take hours, if not days, of discussion and exploration), you now have a basis from which to work. When the director and the consulting director have clear goals in mind, it will be those goals that will guide the process. From this point on, the consulting director becomes the probing, questioning, challenging, and supportive conscience of the director. And like the exploration of character relationships as outlined above, most of the work is done through questions. Your goal is not so much to inject ideas, visions, or solutions, but rather to reveal the ideas, visions, and solutions that already exist within the director. If the director is passionate about telling the story then she will be guided by that passion. It is your job, as the consulting director, to create an environment wherein the director can explore, question, and challenge her own vision and thereby become more articulate, more confident, and stay connected to her passion.

Directing is a very lonely job. But I have found that the more time I spend discussing, debating, and defending my vision with other directors, the stronger I become. I am very often not aware of the depth of my vision until I am challenged to be articulate and specific.

A PANEL DISCUSSION

In an effort to explore the pros and the cons of director-to-director collaboration, I have elected to call upon a few director friends of mine to answer some specific questions about collaborating with other directors. These are all highly accomplished directors with varied backgrounds and experiences. The range of their responses will give you an idea of the complexity of this issue.

Here is a brief background on each director on the panel:

Frederick Johntz
As a consultant and private coach, Fred has worked with numerous writers and directors on projects ranging from independent shorts to big-budget studio features. For the last twenty years, Fred has worked in film, television, and theatre as a writer, director, and producer. He has taught film directing at UCLA Extension, the American Film Institute's Professional Training Division, and the Hollywood Film Institute. Fred has also worked as a film editor and an assistant art director.

After studying theatre at the University of California, Santa Cruz, Fred graduated Magna Cum Laude from San Francisco State University with a degree in Cinema Studies. He has worked and studied with such notable directors as Robert Woodruff, Lee Breuer, and Jedediah Horner. He has studied writing with Robert McKee and Mimi Roth, and acting with Luis Valdez, Jean Shelton, and Lorinne Vozoff.

Asaad Kelada
One of television's most prolific directors, Asaad has directed over 400 episodes for all of the major networks, including such series as *Family Ties*; *The Facts Of Life*; *Who's The Boss?*; *WKRP In Cincinnati*; *In The House*; *Sister, Sister*; *The Michael Richards Show*; *Everybody Loves Raymond*; and *Dharma And Greg*. For the theatre he has directed notable productions for acclaimed professional companies, including South Coast Repertory; Seattle Repertory Theatre; Philadelphia's

Playhouse In The Park; The Mark Taper Forum Lab; The El Portal Center For The Arts; and The Tiffany Theatre in Los Angeles, where he directed the award-winning world premiere of Hyam Maccoby's *The Disputation*. He is a graduate of the Yale School of Drama and a former member of the teaching faculty at Antioch College, Ohio; the American Academy of Dramatic Arts, West; California Institute of the Arts; and U.S. International University, San Diego.

Cyrus Nowrasteh

Cyrus Nowrasteh directed the Paramount/Showtime production *The Day Reagan Was Shot* (from his own script). Produced by Oliver Stone, *The Day Reagan Was Shot* stars Richard Dreyfuss as Alexander Haig and depicts the chaos that occurred behind the scenes that day. Nowrasteh also directed the independent production *Norma Jean, Jack And Me*, which played a number of international film festivals. He has worked extensively as a screenwriter, having written and developed the pilot for the USA-network television series *La Femme Nikita*, as well as the 2002 Showtime production *10,000 Black Men Named George*, starring Andre Brougher.

Rosa von Praunheim

Rosa von Praunheim did over sixty films in thirty-three years. He started around the same time as Fassbinder, Schröter, Wenders, and Herzog and became well known making gay liberation movies. He took the name Rosa to remind us of the pink triangle the Nazis used to mark gay people in the concentration camps. His films have been shown all over the world. His latest works are *The Einstein of Sex*, about the sexologist Magnus Hirschfeld, and *Fassbinder's Women*, a very personal view of the sadomasochistic Fassbinder. He just shot two new movies, *Four Drag Queens and a Hallelujah* and *Cows Fucked by the Fog*, which will be released on his sixtieth birthday.

Michael Wiese

Michael Wiese is an American producer, director, author, and publisher living in Cornwall, England. He is currently writing a DV feature that he will direct on location in Bali.

Here is the letter I sent to each:

Thank you for agreeing to be a part of this discussion. I am aware that we are exposing an aspect of the filmmaking process that is rarely discussed, but I feel that it is important that we open up this discussion in a healthy and supportive manner.

The following questions will be included in my new book, followed by your comments and the comments of others. This structure will bring it as close as possible to the feeling of a dialogue between all of us. Enjoy the discussion and don't worry about being too verbose, provocative, or opinionated.

And now for the questions and responses:

> *1. Besides your regular crew and creative team, what other artists do you usually consult with during the creation of a film?*

Asaad Kelada: The kind of work I do (directing multiple-camera television sitcoms) has a significantly different system than a single-camera show. We're indoors working banker's hours. There's a structure with run-throughs. To a great extent it's a writer/producer's medium and this is one thing the director is battling all the time. It's the gradual and sometimes not so gradual erosion of the role of the director because there is a sense that the director is a functionary, there primarily to carry out what is already prescribed as opposed to being a contributing artist.

We have regular breakfasts at the DGA (The Directors Guild of America). There's one breakfast meeting that is for single-camera episodic television and another that's for multiple-camera. I go to the multiple-camera breakfasts, ultimately to discuss the experiences of the individual directors in this arena, what problems we're all having, and what we can learn from each other's experiences. And also the patterns that are developing wherein the writer/producers are becoming more intrusive and less aware of the creative contribution of the director.

And it's in the sharing of these experiences, challenges, and ideas that we are all developing a better understanding of the process. The director's job is a very lonely one, and it's a very secluded one in a paradoxical way, because at the same time you're talking with a vast network of people. But ultimately the process itself is a very isolated one. We think alone. We have to make our decisions alone. It sometimes can get myopic and it is very important, I feel, to have some kind of outlet where directors can talk with directors and exchange ideas and thoughts and perceptions about what we are doing   not just about the state of the business and the workplace, but about the process itself, our creative role.

Cyrus Nowrasteh: The film's subject, or themes, will often yield the necessity for "consultants" or "experts" in certain areas that can give the film more authenticity. I have worked, for example, with historical advisors and technical consultants, and they can be a great help. As for the creative aspects of the film, I have consulted with Mark [Travis] on two films and have found him a great help in my prep, more often pre-prep, for the film. Mark is an experienced director whose focus is on the dramatic interpretation of the material. We talk about story, character, motivation, and the staging of scenes — the "practical" aspects of directing that are too often ignored in film schools and manuals.

Michael Wiese: On the Bali film, I've met with all kinds of consultants, ranging from ethnomusicologists to government officials and specialists in the village (musicians, shamen, priests, shadow puppeteers, as well as Balinese women who've eloped with Americans, expats, and others who echo similar experiences as the characters in the script.) These meetings help me fill in and substantiate things that the various characters do. Accuracy is important but second to the dramatic requirements of the story.

I have and will meet with others, such as script and directing consultants. On the script side, Chris Vogler's insights into the mythic underpinnings of the material I have found very valuable. On the directing side, Mark [Travis] and Judith Weston (author of *Directing The Actor*) have brought their talents to bear on the material. With Mark we've rehearsed scenes, found new approaches to the characters and their actions, did a complete read-through of an earlier script version with a dozen actors, and worked on individual scenes. With Judith we worked primarily on script analysis (what's really going on in each scene, what each character's spine is, and what I want to accomplish in various scenes.)

Frederick Johntz: I will consult with whatever artists or experts I feel may help me to make my project stronger, deeper, or more accurate. If I am going to be working in a genre that is not my strong suit, like an action or a fight sequence, I will seek out fellow directors who are experienced in this area. One of the exciting aspects of filmmaking is that we get to explore worlds with which we are unfamiliar. When I made *Toast*, a film about mental illness, I did a considerable amount of field research. The main actress and I spent time volunteering at Camarillo State Hospital, meeting and interacting with the young people who were hospitalized there as well as the staff and the doctors. I see no difference between this type of research and consulting with fellow filmmakers about an aspect of the process in which they have expertise. To me it's all about getting the best film possible.

Rosa von Praunheim: I consult with everybody. I love to discuss, talk, and involve people in my projects. I love to improvise with actors and learn from them. I did over sixty films and each process is different. In my documentaries of course I am totally dependent on reality, on research, and that connects me to thousands of people. My narrative films usually are based on real people, biographies. *The Einstein Of Sex* was based on Magnus Hirschfeld, and that required a lot of research. As for other directors, Fassbinder was a power freak and just wanted everybody to submit, so I ignored him. Werner Schröter, who later became very famous, was very available and open, which made it possible to assist each other and help each other in the beginning. Frank Ripploh from *Taxi Zum Clo* was my assistant before he had a huge success with his first film.

> *2. When you consult with another director, are you at all concerned that you may lose your vision, your focus, or your feeling of authority over the story?*

Cyrus Nowrasteh: Since I am a writer director and wrote the screenplays for both films in which I have used Mark as a consultant, "losing the vision" or my "authority over the story" is not a concern. More importantly, I find his consultation enables me to look at my story differently, more fully, explore it in new and fresh ways — to maintain some level of distance. It's very easy when the director has written the screenplay to become inhibited by his original vision, too narrow in his interpretation, and lose sight of the many and varied ways to interpret his own story. One has to maintain a level of distance from the script, to see it anew as a dramatic event, to see it with fresh eyes. This is the most useful aspect of having another director to consult with, to try different things, to hear suggestions, and explore alternative approaches. The final decision on which approach will actually be used is always mine, but it's so beneficial to have tried other ideas, to have tested the entire palette, if you will. Also, too often the creative team around a director can be "yes" men/women focused on their own jobs and not necessarily able to comprehend the overall vision of the film. When I consult with Mark he is urged by me, and is well able on his own, to question my choices, to fully explore why I'm making the choices that I am, to push me.

Michael Wiese: My feelings range from total paranoia (that I am a complete failure for failing to grasp the greater dimension that my colleagues so easily bring to the material) to thanking the drama gods that I know Mark and Judith and they are willing to help!

I have to fight my ego (that says I must be responsible for and get the credit for everything), which hinders me from the collaborative process. Once on the other side of that I am delighted to be in the filmmaking "jazz band," where we simply play with ideas, gather suggestions, refine the performances, and innovate on how to record them.

I don't feel I am losing focus but rather gaining clarity when I can bounce ideas off someone such as Mark. I am not threatened by Mark or Judith because I know they are trying to find the best ideas for the material and are not trying to take over the project.

On my Bali film project, which I've been working on for several decades, there is so much material, and I'm so invested in it, that working with someone from the outside is illuminating and helps separate the wheat from the chaff.

Frederick Johntz: This is a real concern. I believe that if you don't have passion for the story you want to tell and a firm grasp of your personal connection to it, you run the risk of getting lost. Especially interesting for me are the times I have been led astray from my vision, the times I went against my instinct. This is a time to trust how you feel. The intellect is a very important aspect of directing but it can get you into trouble. Bottom line is that it's an art form and you have to trust your instinct.

Asaad Kelada: Not at all. When I was first beginning I had done just one episode, an episode of *Rhoda*, and my very next episode was *Phyllis* — it so happened that it was a huge episode, with a big wedding. It was a definite challenge. I had been working on the MTM lot and Jay Sandrich (renowned sitcom director) was one of the directors that I had been observing, and he was always very generous with me. So I went to Jay and I told him that I have this big episode and can I impose on him and could we walk on the set and maybe he could give me some ideas, or guide me in the shooting of it or just how to approach it. And he came on his lunch hour and we walked on the set and we talked through some of the scenes. And it was very helpful. Just the support and the sense that this established giant in the medium, who helped define the style of sitcoms, was taking the time with a novice who had only one episode under his belt. And we talked as co-directors. He never talked in a patronizing way. We talked as two directors. I'll never forget that. It was invaluable. It is what we all should be doing — helping each other.

> *3. Do you feel at all threatened if you are consulting with a director with much more experience?*

Cyrus Nowrasteh: The only director worth consulting with is a director who has more experience. Why consult with a beginner?

Asaad Kelada: I have never found myself threatened in any way by talking to another director — either to provide what I know or to feel that I'm diminishing myself by asking what I don't know. It would be rather foolish not to take advantage of someone's strength and someone's insight.

We work in a very competitive medium. And the tendency is to try to protect our turf and territory — and I have come to the point where I really do believe that there is room for everybody. It ends up being survival of the fittest here also. It is not about me versus you or me instead of you. The more there is collaboration, the sharing of knowledge and experience and insights, the better off I will be. I have been the beneficiary of some very generous directors who have shared their knowledge with me. I have tried to reciprocate by passing it on. If I am in a position where I have something that can be of support to someone else, it's foolish not to pass it on. I love my work and what it represents and I want it to continue and to be something I can be proud of. So if I can help somebody who is following me to do the best work he or she can, then I am only serving what I have chosen to do in my life.

Michael Wiese: In a consulting session, no. On the set, probably. With the added pressure of having a visiting director on the set, I may lose some brainpower thinking about them rather than getting the scenes on their feet. There is the inclination to want to perform and impress, especially when you are not secure in what you are doing. I'm not secure in my directing abilities and that's why I come to folks like Mark.

Frederick Johntz: This of course can create problems, as I look up to directors with more experience. Their experience can be of great value, but it can also create self-doubt in my mind. What I have to remember is that it is my film and if I don't make it to please myself, it will never please anyone.

Rosa von Praunheim: I don't believe in learning. Nobody is more experienced then I am. My experience is my life and my life experience. I tell my students to be very personal, so you don't have competition. How can you learn from famous directors? You shouldn't imitate them. Do your own thing, just do it. It might be good if somebody pushes you and tells you how important it is to be active, to take the camera and do it. I get inspired by life and that includes everything.

> *4. Looking at the four phases of the creation of a film (preparation, preproduction, production, and postproduction), what do you look for in the collaboration with another director during any or all of these phases?*

Cyrus Nowrasteh: In my experience I have consulted with Mark primarily in the preparation phase. This I consider my private prep, my time to explore the material before the creative team arrives for preproduction. By the time they arrive I want to have done a good deal of my own prep so that I'm better able to translate my ideas and vision to them. Once in preproduction or rehearsal with the cast, I may call Mark on the telephone, raise questions and ideas with him, but not too often. Also, in postproduction I will show Mark scenes and different cuts of the film to get his feedback. I find the collaboration most intimate and productive in the preparation phase where it's usually just Mark and myself discussing the script, the creative vision, and — most beneficial — workshopping with professional actors.

Frederick Johntz: During the preparation phase I am interested in getting feedback on the story. Is it well structured? Where are the places I need directorial solutions for script problems? During preproduction I am usually looking for help in solving the more technical aspects of production and a fellow director can be of great help during this phase. During production it's usually more of an emergency-type call. Actors that are causing problems, performances that aren't working, crew people who are not giving me what I need, etc. Postproduction is the time to get a fresh set of eyes to look at the cut picture. By this point I've spent so much time with the film I am often blind to inherent problems. A good director can see these things almost better than anyone else and this feedback can be invaluable.

Michael Wiese: During the preparation there is script analysis, new ways to think about the characters, their spines, the actions they take, their emotions, and what's going on in each scene.

During preproduction there are rehearsals, finding the best ways to communicate with different actors' styles, different things to try out, to open them up to playing with a part, to building bonds and building trust between the actors and myself. We may explore improvisation or find other ways to block difficult scenes. Once the blocking is determined we may think about how to cover the performance (with the camera) and then, given the reality of the set, end up throwing this all away, but at least we have a base to work from.

It's the same with postproduction. Sometimes I'll bring in an outside editor or director to look at a cut, usually towards the end of the editing process.

Asaad Kelada: For me (directing episodic television) it is primarily in the preparation stage. I do that a lot. I try to familiarize myself as much as I can with a new show I'm going to be working on. When I started directing television it was a result of spending years of observing other directors to see how it is done. Now, even though I've done it for many years, before I first directed *Dharma & Greg*, I spent a week watching how the show was done and I talked extensively with the director. And I do reach out to other directors, especially if it is a new show. And when I'm working there are often other directors who are preparing to direct and I share my insights with them.

> *5. In your next project, do you see yourself exploring the collaboration with another director in a different way than in the past?*

Cyrus Nowrasteh: I expect to collaborate again with Mark, although I wouldn't hesitate to also collaborate with another director.

Frederick Johntz: On my next film I will want to have a director who I can consult with throughout the project. Of course for me that's easy. Since I'm partners with Mark, I'm offering him the job.

Asaad Kelada: Given the assumption that there is a next project... actually my next project is an episode of *Dharma and Greg*. I would like to direct a feature and to be able to explore that imagery and that process to tell a story. And I hope when the opportunity comes, I will choose to have a collaborative relationship with a director.

Rosa von Praunheim: Yes. I am preparing a film called *Hollywood Cannibals* with Lawrence Elbert , who also helped on my film *Can I Be Your Bratwurst Please?* with Jeff Stryker. Lawrence has a great Underground taste; he works with great drag queens and we share a strange humor.

6. What about the perception of the rest of your staff (producers, writer, creative team members) if they know that you are seeking the input of another director? Is that a problem?

Cyrus Nowrasteh: I have told my producers about using Mark as a consultant, and they seem to have no problem with it. Although when they've inquired about sitting in on our sessions, I have discouraged the idea. When Mark and I workshop, I want it to be a loose environment, a risk-taking endeavor without consequences, not something for others to judge or interpret. As for other members of the creative team, my work with Mark is usually done before they even come on. My job is to communicate my vision (that I have developed in collaboration with Mark) to them once they arrive.

Frederick Johntz: As for perception I think it's a matter of how it's handled. If you exude confidence as a director and have someone with you who has the title of assistant or producer, I think you can consult with them as much as you want without any perception problem. It worked for us on *The Baritones*. Mark was the director and I was a producer and we talked endlessly without his authority ever being eroded.

Michael Wiese: Probably not if the roles are clearly defined. I just finished a co-directing project. Going in, I originally thought there would be great problems between us but there were not. My job was to primarily work with the actors and with performance. My co-director worked with the camera setups. We had collaborated on the storyboards, although he took primary responsibility for this. If I saw a shot I didn't think was working I would tell the co-director and cameraman and we'd discuss it. If the co-director thought of some other performance aspect he wanted to see or something he wanted me to try, he would tell me and I'd do it. We both welcomed each other's input. Only once was their a small disagreement over a shot setup. We both told the cinematographer how we saw it and he found a terrific compromise that worked for both of us. So yes, it can work very well and it enables each to focus even more on one area of production, knowing that the other end is covered.

Asaad Kelada: I think it's a very tricky thing because ultimately I have to be very careful I don't shake my co-workers' confidence in my ability to carry out my functions and that they are in safe hands. It has to be very carefully handled, if I am consulting with another director, as to how that appears. Is it because I don't know what I'm doing or is it to make what I'm doing even better? It is really part of the director's private homework. I don't think it belongs in a public venue. It's not doing it secretly. Because if it is done secretively then it will be known that I am doing it out of weakness. So for me, the timing of it is important and what I want to accomplish from it. For me it is part of the preparation, before I go in and become the Alpha. And once I am in the leadership position I have theoretically answered all the questions I needed to have answered. I don't think it would be a good idea to have another director on the set. Because I know it would undermine me because in that context I know somebody is looking over my shoulder.

> 7. *What about the actors knowing that you are collaborating with another director?*

Cyrus Nowrasteh: I don't think it's necessary for the actors to know that I have collaborated with another director. They weren't present during the collaboration, nor should they be. It's a time of exploration and experimentation, like writing different early drafts of a script that are unnecessary for them to see. Once the actors have arrived it's important for me to work with them as their director and adapt the preparation I've done with Mark and others to my principals, and find anew what works best. That preparation, that collaboration, makes me that much more prepared to "see" what's best at this crucial time, because I've already done my homework.

Frederick Johntz: This is probably touchier than any other relationship, but I think it is fine so long as I am the only one working directly with the actors. As soon as any outside person, be it my assistant, other actors, the cinematographer, or anyone else begins to give character direction to an actor I could be in trouble. I just don't allow it.

Michael Wiese: One person has to establish the relationship with the actors. After that, there are lots of people on a set doing lots of different jobs. No big deal. And certainly in the workshops I've done with Mark, the actors listen to the student director even though Mark may make many comments. As long as everyone knows what's going on and there is respect in all directions there shouldn't be a problem.

If, on the other hand, the director is really insecure and trying to hide the consultant ("It's just my cousin Louie in from Jersey for a few days") in order to take full credit, then this could quickly undermine the director's authority. If you are upfront with people about what's going on, any configuration can work.

In the end, you are bringing together a whole production circus whose goal is to make the best movie you can. Everyone has their job and the end purpose is the same: Work hard, have fun, make a great movie.

Rosa von Praunheim: No problem. I worked with other directors who did camera for me. Elfi Mikesch, for example, is a great filmmaker herself. So that makes it easier, because she is very precise in telling actors what she wants in terms of walking in the light, in keeping the frame, and has very precise visual ideas which involve acting precision. Because I respect Elfi's work a lot, I let that happen and I am thankful for her ideas. Mike Kuchar is the same, a famous Underground director himself. He did the camera for *Red Love* and others, and I love his visual ideas and his knowledge about acting. I guess my staff loves that too, but I have no idea what they say behind my back. I guess it's very difficult for most people on the set to understand what the film is fully about. What matters is the result.

8. Any other comments you would like to have included in this discuss of the Ultimate Collaboration?

Cyrus Nowrasteh: Working with a consultant is a very rewarding, but also delicate endeavor. One has to completely immerse themselves in this process, to probe, question, and discover with another creative voice. This means to risk displaying how little they know, how lost and alone they can be in trying to develop a drama. We don't have all the answers; we don't all know what is best months before we arrive on the set to make a film. And we certainly don't know what's best just because we wrote it. We have to find it. The consultant who aids in this process must truly be selfless and thinking how best to help the director find the film he wants to make. Such persons are hard to find because such qualities (generosity, selflessness, etc.) are rare. It helps that Mark has done so much directing in his career and received much acclaim for his book and workshops. He's a very secure individual. He isn't out to "show-up" the director, or to get a job, or to prove to anyone that he made the film.

Frederick Johntz: I would just like to encourage the directors out there reading this to give themselves the freedom to seek advice and input from other directors. Directing is a lonely business and there is a prevailing myth that the director must by definition have all the answers. Well, nobody has all the answers. Not even our greatest directors have all the answers. So why not open yourself up to input from others? After all, you are the director and you can pick and choose what works and what doesn't, and if it works, you get the credit.

Rosa von Praunheim: Yes, I love ultimate collaboration, especially as a professor. I love to work with my students and encourage them to get involved with each other, personally, professionally. Film is team-work, but most of all I have them get involved with life itself. Life, living, intensely living, learning from life, watching life — that's what should inspire you. Be spontaneous, forget about your mind, your intellect, just feel, let go, use automatic writing, do small films quickly, just do them — the more you do, the better you get. It's not you who controls, it's the *film*. Just listen to your subjects, to your material, and learn from it. *It* tells you what to do, much more then any teacher can. I take my students to autopsies, to S&M clubs, to Hollywood, and the next time to Calcutta, and I teach them to love drama. Happiness is dull, but whatever goes wrong is what you should be thankful for. Then you live. Then you grow.

Michael Wiese: My worst experience and what I learned: Years ago, I directed a low-budget movie. I was very insecure about my own abilities. I had produced lots of other kinds of films and videos but not assumed a sole director role on a dramatic feature. I found a producer who talked the talk and appeared like he would support me. He told me that he'd helped several first-time directors and even had taken over a project when it got into trouble. I didn't feel entirely right about this guy, something in my gut trembled whenever I was around him, but I didn't heed the warning. I needed a producer and the shoot was only weeks away.

He offered to solve all my problems and to even put some money into the production (never happened) if he liked what he saw. So I fell for it. He had lots and lots of ideas of about how we should do everything. He made sure everyone knew that he worked with lots of famous actors and on many well-known television shows. On paper it sounded good: He would produce and I would focus on directing the performances.

He was loud and very different from anyone else on the set. He stood out immediately with his Hollywood-set lingo. Many small problems started to arise, which I overlooked. I was glad that someone, besides myself, would watch over the production. I just wanted to direct.

But alas, I didn't move as fast as he wanted. He'd worked with TV directors who as soon as they say, "Cut," shout out the next camera position. One night I was thinking about the next setup. Though the lights were not even out of the grip truck and the actors had not yet arrived on the set, he demanded that I tell him where the camera was going to be set up. I told him we had at least half an hour before we have to know that and that I was still thinking about how to open the scene. (We were going to have to restage a love scene because I'd just learned the male actor had a herpes sore on his lip). I told him I hadn't decided what I wanted to do but I had it narrowed down to two choices.

This was not the response he wanted to hear. He went ballistic. He berated me for being so slow, said that I couldn't direct for shit, that I was ruining the movie, and he began shoving me around. He got himself so worked up that he hauled off and punched me! He said that unless he took over directing the movie immediately, he was going to quit. He said he would be in his hotel room and if I didn't call within the hour and pass over the directing reins, he would go home. I told him he didn't have to wait. I already had made up my mind. I was directing and he should go home. He took his gear (some lights, a camera body, and lens) and I never saw him again (but he did e-mail a few months later during postproduction to make sure he'd still be credited as producer on the film).

His agenda all along had been to undermine me and take over the production, even though I had developed the story, overseen the script writing, brought in the actors, picked the crew, and made the financing/deferral deals.

Minutes after he left, a sudden clarity came over me. It was as if a cloud had uncovered the sun. The morale on the set improved immediately. My communication was great with the actors and crew. They too no longer had to put up with his ranting and raving, his Hollywood posturing (even though he lived in Chicago), and his coming on to the actresses. I didn't have to cringe every time I said "Cut" while he was waiting to rush the camera to the next position. It was a whole new ballgame and we had a great time finishing the film. The number of setups accomplished each day picked up by about 40%!

I learned several very important lessons:

1. Don't get desperate and think you are not enough. If you do, you will make wrong choices. You have to work out of your own integrity. Inside I knew this guy wasn't right but I talked myself out of it because I thought I "needed" a producer.

2. Give yourself time to shop around. Say "No," even to money, if it doesn't feel right.

3. There are always people around to support you. Pick them carefully. Use all your senses in interviewing. Discover any hidden agendas early on. One person can infect a whole production. The secret is when you have to cut bait, cut!

4. A successful production depends on the skills and interpersonal workings of a lot of people. If anyone pulls a Darth Vader and negatively influences the tone of the set, get people that complement you, rather than supplement or duplicate your abilities. Gather together people that you like and respect and are willing to take the collaborative journey with you.

Asaad Kelada: I got a call a few years ago from a feature-film director. He was going to do his first comedy and he wanted to talk to me about directing actors. He wanted to know if there were any insights I could give him. We had a long talk and he said it was very helpful. It was an interesting juxtaposition because I was talking about something with which I had experience (directing multiple-camera sitcoms) but in a medium with which I did not have experience (single-camera feature films). Now he was obviously not threatened in calling me and I was certainly not threatened in talking to him. We both came from two different areas of strength. It was a very energizing experience for me. Ultimately we're still telling a story, still asking what makes a scene funny. We were talking about all of these approaches and techniques… and it was wonderful to be able to do that. And that's why I think what you're doing, adding this focus to your book is really important as part of the director's journey. We are part of a larger continuum in the work we do, and to be able to exchange those thoughts is really essential.

IT'S A WRAP – FOR THE MOMENT

It's always difficult to know how to end a book. Especially a book where there is no specific storyline. In *The Director's Journey* I ended with the Bumblebee Story. That felt good. It gave me a sense of closure and completion.

The truth is, there is no ending. There is no closure. This "conversation" that we are engaged in still has many unresolved questions and issues. There are still many aspects of the filmmaking and the storytelling process that need to be explored and examined. It will always be that way. You and I are in a process, a dialogue, a debate, a relationship. And now it is your turn. I've been talking non-stop for almost 400 pages and it's time for me to take a break and listen.

One of my greatest joys as an author has been the dialogue that has been initiated by *The Director's Journey*. I am in continuous conversations with filmmakers all over the world in heated debates and discussions. As I travel lecturing and teaching and directing, I invariably run into directors who have questions, insights, and responses that thrust me back into the dialogues that I find so invigorating, refreshing, and informative.

Now it's your turn to join the discussion if you like. All it takes is one e-mail and you are part of my International Director's Roundtable.

Mark Travis
Travis Johntz Productions

marktravis@sbcglobal.net
www.travis-johntz.com

We look forward to hearing from you.

Take a moment. Spread your wings. And fly.

APPENDIX

There are many fine books on the crafts of filmmaking, directing, writing, and acting. Here are a few that I have found inspirational.

Directing
- Ball, William. *A Sense of Direction*. Drama Book Publishers, 1984.
- Brook, Peter. *The Empty Space*. Avon Books, 1968.
- Clurman, Harold. *On Directing*. Macmillan Publishing Company, 1972.
- Cole, Toby, and Helen Krich Chinoy. *Directors on Directing: A Sourcebook of the Modern Theatre*. Bobbs-Merrill Company, 1953, 1963.
- Geduld, Harry M. *Film Makers on Film Making*. Indiana University Press, 1967.
- Gelmis, Joseph. *The Film Director as Superstar*. Doubleday and Company, 1970.
- Katz, Steven D. *Film Directing Shot by Shot: Visualizing from Concept to Screen*. Michael Wiese Productions, 1991.
- Lumet, Sidney. *Making Movies*. Alfred A. Knopf, 1995.
- Pincus, Edward, and Steven Ascher. *The Filmmaker's Handbook*. New American Library, 1984.
- Sayles, *Thinking in Pictures: The Making of the Movie Matewan*. Houghton Mifflin Company, 1987.
- Seger, Linda, and Edward Jay Whetmore. *From Script to Screen*. Henry Holt and Company, 1994.
- Sherman, Eric. *Directing the Film: Film Directors on Their Art*. Little, Brown and Company, 1976.
- Sherman, Eric. *The Director's Event*. Signet, 1972.

Acting

- Chekhov, Michael. *To The Actor*. Harper and Row, 1953.
- Hagen, Uta. *Respect for Acting*. Macmillan Publishing Company, New York, 1973.
- Lewis, Robert. *Advice to the Players*. Theatre Communications Group, New York, 1980.
- Meisner, Sanford, and Dennis Longwell. *Sanford Meisner on Acting*. Vantage Books, 1987.
- Shurtleff, Michael. *Audition*. Walker Publishing Company, 1978.
- Spolin, Viola. *Improvisation for the Theatre: A Handbook of Teaching and Directing Techniques*. Northwestern University Press, 1963.
- Weston, Judith. *Directing Actors*. Michael Wiese Productions, 1996.

Writing

- Egri, Lajos. *The Art of Dramatic Writing: Its Basis in the Creative Interpretation of Human Motives*. Simon and Schuster, 1946.
- Seger, Linda. *Making a Good Script Great*. Samuel French, 1987.
- Field, Syd. Screenplay: *The Foundations of Screenwriting*. Dell, 1979.
- Volger, Chris. *The Writer's Journey: Mythic Structure for Storytellers & Screenwriters*. Michael Wiese Productions, 1992.
- Goldman, William. *Adventures in the Screen Trade*. Warner Books, 1983.

Miscellaneous

- Arijon, Daniel. *The Grammar of Film Language*. Focus Press, 1976.
- Cameron, Julia. *The Artist's Way: A Spiritual Path to Higher Creativity*. Tarcher/Putnam, 1992.
- Cheshire, David. *The Book of Movie Photography*. Alfred A. Knopf, 1979.

- Maltin, Leonard. *Behind the Camera: The Cinematographer's Art*. Signet Film Series, 1971.
- Rosenblum, Ralph, and Robert Karen. *When the Shooting Stops... the Cutting Begins, A Film Editor's Story*. Viking Press, 1979.
- Schaefer, Dennis, and Larry Salvato. *Masters of Light: Conversations with Contemporary Cinematographers*. University of California Press, 1984.

ABOUT MARK TRAVIS

Photo by Geraldine Overton

MARK TRAVIS is a graduate of the Yale School of Drama and a former creative consultant to film director Mark Rydell. His highly-praised direction of *A Bronx Tale*, *Survival of the Heart*, *Undressing New Jersey*, *Once A Man Twice A Boy*, *Wings*, *The Coming of Stork*, *Equus*, *Linke vs. Redfield*, *Verdigris*, *What Does the Sun Sound Like*, *They Call Me Mr. Fry*, *Getting It Wrong*, and *In the Now* has garnered a total of twenty-eight *Drama-Logue*, *L.A. Weekly* and Drama Critics Circle awards.

Mark's television directing credits include *The Facts of Life*, *Family Ties*, *Capitol*, and the Emmy Award-winning PBS dramatic special, *Blind Tom: The Thomas Bethune Story*. In 1990 he completed his first film, *Going Under*, for Warner Bros., starring Bill Pullman and Ned Beatty. In 1999 he directed the documentary, *Earlet*, and in 2001 he wrote and directed *The Baritones*.

In 1992 Mark opened The Travis Group (now Travis-Johntz Productions), a consulting company for directors, writers, and producers. Mark has been sharing his techniques on writing, acting, and directing at The Directors Guild, American Film Institute, UCLA Extension, Taos Talking Pictures Film Festival, Denver Film Festival, Pittard-Sullivan, Hollywood Actor's Workshop, and Hollywood Film Institute in the U.S.; in Japan at Film & Media Lab and Vantan Film School; and in Germany at UW Filmseminares, ActionConcept, IFS, and the Munich Film School.

He has served as a directing consultant on such feature-length films as *Men of Honor*; *The Day Reagan Was Shot*; *How to Go on a Date in Queens*; *The Killing Jar*; *Tear It Down*; *Norma Jean, Jack and Me*; *The Hunt for the White Tigers*; *The Red Team*; *Road Dogz*; and such television series as *Lois and Clark*; *The Pretender*; *Picket Fences*; *Beverly Hills, 90210*; *Melrose Place*; *The Practice*; and *Ally MacBeal*.

The first edition of this book, *THE DIRECTOR'S JOURNEY: The Creative Collaboration between Directors, Writers, and Actors*, was #1 on *The Los Angeles Times* non-fiction best seller list.

Mark is currently writing a new book, *LIFESTORIES: The Art and Craft of Autobiographical Storytelling*.

FILM DIRECTING: SHOT BY SHOT
Visualizing from Concept to Screen

Steven D. Katz

This classic with the famous blue cover is one of the most well-known books in the business, and is a favorite of working directors as an on-set quick-reference guide. Packed with visual techniques for filmmakers and screenwriters to expand their stylistic knowledge, this international best seller contains in-depth information on composition, previsualization, camera techniques, and much more. Includes over 750 storyboards and illustrations, with never-before-published storyboards from Spielberg's *Empire of the Sun*, Welles' *Citizen Kane*, and Hitchcock's *The Birds*.

$27.95
Order # 7RLS
ISBN: 0-941188-10-8

Both Katz Books Only $47

Save 12% when you order both books
Order #KatzB

FILM DIRECTING: CINEMATIC MOTION
A Workshop for Staging Scenes

Steven D. Katz

This follow-up to the phenomenally popular *Shot by Shot* is a practical guide to common production problems encountered when staging and blocking film scenes. Includes discussions of scheduling, staging without dialogue, sequence shots, actor and camera choreography, and much more. Also includes interviews with well-known professionals such as director John Sayles and visual effects coordinator Van Ling (*The Abyss*, *Terminator 2*).

$24.95
Order # 6RLS
ISBN: 0-941188-14-0

DIRECTING ACTORS
Creating Memorable Performances for Film & Television

Judith Weston

The most important relationship on a movie set is between director and actor. The director is responsible for telling the story and the actors are responsible for bringing the story to life. *Directing Actors* is a method for establishing creative, mutually beneficial relationships between actors and directors. Using simple, practical tools that both directors and actors can use immediately, this book will show you how to get the most out of rehearsals, troubleshoot poor performances, and give directions that are clear, succinct, and easy to follow.

$26.95
Order # 4RLS
ISBN: 0-941188-24-8

SETTING UP YOUR SHOTS
Great Camera Moves Every Filmmaker Should Know

Jeremy Vineyard

Written in straightforward, non-technical language and laid out in a non-linear format with self-contained chapters for easy reference, *Setting Up Your Shots* is like a Swiss army knife for filmmakers! Using examples from over 140 popular films, this book provides detailed descriptions of more than 100 camera setups, angles, and techniques. An excellent primer for beginning filmmakers and students of film theory, as well as a handy quick-reference guide for working filmmakers.

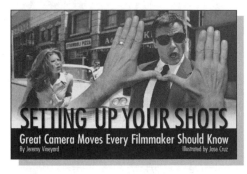

Contains 150 references to the great shots in your favorite films, including *2001: A Space Odyssey*, *Blue Velvet*, *The Matrix*, *The Usual Suspects*, *Vertigo* and more.

$19.95, Order # 8RLS, ISBN: 0-941188-73-6

24 HOURS | **1.800.833.5738** | **www.mwp.com**

FILM & VIDEO BUDGETS
3rd Updated Edition

Deke Simon and Michael Wiese

For over 15 years *Film & Video Budgets* has been THE essential handbook for both beginning and professional filmmakers. Written by two pioneers of do-it-yourself filmmaking, this book outlines every element of production.

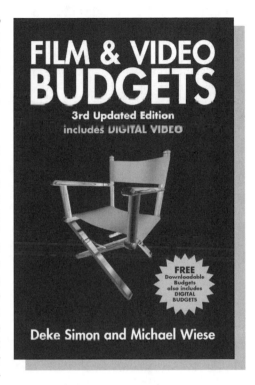

Updated and revised for digital video productions (and video-to-film transfers), this definitive book contains detailed formats and sample budgets for many different kinds of productions, from "no budget" digital movies to documentaries to a $5 million feature—along with all the crucial practical information that's made it an industry bible. Also includes new and highly useful materials, such as a comprehensive master list of line items for just about everything that could possibly be put into a production, and information-packed chapters on handling pre-production and setting up a production company. Also includes Excel sample budget templates downloadable for free from the Web.

Deke Simon and Michael Wiese are veteran filmmakers who have had extensive experience in film, TV, and video.

$26.95
Order # 9RLS
ISBN: 0-941188-34-5

Budget samples include:
- $5 Million Feature Film
- Documentaries
  (both film and video)
- Industrial
- Music Video
- Student Film
- No-Budget Digital Feature
- Digital Video Feature
- Video-to-Film Transfer
- And more!

FROM WORD TO IMAGE
Storyboarding and the Filmmaking Process

Marcie Begleiter

Whether you're a director, screenwriter, producer, editor, or storyboard artist, the ability to tell stories with images is essential to your craft. This remarkable book is engineered to help both word- and image-oriented artists learn how to develop and sharpen their visual storytelling skills via story-boarding. Readers are taken on a step-by-step journey into the previsualization process, including breaking down the script, using overhead diagrams to block out shots, and creating usable drawings for film frames that collaborators can easily understand. Also includes discussions of compositional strategies, perspective, and figure notation as well as practical information on getting gigs, working on location, collaborating with other crew members, and much more.

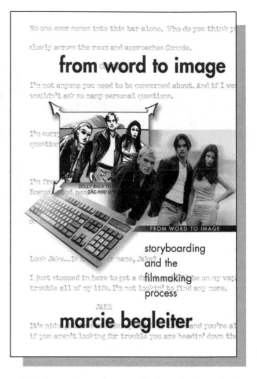

Marcie Begleiter is a writer and educator who specializes in pre-visualization. She has worked extensively in the film, television, and interactive industries and is currently on the faculties of the Art Center College of Design and the American Film Institute.

$26.95
Order # 45RLS
ISBN: 0-941188-28-0

THE WRITER'S JOURNEY
2nd Edition
Mythic Structure for Writers

Christopher Vogler

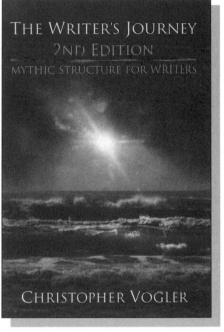

See why this book has become an international best-seller and a true classic. First published in 1992, *The Writer's Journey* explores the powerful relationship between mythology and storytelling in a clear, concise style that's made it required reading for movie executives, screenwriters, scholars, and fans of pop culture all over the world.

Both fiction and nonfiction writers will discover a set of useful myth-inspired storytelling paradigms (i.e., "The Hero's Journey") and step-by-step guidelines to plot and character development. Based on the work of Joseph Campbell, *The Writer's Journey* is a must for all writers interested in further developing their craft.

The updated and revised 2nd Edition provides new insights, observations, and film references from Vogler's ongoing work on mythology's influence on stories, movies, and man himself.

Christopher Vogler, a top Hollywood story consultant and development executive, has worked on such high-grossing feature films as The Lion King *and* The Thin Red Line *and conducts writing workshops around the globe.*

$24.95
Order # 98RLS
ISBN: 0-941188-70-1

24 HOURS | **1.800.833.5738** | **www.mwp.com**

INDEPENDENT FILM & VIDEOMAKER'S GUIDE
2nd Edition
Expanded & Updated

Michael Wiese

The new, completely expanded and revised edition of one of our best-sellers has all the information you need, from fundraising to distribution. This practical and comprehensive book will help filmmakers save time and money and inspire them to create successful projects.

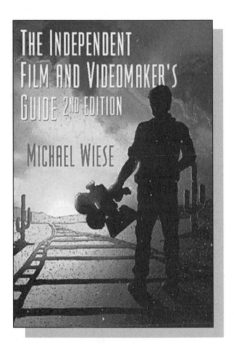

Contents include:

- Writing a business plan
- Developing your ideas into concepts, treatments, and scripts
- Directing, producing, and market research
- Understanding distribution markets (theatrical, home video, television, international)
- Financing your film
- Making presentations and writing a prospectus

Plus, an appendix filled with film cash flow projections, sample contracts, valuable contact addresses, and much more.

Using the principles outlined in this book, Wiese recently co-directed the short film *Field of Fish*, and is currently preparing his Bali feature. Additionally, Wiese is national spokesperson for Kodak's Emerging Filmmakers Program. He has conducted workshops on independent filmmaking in England, Germany, Finland, Indonesia, Ireland, Canada, Australia, and throughout the U.S. Contact Wiese at mw@mwp.com.

$29.95
Order # 37RLS
ISBN: 0-941188-57-4

DIGITAL MOVIEMAKING
A Butt-Kicking, Pixel-Twisting Vision of the Digital Future and How to Make Your Next Movie on Your Credit Card

Scott Billups

You've got the script. You've got the vision. Now all you need is a deal to get your film made. But what if the powers-that-be say no? Do you have to give up your dream? Not any more. The digital revolution has made it cheaper and more possible than ever before for people to shoot and edit their own professional-quality films. This book will show you how to grab the bull by the horns and make your dream a reality.

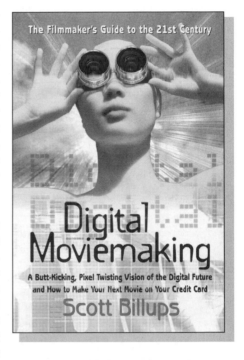

Written for both experienced film and video directors who are new to the digital format and up-and-comers new to filmmaking in general, video guru Scott Billups' guide takes you through the brave new world of digital moviemaking. All the nuts-and-bolts information you need is right here, but technophobes need not fret. Billups explains in clear, concise, plain English what all these new terms and tools mean, and why it's not as hard as you think. He'll show you how to choose the technology that best fits your needs (and budget!) and how to get the maximum effect out of your equipment. Learn about different formats, effects tools, and cameras, as well as issues and challenges unique to shooting digitally.

Scott Billups has produced, directed, and written feature films, television programs, and commercials.

$26.95
Order # 2RLS
ISBN: 0-941188-30-2

ORDER FORM

TO ORDER THESE PRODUCTS, PLEASE CALL **24** HOURS - **7** DAYS A WEEK
CREDIT CARD ORDERS **1-800-833-5738** OR FAX YOUR ORDER **(818) 986-3408**
OR MAIL THIS ORDER FORM TO:

MICHAEL WIESE PRODUCTIONS
11288 VENTURA BLVD., # 621
STUDIO CITY, CA 91604
E-MAIL: MWPSALES@MWP.COM
WEB SITE: WWW.MWP.COM

WRITE OR FAX FOR A FREE CATALOG

PLEASE SEND ME THE FOLLOWING BOOKS:

TITLE	ORDER NUMBER (#RLS _____)	AMOUNT
_____	_____	_____
_____	_____	_____
_____	_____	_____
_____	_____	_____
_____	_____	_____

SHIPPING _____

CALIFORNIA TAX (8.00%) _____

TOTAL ENCLOSED _____

SHIPPING:
ALL ORDERS MUST BE PREPAID, UPS GROUND SERVICE ONE ITEM - **$3.95**
EACH ADDITIONAL ITEM ADD **$2.00**
EXPRESS - **3** BUSINESS DAYS ADD **$12.00** PER ORDER
OVERSEAS
SURFACE - **$15.00** EACH ITEM   AIRMAIL - **$30.00** EACH ITEM

PLEASE MAKE CHECK OR MONEY ORDER PAYABLE TO:

MICHAEL WIESE PRODUCTIONS

(CHECKONE) _____ MASTERCARD _____VISA _____AMEX

CREDIT CARD NUMBER _____

EXPIRATION DATE _____

CARDHOLDER'S NAME _____

CARDHOLDER'S SIGNATURE _____

SHIP TO:

NAME _____

ADDRESS _____

CITY _____ STATE _____ ZIP _____

COUNTRY _____ TELEPHONE _____

ORDER ONLINE FOR THE LOWEST PRICES
24 HOURS | 1.800.833.5738 | www.mwp.com